CO
PR

COACH PRIME

DEION SANDERS AND THE MAKING OF MEN

Jean-Jacques Taylor

MARINER BOOKS

New York   Boston

HarperCollins books may be purchased for educational, business, or sales promotional use. For information, please email the Special Markets Department at SPsales@harpercollins.com.

FIRST EDITION

Designed by Chloe Foster

Library of Congress Cataloging-in-Publication Data has been applied for.

ISBN 978-0-06-330691-2

23 24 25 26 27 LBC 5 4 3 2 1

To my parents, Doris and Henry, who encouraged me to chase my dream of being a writer from the moment I spoke it into existence.

To my mom's parents, William and Alberta, and my dad's parents, Henry and Ruth, for blessing me with wonderful parents.

CONTENTS

Contents

PART IV

PROLOGUE

It was less than ten minutes before kickoff when Jackson State football coach Deion Sanders—Coach Prime to his players, fans, and media—stood atop a two-foot-high blue crate and addressed his players in the locker room.

Coach Prime knew that if the Tigers didn't beat Southern University in the Southwestern Athletic Conference Championship game at Mississippi Veterans Memorial Stadium, this would be the last time he'd ever address these players before a game.

A loss would end Jackson State's quest for perfection and an opportunity at redemption for their embarrassing performance the year before, at the 2021 Cricket Celebration Bowl.

Coach Prime glanced at his iPhone, where he typically types a few words or phrases in the Notes app to remember his talking points. He prides himself on authenticity and, at times, speaks with an old-school Baptist preacher's cadence and passion. But he likes to stay on message, often speaking in repetition, for emphasis. This time was no different. Every word that came from Coach Prime's mouth was not only intentional but loaded. Everyone knew he'd already agreed to terms to become the University of Colorado Buffaloes' head football coach. This was his last season with JSU and, if the Tigers didn't win, his last game.

Coach Prime's words of the week changed often, depending on the team's opponent and whatever outside noise the players needed to ignore. This week, it was "focus and finish." They'd been hearing it from him for days and knew what to do when they heard it.

"Focus and finish!" the players repeated in one loud, deep voice.

"I can, I will, I am!" Coach Prime called out.

"I can, I will, I am!" his team responded.

The call and response of "I can, I will, I am" continued twice more. Then silence. The players felt the tension.

"Come on now," one said.

"Yes, sir," said another. Coach Prime rarely, if ever, showed his players this type of emotion. For once, he needed them. They happily encouraged him.

"I want this, man," Coach Prime said softly, referring to winning the game. "I'm not thinking about me right now, I'm thinking about Amari. Where you at?"

Amari Ward walked to the front of the locker room and faced his teammates. Coach Prime placed his left arm around Amari's shoulders.

"What he dealt with. What he witnessed. What's in his spirit is traumatic. If you don't do it for you. If you don't do it for your teammates. If you don't do it for your family, do it for him. He has a long-lasting memory that will never be erased." Coach Prime looked Amari in the eye. "You need to know how much we love you, how much we appreciate you, and how much we got you."

As Amari walked back to his teammates, Coach Prime looked at his phone, cleared his throat, and again stared out at his players. He talked about how he is intrigued by history but doesn't let it define him. How history can discourage those who see the world through a different prism. How history said a person can't play professional football and baseball at the same time. How history said a person can't score a touchdown in a National Football League game and hit a home run in a Major League Baseball game in the same week. How history said a cornerback would never be one of the NFL's highest-paid players. How he never let history stifle his dreams and how the team should not allow history to stifle theirs. He ended his speech-sermon with classic repetition.

"History intrigues me, but his story compels me. His story compels me. His story compels me. *Your* story compels me. His story compels me. His story compels me."

Coach Prime didn't specify what Amari's story compelled him to do or to feel. But he didn't need to. The events around Amari's roommate had shaken the whole team and was simply the latest compelling story, among a roster of players full of them.

Coach Prime could've been talking about Hayden Hagler, who had siblings die in three separate incidents. He could've been talking about Quay Davis, who experienced the death of a child, and fathered four children before graduating high school.

Maybe he was about talking Charlie Goodell, the NFL commissioner's nephew, who has narcolepsy. Or Matt Vitale, who battles Crohn's disease and spent several months in the hospital after a perforated bowel led to an infection and resulted in several inches of his small intestine being removed. Or Jeremiah Brown, who was homeless for a year and a half.

Perhaps he was talking about Jurriente Davis, whose father was murdered before he knew him. Or Tre'von Riggins, whose dad died from complications from a stroke. Or Kirk Ford, who's allergic to pretty much everything you can name and spent much of his childhood in the hospital for a variety of ailments.

Coach Prime could've literally been talking about thirty or forty other players who overcame their circumstances to become part of the Jackson State football team that appeared on ABC's *Good Morning America* and ESPN's *College GameDay* in the midst of their quest for perfection.

Coach Prime, of course, was dealing with his own story of triumph and tragedy.

The Pro Football Hall of Fame cornerback nearly died in 2021, his second season at Jackson State, because of blood clots. Complications led to a hospital stay of nearly a month in the ICU—he missed three games—and he endured nine surgeries and the loss of the first two toes on his left foot.

Now, though, he needed to keep his players focused, so that they could finish strong.

They had seen and heard the rumors about Coach Prime's future at Jackson State on *SportsCenter* and social media all week. Friends and family called and texted nonstop with questions.

"I had my phone on do-not-disturb for four days," offensive coordinator Brett Bartolone said.

Grad assistant Brandon Morton said that when word that Coach Prime was headed to Colorado leaked the night before the SWAC Championship, it worried him.

"As a young kid, that's going to affect you, especially a dude like Prime," he said. "A lot of these kids came to play for Prime. That's the only reason they came down here. Before the SWAC Championship, there was this elephant in the room."

Still, Morton was optimistic about the Tigers winning. They had beaten Southern University 35–0 a month earlier, and he believed they would win as long as they didn't implode. After all, JSU had the nation's No. 1 defense, allowing only 11.1 points and 255.9 yards per game. Their offense, averaging 37.8 points per game, had only six scoreless quarters all season.

Quarterback Shedeur Sanders was the SWAC's offensive player of the year, linebacker Aubrey Miller Jr. was the defensive player of the year, and receiver Kevin Coleman Jr. was the newcomer of the year.

JSU had everything it needed to dominate, which had been its mission all season. Coach Prime had established a culture of work and discipline, and a disgust for mediocrity and complacency.

Now it was time to see if the players truly embraced all the lessons he had preached about consistency, discipline, and focus. He had drilled into them all season that men ignore distractions and focus on the task at hand.

"Let's go out there today and write his story," he said, "and we'll deal with the history later. You with me?!"

"Yes!" they replied.

PART I

CHAPTER 1

It was just the grace of God.
—JSU president Thomas K. Hudson

The union between Jackson State and Deion Sanders was a symbiotic relationship from the start.

Jackson State needed Coach Prime to resurrect its moribund football program and Coach Prime needed Jackson State to become a head football coach. Jackson State, one of the SWAC's premier football programs, had fallen on hard times after hiring four head coaches and four athletic directors in eight years.

The program had not won a SWAC Championship since 2007. It hadn't had a winning season since 2013, going 23-44 in that span. In 2019, Jackson State went 4-8 and finished fourth in the East Division.

From 1971 to 1999, JSU won nine games 11 times. In 1978 and 1996, they won 10 games, the most in school history.

Four players—Walter Payton, Jackie Slater, Lem Barney, and Robert Brazile—are in the Pro Football Hall of Fame, and JSU has 18 SWAC football championships.

W. C. Gorden, 119-48-5 in 16 seasons, won eight SWAC titles, including seven in the 1990s.

Jackson State wanted Coach Prime to return the Tigers to the glory days.

Athletic director Ashley Robinson, a Jackson native, arrived in 2018 with the slogan "Building on Tradition, Blazing New Trails."

Like most folks who grow up in Jackson, Robinson attended football games at the Vet, which is what the locals call JSU's stadium, as a kid, and the university had been a presence in his life for as long as he could remember.

Robinson averaged a double-double as a high school senior, but it wasn't good enough to get a scholarship offer from the one school he wanted: Jackson State. The 6' point guard played at Mississippi Valley State and became Valley's all-time leader in assists.

After his athletic career, Robinson began a career in compliance and administration. Valley named him athletic director in 2012. Jackson State passed on him again in 2015, when it didn't hire him as athletic director.

In 2018, Jackson State fired Wheeler Brown and the prodigal son returned home.

Athletic directors are judged by their hires in football and men's basketball. Robinson's football hires at Prairie View A&M University—Willie Simmons and Eric Dooley—were excellent.

Simmons led Prairie View to consecutive winning seasons for the first time in fifty-one years. That gave JSU confidence Robinson could find the right coach to make the program strong again. Robinson didn't give John Hendrick a new contract at the end of the season, so he needed a coach. He was watching the NFL Network one fall afternoon in 2019 when he saw Coach Prime say he wanted to be a head coach in college football.

"I was sitting here with my assistant VP of business operations and I said, 'What do you think about Deion Sanders?'" Robinson remembered.

Robinson's first conversation with Coach Prime was a doozy. He had researched JSU's recent football struggles and he provided solutions for its problems, while sharing his vision for how to make JSU an elite program built on old-school principles.

Hiring Coach Prime would ensure Robinson went down in the annals of Jackson State and college football history as the man bold enough to make college football's most innovative hire.

The scrutiny would be intense, and if Coach Prime didn't work out, the criticism would be searing. Robinson, though, ain't never been scared. Or passive. And if hiring Coach Prime worked the way he envisioned, each man would elevate.

Coach Prime had learned from his successes with TRUTH, his youth football and baseball organization, which he patterned after the Fort Myers Rebels he played for as a kid. TRUTH stood for: Trust in God, Respect myself and others, Understand I have unlimited possibilities, Try my best and never give up, Honor myself and the TRUTH creed at all times." He also learned his failures with Prime Prep Academy, a charter school focused on elite football and basketball.

Prime Prep, which he cofounded in 2012, closed in 2014 because of a litany of financial, legal, and regulatory issues. Patience is the one thing he learned from the Prime Prep experience. He was in such a hurry to make an impact, Coach Prime rushed through some steps in the vetting process that would've prevented Prime Prep's issues.

"When I see what needs to be done, I think, oftentimes, everybody sees it the way I see it," he said. "Not oftentimes they do, so that affects your patience because you got vision."

Aside from the coaching opportunity, being at an HBCU intrigued Coach Prime because of America's turbulent times.

George Floyd, an African-American man, had been murdered in Minneapolis on May 25, 2020, during an encounter with police.

The forty-six-year-old Floyd had been arrested after a store clerk accused him of using a counterfeit twenty-dollar bill. While Floyd was being detained, Officer Derek Chauvin, who is white, knelt on Floyd's neck with his knee for more than nine minutes.

Two other officers—J. Alexander Kueng and Thomas Lane—helped restrain Floyd. Another officer, Tou Thao, kept witnesses from coming to Floyd's aid, despite his obvious distress.

Chauvin eventually received a federal sentence of twenty-one years for second-degree murder. Kueng was sentenced to three years,

Lane received three years, and Thao received three and a half years for their part in the crime.

Floyd's death coincided with a rise in attendance at HBCUs across the country. Coach Prime has always had a soft spot for helping young Black men find their way in a society filled with obstacles.

His mom had been a foster parent for decades and she had passed on that love for helping kids. Helping one person can change the trajectory of lives and generations, so Coach Prime viewed coaching as a way to do that.

His daughter, Shelomi, would be the last of his kids in high school, and she lived with her mom in suburban Dallas. All of those factors combined with the opportunity to run a college program persuaded Coach Prime to take the job when Ashley Robinson, in his new role as JSU athletic director, approached him about it.

After speaking every day for about ten days, Coach Prime finally told Robinson to call his agent and make a deal.

Robinson called interim president Thomas K. Hudson to make sure he was on board. He was.

"My mind wasn't focused on Deion the celebrity. It was focused on Deion Sanders the prospective football coach for Jackson State," President Hudson said. "Why not? Isn't this the time, isn't this the moment, isn't this what's needed? It's a match made in heaven. This is a God move."

President Hudson and Robinson hired a private driver and made the 345-mile trip down Interstate 20 West to Canton in a black Mercedes Sprinter van.

Coach Prime agreed to a four-year deal worth $1.2 million. He reportedly received 10 percent of all sales after 30,000 tickets were sold as well as 10 percent of all season ticket revenue after the first 10,000 bundles.

"When they pulled up, I said for me to leave [my house], it has to be God," he said. "God called me to Jackson State and me to these men."

Coach Prime announced the deal on his podcast *21st and Prime* on Barstool Sports.

"He's not just going to make them better football players. He's going to make them better men," NFL commissioner Roger Goodell said on the broadcast.

Coach Prime wasn't for everybody. He changed the atmosphere wherever he went, while understanding change wasn't easy or convenient.

Coach Prime provided cachet and attention no other coach would. His combination of charisma, personality, and fame meant media would flock to Jackson, initially just to see why he took the job.

But to make Jackson State football relevant again, Robinson needed to make a bold move and he needed the three most important men on campus to be aligned philosophically and work together.

"It's not about egos. It's not about who's managing who. It's not about control," Robinson said. "We're going to work together."

Coach Prime knew critics and haters wouldn't give him time to acclimate to the job or take a few years to flip the roster. If he didn't win, they'd eviscerate him. Luckily, he's always been a person who doesn't care what others think.

"This is what I've been doing my whole life. Man, I've been called to take things to another level," Coach Prime said. "To challenge, to convict, to engage, to love, to chastise . . . to do what God is calling me to do now, I'm ecstatic. It's my people. I get to touch."

Coach Prime spoke passionately about how he was going to change the program. In the process, he introduced the phrase, "I believe," which would become one of the program's mantras.

Nothing happens without belief. His entire life is built on the concept.

He believed he'd be a professional athlete. He believed he'd eventually coach a college football team.

Several times, he asked the crowd at his introductory news conference, "Do you believe?"

"We believe!" they responded every time.

Everybody could laugh about Coach Prime's first season once it ended.

The Tigers played only six games because of COVID-19 protocols. The season started February 21, about six weeks after Coach Prime and his staff arrived on campus.

They went 4-3 with a forfeit win over Alcorn State University to end the season. The abbreviated 2020 season set the foundation for the championship seasons in 2021 and 2022.

In his first team meeting, Coach Prime told the players his job was to make them quit and their job was to survive.

"He said, 'If you suck, you suck. I came here to win. I'm loyal to winning and if you're not helping me win, you're out,'" holder Lane McGregor remembered. "He changed the whole culture around. You hear the same thing from every new coach, but he really meant it."

Coach Prime needed to know which players, if any, would be good enough to have a role on a championship team.

"He was straightforward," K. J. Arrington said. "He was telling us, 'Half of y'all aren't going to be here. I'm trying to get all y'all out of here. This season is like your tryouts.'"

Only five players—Arrington, D. J. Stevens, Justin Ragin, Christian Allen, and Tyson Alexander—remained from Hendrick's two seasons. The previous staff recruited Anthony Petty and Devonta Davis.

"The standards changed. You used to be able to talk back to coaches and still play," Arrington said. "Now, you might not play for a quarter or a half."

Coach Prime changed the team's mentality by making everyone compete for starting jobs, playing time, and spots on the travel roster.

"I'm putting checks by some names. I want him. I don't want him. I want him," Coach Prime said after their third straight loss and final game of the season. "That's the evaluation process and it has to happen. Everybody gets held accountable. I'm going to hold you accountable—not just the players but the coaches as well."

CHAPTER 2

I call it the Prime Time effect.
—SWAC associate commissioner, media relations
Andrew Roberts

Deion Sanders, Shedeur Sanders, and Travis Hunter made the 238-mile drive from Jackson, Mississippi, to Birmingham, Alabama, for SWAC Media Day in a customized black Sprinter van.

Shedeur was the 2021 FCS freshman of the year, and Travis was the only five-star player to ever sign with a FCS school. There are 128 FCS schools (formerly Division 1-AA) in 14 conferences. It is the second-highest level of college football.

They were Jackson State's two player representatives for Media Day, which surprised no one. Coach Prime made it clear at a team meeting in July that Shedeur and Travis were the only players he considered starters.

Every other starter would be determined in fall camp.

The Tigers placed eight players on the preseason All-Conference team, which is voted on by the SWAC's coaches and sports information directors. Five players, including left tackle Tony Gray, made the first team. Players named first-team All-Conference were deemed the best in the league at their position. Tony and Malachi Wideman, who was named to the second team, each possessed NFL talent, but would have to compete for playing time because they had angered the coach. Coach Prime is old-school, a collage of the stern, disciplined coaches who shaped him as a player and a man.

He despised lazy players and excuse-makers. In his mind, Tony fell into the latter category, while Malachi was the former.

Tony, like others, played poorly in the 2021 Cricket Celebration Bowl, when South Carolina State blew out Jackson State, 31–10. Tony, as part of the fallout, lost his starting job in the spring. He'd compete with Southern Methodist University transfer Demetri Jordan for a starting job.

"Tony is the same-old Tony. When I ask the strength coach who's not giving it to you, it's Tony," Coach Prime said. "When I ask the [offensive line] coach who's not showing toughness, it's Tony. It's going to be tough for him to start."

Tony, 6'5" and 310 pounds, had an NFL frame and athleticism, but JSU was his third school. He talked more than he listened, which pissed off the coaches.

"The most important thing was impressing the offensive line coach," Gray said. "That's how I felt. When you talk to the head man, it usually means you're in trouble or something."

Malachi, a four-star recruit, signed with Tennessee but caught just one pass for 24 yards in 2020. He entered the transfer portal and joined JSU.

Malachi struggled to learn the playbook and started slowly. In Week 5, Coach Prime told then offensive coordinator T. C. Taylor to do whatever it took to get the 6'5" 190-pound receiver on the field.

He responded with 12 touchdown catches in the last nine games. Twenty-four hours before media day, Coach Prime saw Malachi for the first time since summer workouts began.

"He came into my office with a bunch of excuses and lies," Coach Prime said. "I said, 'Malachi, we have 115 players in the program. Why are there just two of y'all in the situation you're in?'"

Coach Prime walked to the whiteboard, grabbed a black marker, and scribbled "IDA" in capital letters.

"You know what this means?" he asked.

"No," Malachi replied.

"The greatest players are never in the league. They're 'ida been this' or 'ida been that' or 'ida been here' or 'ida been there,' but they never did this or that or went here or there," said Coach Prime, "because they weren't disciplined enough to stay on their path.

"That's where you're headed. Get it together. The coaches ain't chasing you no more. They're not calling you and they're not looking for you. It's up to you."

Media Day, held in the downtown Sheraton's Grand Ballroom, signaled the start of football season. It's a chance for the TV, radio, and print media to speak with all of the SWAC's coaches and its most prominent players. Each school brought its head coach and two players.

It's a much different experience since Coach Prime arrived.

"I call it the Prime Time effect," said Andrew Roberts, associate commissioner, media relations.

In 2021, 125 accredited media attended Media Day, the most ever. In 2022, the SWAC issued 175 media credentials.

The players and coaches kept a tight schedule that featured a nonstop string of interviews. ESPN3 carries live coverage of Media Day, and ESPN broadcasters Tiffany Greene and Jay Walker did ten-minute interviews with each school's representatives.

Before the TV interviews, Coach Prime, Shedeur, and Travis sat at a table with a chrome JSU helmet, name cards, and a mannequin wearing a white jersey with blue numbers and spoke to print reporters.

After a few minutes they moved into the TV room adjacent to the main ballroom. First, Coach Prime did an internet interview. Next Coach Prime and athletic director Ashley Robinson spent twenty minutes on *Roland Martin Unfiltered*. Martin, one of the country's leading Black journalists, streamed his own show and had 665,000 followers on Twitter.

Coach Prime and the players conducted several more TV interviews before they headed to the main stage. That's the moment Coach

Prime told the world that the 2022 season was about dominating the SWAC and winning the Black college national championship.

It's the reason he hired Georgia's assistant strength coach Mo Sims to make his team bigger, faster, and stronger. And why he hired Brett Bartolone, an offensive analyst at Nevada, as offensive coordinator to run an Air Raid offense designed to maximize Shedeur's intelligence and accuracy.

And why he added Tim Brewster to coach tight ends. Brewster, Florida's tight ends coach in 2020–21, was widely considered the nation's top tight ends coach.

"We've won," Coach Prime told the ESPN3 audience. "Now, we want to dominate. We want to dominate everything."

In the SWAC Preseason Poll, Jackson State received the most first-place votes. The vote total went as follows:

EAST
Jackson State 116 pts (12 1st)
Florida A&M 108 (7)
Alabama A&M 87 (2)
Alabama State 60 (1)
Bethune-Cookman 56
Mississippi Valley 35

WEST
Southern 111 (11)
Alcorn State 110 (5)
Prairie View 82 (5)
Grambling 77 (1)
Arkansas–Pine Bluff 42
Texas Southern, 40

Shedeur was named preseason offensive player of the year and Florida A&M University (FAMU) linebacker Isaiah Land was named defensive player of the year.

Shedeur talked about finishing the season, while Travis pointed at the championship trophy.

"If we don't have that at the end of the season," he said, "we haven't done our job."

Travis spoke while wearing a boot on his right foot. He recently had had surgery to repair a nagging ankle injury he originally suffered in high school. No one knew if the nation's highest-profile freshman would be ready for the opener in forty-six days.

Coach Prime also used his platform to drop subtle messages about how the SWAC needed to change its business practices. He wanted better housing and dining for players, and he'd like fewer classic games—JSU played in three—so schools could make more money and spend it on their programs instead of making "classic" promoters rich.

"If you want change you have to talk about it," he said. "God has given me the authority to talk about it."

After the ESPN interview, Coach Prime conducted a series of radio interviews. Wearing a JSU blue double-breasted suit with red buttons and white tennis shoes with tiny spikes on the toes, he was so clean he was dirty, as he often says.

Coach Prime gave the local media a few minutes before he left. He stepped into a group of ten reporters and four minicams and answered one final round of questions.

He was still smiling. When the questions ended, his smile faded. Coach Prime had successfully spread the gospel of JSU football for three harried and exhausting hours.

CHAPTER 3

I fathered my fathers pretty much.
—Deion Sanders

To understand Deion Sanders—the man, the father, the friend, and the coach—you need to learn about the kid who grew up in Fort Myers, Florida.

You need to know about his mama's work ethic. You have to understand his father's drug addiction and his stepfather's relationship with alcohol. If you examine his relationship with Jamie Chaney, you'll grasp why his circle is tight.

And you need to know about the discipline youth football coach Dave Capel instilled in him with the Fort Myers Rebels, and how North Fort Myers football coach Ron Hoover reinforced it.

Sanders was born August 9, 1967, in Fort Myers, to Mims and Connie Sanders.

He's always been a person who danced to a beat only he could hear. What else can you say about a kid who'd rather play baseball than have a birthday party?

"All he ever did was focus on sports," Connie said. "He never cared about anything else."

Connie grew up in Albany, Georgia, where her dad worked construction and her mom cleaned homes. After high school, she moved to Fort Myers to live with a cousin, attend junior college, and explore the world.

She wasn't in Florida long when she met good-looking, charismatic Mims Sanders at a "get acquainted" dance.

"He was a little skinny man, but he was very sporty," Connie said. "Like Deion dresses, his daddy dressed the same way. He walks like him. He dresses like him and he acts like him."

Connie and Mims, Daddy Buck to most folks, were only married for a couple of years.

"Buck didn't want to be married. He's a good person, but he just wanted to have a good time," she said. "It's not like he had a bunch of women, he just liked to party."

Connie and Daddy Buck stayed close even after their divorce.

"When he got on drugs, I still looked out for him. I'd see him on the streets dirty and I'd stop and I'd take him to my house, so he could bathe and put on some clean clothes and then I'd take him back to the streets," she said. "And they had a restaurant on the main drag, and I'd pay the lady so much at a time so she could feed him every day."

Daddy Buck maintained a sporadic presence in his son's life. Doing so, he taught the son what not to do.

"Daddy Buck had a great personality. He used to light up a room. He was hilarious," said Coach Prime, who can rattle off a string of humorous stories about his father when the mood is right. "I don't ever remember a serious conversation with Daddy Buck unless I was having it with him—not him having it with me."

Coach Prime learned the importance of independence early because it was just Connie and him. Connie ran an orderly household because she usually worked sixteen hours a day between her jobs at the hospital and a nursing home.

Coach Prime dressed himself for school—Connie pinned his keys to his pants pockets—and heated up the dinner she had prepared and left in the stove after school. Seeing his mom work so hard motivated Coach Prime. At seven, he promised Connie that one day he'd buy her a big house and she wouldn't have to work anymore.

A few years later, Connie married Will Knight, whom she met grocery shopping. Will, a supervisor at Wickes Lumber, was the kind of man who never called in sick. They had a daughter, Tracie, who's nine years younger than Coach Prime.

The couple bought a three-bedroom home at 1625 Henderson across from Oak Ridge Cemetery, which Coach Prime claimed made him fast since he'd sprint through the graveyard after dark to get home.

Will, a man of few words, taught his stepson how to fish. On Saturdays, they sat on the bank for hours with their cane poles and waited for the bluegill and mullets to bite. Sometimes he took Coach Prime to the lumber yard and made him pull weeds, so he learned about hard work.

"He treated him like a son," Connie said, "and Deion treated him like a father."

Coach Prime used the time fishing to fantasize about having a lake at his home and owning a boat, so he could always find the best fishing holes.

"Fishing in this one spot ain't doing it because if you have a boat you can go everywhere. We just sitting on the bank, but I loved it," he said. "I like challenges. It was a challenge to catch what was under that water."

On Fridays, while Coach Prime starred at North Fort Myers High School, Will took Tracie, the ultimate daddy's girl, to McDonald's for a cheeseburger Happy Meal and a cherry slushy from 7-Eleven, after cashing his paycheck. Once Will settled in, he'd start drinking until Sunday evening, when it was time to prepare dinner and get ready for work on Monday morning.

"Will was a good man. He had his faults. He drank, but he didn't take a drink every day," Connie said of the man she loved enough to marry twice.

"He started drinking on Friday. Friday to Sunday. On Sunday evening, he'd sober up so he could go to work on Monday morning. He didn't play about his job."

On Saturdays after his shift at Bojangles, Coach Prime often took Daddy Buck a box of fried chicken to his apartment. Occasionally, he walked in on Daddy Buck getting high.

"You walk in there and see your daddy shooting up and that's a daunting thing to see, but it was what it was," he said. "That was normalcy back then.

"I had to sit Daddy Buck down and check him. You too old for this. I always fathered my fathers pretty much."

Coach Prime had seen the effects drugs and alcohol had on his fathers, which meant he had no interest in experimenting with drugs. He's never tried alcohol or smoked a blunt. It never bothered him if friends smoked weed or drank alcohol, and he certainly knows that some of his players fire up regularly. He discourages their behavior without judging them for it. Everyone, he's said, must ultimately make their own choices.

Coach Prime began playing T-ball at five and football at eight. A year later, he joined the Rebels to play football.

"You could see he was special right away," his mom said. "Deion was one of a kind."

He starred for the Rebels, and Coach Capel introduced him and Jamie Chaney to discipline. Jamie's dad and Daddy Buck were tight, which made their sons close friends, even though Coach Prime was three years older.

Like Coach Prime, Jamie played for the Rebels, North Fort Myers High School, and Florida State.

The Rebels were a predominantly white organization whose fans waved the Rebel flag during games. Players addressed adults as sir or ma'am, arrived for practice and games on time, and maintained As and Bs. They wore blazers and church shoes to out-of-town games.

"It was like an oasis," said Jamie.

The athletics were good, but playing for football and baseball organizations on the other side of town let Coach Prime dream about another life. Every house he's ever built has a long driveway because the large homes on McGregor Boulevard had long driveways.

"I used to think the longer your money," he said, "the longer your driveway."

He starred in football, baseball, basketball, and track at North Fort Myers High School. Daddy Buck occasionally showed up to his games, but there was no rhythm to his attendance.

Will, who favored baseball over football, never came, either. Neither did Connie. She worked.

"I was always that dude so I never needed no claps. It ain't never occurred to me that nobody was there," said Coach Prime, "because if you give me enough time I'm going to turn the whole stadium up and they'll be clapping for me and the applause and the adoration will be there.

"Now, you want to identify with your folks. My mama seen me play one all-star game in basketball. She was working. I couldn't get mad at that."

When it came time for college, Coach Prime picked Florida State over Florida and Georgia because the Seminoles didn't promise him anything but opportunity. Everything else, he'd have to earn. He didn't want anything given to him, so strong was his work ethic.

He didn't like the dorms or the community bathrooms at Florida, and when they put his jersey number in multiple lockers it turned him off further because, to him, if two players had the same number on the same team it meant they weren't good. Georgia coach Vince Dooley told him he'd have to red-shirt as a freshman and Coach Prime told the legendary coach he wouldn't be playing at Georgia.

Coach Prime started fall practice as the sixth-string cornerback at Florida State. When the season began, he was part of a three-man rotation. By Week 3, he started.

Connie never missed a game.

"Back in the day they didn't want you to take off, so I didn't. I just did what they said," Connie said. "Once he got to college, I never missed a game. I was there every Saturday in Tallahassee. Me and his daddy."

Buck would ask Connie to scoop him up on game days in Tallahassee and they'd make the four-hundred-mile trip laughing and talking about the good old days along the way.

"He'd walk into the games at Tallahassee and say, 'Prime Time Sr. is here.' The coaches loved him," Connie said. "He didn't even need a ticket."

One time, when he was home from Florida State, Coach Prime took his father into Legions, a nightclub.

"It ain't right," Daddy Buck said. "A son can't be in the same club as the father. It ain't right."

Daddy Buck told Coach Prime two things he'll never forget. One was about the nightclub. The other occurred on a limo ride home after a game he played for the Falcons.

"'I don't see the need. Earrings and football players don't go together,'" Coach Prime remembered Daddy Buck telling him. "I never wore an earring on the football field again."

At Florida State, Coach Prime became one of the nation's most electrifying players. He intercepted 14 passes, returning three for touchdowns. He also returned three punts and one kickoff for touchdowns.

A couple of summers, he let his little sister Tracie hang with him in Tallahassee. She loved it.

"I liked spending time with him and his friends," she told me. "He swears he took me to church and spanked me, but I just remember he got mad because I ate all of his [Frosted Flakes] and he sent me home."

At Florida State, Coach Prime began promoting himself as Prime Time—a nickname he earned in high school for his exploits on the basketball court—because he believed marketing himself as a brand would increase his value as a player since cornerbacks were near the bottom of the NFL pay scale.

It worked and helped him control the 1989 NFL draft.

He knew Troy Aikman was going to Dallas, and he told Green

Bay and Detroit that he wasn't going to play for either team. He had already signed a contract with the New York Yankees, so baseball was a viable option.

The Packers picked Tony Mandarich and the Lions selected Barry Sanders. Kansas City was more interested in Derrick Thomas and picked him fourth. That left Coach Prime for Atlanta, which is where he wanted to play.

"He always wanted to be in charge," Connie said. "He always wanted to run things."

CHAPTER 4

That was like a dagger in my chest.
—tight ends coach Tim Brewster

Coach Prime was an elite high school and college player. His sons were elite high school players, who received college scholarships. He understands the importance of recruiting and that's why he has a staff of coaches committed to doing it at the highest level.

Ray Forsett, the man they call Pretty Tony, and Otis Riddley—Coach O to JSU players and staff—believed they had an opportunity to add another game-changing recruit to their roster.

Forsett, one of Coach Prime's confidants, serves as JSU's unofficial chief of staff. They've been tight for more than a decade.

Forsett is the only person who knows what the players are doing in the dorms, around campus, and in the streets. When players screwed up, sooner or later somebody phoned or texted Forsett with the details and he'd relay the info to Coach Prime.

The former high school basketball coach is 6'3" and a couple of fried pork chops past 300 pounds. He has a bald head that's always covered by a baseball cap, an easy smile, and a bushy beard, and he's the kind of guy who could sell hay to a scarecrow like Big Yavo rapped in "Him."

Riddley, JSU's director of player personnel, is one of two hold-overs from the previous regime. T. C. Taylor, the receivers coach, is the other.

Coach Prime didn't want anything or anyone from the previous regime affecting his ability to create a new culture at JSU, which is standard coaching protocol. He kept them as a goodwill gesture to Robinson, who was partial to each man.

He loved Taylor's potential as a future head coach and he had been a star receiver at Jackson State from 1998 to 2001. Riddley, a Jackson native, earned a strong recommendation from Robinson's stepfather, who had seen his work up close as a high school coach.

Taylor was named tight ends coach, while Riddley was put in charge of recruiting, though he insisted on a fancier title.

"Director of recruiting can't be my title. I need to be director of player personnel," Riddley said. "I knew as a Black man my title is very important. Director of recruiting looks very different than director of player personnel.

"If I'm going to do this and pigeonhole myself, I'm going to set it up right from the start."

Forsett and Riddley stood on the sideline while the players stretched before an August practice, their hearts filled with optimism. They wanted Miles McVay, a four-star recruit from East St. Louis, Illinois, who would have every bit the impact Travis's signing had when he committed to JSU. When Travis, the No. 2 player on ESPN's 300 list of top recruits, signed with JSU, it meant no players were off-limits for JSU and other FCS schools. If FCS schools could compete with FBS schools for elite players, it would eventually close the gap between the two levels.

Signing McVay would prove getting Travis wasn't a fluke.

There are 133 FBS schools, which is the highest level of college football, and ten conferences. The five most powerful conferences—the Atlantic Coast Conference, Big Ten, Big 12, PAC-12, and Southeastern Conference—are nicknamed the Power 5 conferences. The other five FBS conferences are referred to as the Group of 5 conferences.

Schools in FBS can have 85 scholarship players, while FCS schools are limited to 63 scholarships.

McVay stood 6'7" and weighed 335 pounds. Sure, he had too much baby fat but you can't coach those long arms or that NFL body. Brewster, who recruited quarterback Vince Young to Texas, was McVay's lead recruiter.

Brewster is a relationship builder, a man who spends hours learning what motivates his players. He loves recruiting and being the underdog. Competing against Alabama for a player was the ultimate David-versus-Goliath story.

In this age of name, image, and likeness and collectives, the school with the most money usually gets its man. Getting McVay was always going to be a long shot, but the Tigers were in the conversation.

McVay was living with his father, but in the weeks leading up to his commitment he returned to his mom's house.

"I called mama at five this morning," said Brewster, walking off the practice field.

"It's her birthday, and I wanted to be the first one to wish her a happy birthday. We've got the mama and the uncle and everybody else who matters except the dad.

"I feel good about Miles. I called him last night and he picked up on the first ring. He wouldn't have done that if he wasn't interested."

Signing McVay would elevate JSU's program because the primary difference between FCS and FBS programs is on the line of scrimmage. Their linemen are bigger, faster, stronger, and more athletic at the FBS level. Getting McVay would be the catalyst for other offensive and defensive linemen to head to Mississippi's capital city.

At SWAC Media Day, a reporter asked Coach Prime if JSU would ever play Alabama.

"We're not ready to play Alabama right now," Coach Prime said, looking into the camera. "We have to get our trenches right first. When we do, we'll be ready to play them."

Clearly, he wanted McVay to hear that.

"Right then," said Riddley, "he was saying we need you."

Brewster attacked recruiting like a game.

"I love a recruiting battle like this," he said. "It gets my juices flow-ing. I'm in it to win it. There's no second place."

McVay held a press conference and announced his decision to attend Alabama.

"What did I tell you about there not being a second place in re-cruiting? That was like a dagger in my chest," Brewster said the next morning after practice. "But guess what? I'm back on that horse again. At the end, when he said it was a tough choice between Alabama and Jackson State, I can live with that."

In 2021, the Tigers had the top-rated recruiting class in FCS, as Shedeur became the highest-rated prospect to ever sign with Jack-son State. In 2022, Jackson State once again had the top-rated class in FCS, topped by Travis, the first five-star recruit to ever sign with an FCS program.

Jackson State uses a 40-40-20 philosophy. They want 40 per-cent of their recruits to come from the transfer portal, 40 percent graduate transfers, and 20 percent high school players.

Coach Prime likes transfers because they already know how to play. He likes grad transfers because those players are mature and play with urgency since they typically only have a year left. He only wants elite high school players or linemen they can develop for a couple of years.

Coach Prime lets position coaches pick their own players, which is unusual. Most schools have a recruiting board and they decide as a team who to recruit. Coach Prime lets his position coaches deter-mine the types of players they want to recruit.

"We don't recruit like you have this state or that state," he said. "Go get what you want."

Riddley works with Coach Prime to figure out how many players the Tigers want at each position group. Then he tells each assistant how many scholarships or how much scholarship money that posi-tion group has to spend.

When an assistant coach likes a player, he recommends him to Forsett, Riddley, and the coordinators. If they sign off on the player, he's presented to Coach Prime, who typically rubber-stamps the player because he trusts the coaches he hired and he wants them to have the tools they deem necessary to succeed.

"It's on you," Coach Prime will say if he's conflicted about a player. He almost always defers to the coach.

Riddley developed his own system for putting a recruiting board together. An FCS school with a $2.4 million football budget—Georgia's budget is $162.5 million—doesn't operate like a Power 5 program.

Players don't make JSU's recruiting board unless they make an official visit. On their visits, recruits heard about crowds of more than 50,000 at the Vet. They heard about the Sonic Boom of the South playing Mel Waiters's "Got My Whiskey" while the crowd sang along and they wanted to visit. The Tigers had 250 recruits at homecoming and nearly 350 for their regular-season game against Southern.

Clearly, Coach Prime's star power drew recruits to Jackson State. His social media presence provided a huge advantage. Coach Prime had 1.5 million Twitter followers. Only Michigan coach Jim Harbaugh had more, among college football coaches, with 1.9 million followers. Ole Miss coach Lane Kiffin was third with 629,700.

Coach Prime set himself apart on Instagram and that's the demographic he wanted because high school and college kids hang out on IG watching Reels for hours at a time.

He had 3.2 million IG followers, nearly ten times more than Kiffin (62,000), Harbaugh (68,500), Georgia's Kirby Smart (61,700), the University of Southern California's Lincoln Riley (61,500), and Ohio State's Ryan Day (49,900) combined.

In 2019, JSU had zero interactions—two-way communications—on Instagram, 20,276 on Twitter, and 4,247 on Facebook. At the end of the 2022 season, JSU had 901,538 Instagram interactions, 114,530 Twitter interactions, and 20,276 Facebook interactions.

"Before I even knew him, I was reading his tweets. I used to really like it and it used to help me," said reserve quarterback Matt Vitale. "I used to try to find purpose for why I'm going through what I'm going through. I never knew he could be my football coach, but I was like, I gotta see what it's all about and I gotta be in this environment."

Coach Prime's eldest son, Bucky, posts virtually all of his dad's IG content. Coach Prime asked Bucky to work for him a couple of months before the 2022 season. Bucky readily agreed. He already owned an apparel company and YouTube channel (Well Off Media) that he used to showcase his own rap videos as well as local Dallas talent. If he didn't enjoy working for his father he'd just return to Dallas.

"It's very hard working for him, but it's only hard when you don't know what to expect. When you know what to expect it is what it is," Bucky said. "You know he's just going to get mad and yell for a few seconds. You can't be weak or take stuff personal."

For Bucky, it's about controlling the season's narrative with videos that depict what's actually happening at JSU.

In addition to all the social media content, Amazon Prime Video has filmed a multi-episode documentary on the team each year. You can't play for this team if cameras bother you.

"These young dudes just want to be famous," Bucky said. "They want to be seen. We can gain you new followers."

Coach Prime demands as much from Bucky as from anyone else in the program. He's been praised and criticized in front of the team. Coach Prime approves every post, often making suggestions about the type of music bed he wants to accompany a post.

"At the end of the day, it's all about the goal of just being great. If you don't know that, it's going to be very hard," Bucky said. "You just have to fix your mind that when you're doing good enough it's not enough. You might think you're doing a good job, but you could actually do better and he's going to get that better out of you.

"He has to apply the same pressure to everybody, so everyone understands the tone and he don't play games. He can't show weakness to me. He has to show he can get on everybody's ass."

The result is college football's best social media presence.

Giving folks a look inside the program lets recruits and their parents see Coach Prime's range of emotions, humanizing him. At times he's a father, big brother, uncle, friend, mentor, motivator, counselor, confident, ass-kicker and problem-solver.

Coach Prime's IG page and Twitter posts drew recruits to the program because it's authentic content. Unlike most football coaches, who shroud their programs in secrecy and hide their players as though they might reveal state secrets, Coach Prime opened his football team to the world.

"We show the good, the bad, and the ugly. Him yelling in the locker room or him congratulating them in the locker room," Bucky said. "Behind-the-scene interactions between him and the players and him and the coaches. We just show more than people are used to seeing."

Coach Prime also gives Chris Neely, Charles Bishop and *Thee Pregame Show* access to the team. Neely posts content on Coach Prime's IG page and *Thee Pregame Show*'s social media platforms.

"I literally grew up on Pearl Street. I walked to middle school, I walked to high school, and I walked to college," said Neely, a lifelong Jackson resident, who once ran for mayor. "My entire life is within about two hundred to five hundred yards of Jackson State."

Everything in Jackson is better when the football team is winning and doing well. The team belongs to the city, something Coach Prime quickly figured out.

Instead of keeping the team to himself, he shared the program with the people who loved it. He invited former players to attend practices at specific times. He used social media to welcome fans and alums into the program. Doing so brought new fans who were unfamiliar with Jackson State before he became head coach.

There are many ways to share joy. Coach Prime does it with football.

CHAPTER 5

You go. I go. We go. That's kind of his deal.
        —tight ends coach Tim Brewster

When it became clear that Deion Sanders would get the Jackson State job, he told Andre' Hart and Kevin Mathis that he wanted them to join him.

They agreed without knowing exactly where they'd be working. Or how much they'd be making.

"I know his heart. He's not going to put you in a messed-up situation, and if it is, he's going to get your ass out of it," Mathis said. "His vision is different than everybody else's.

"If you ain't rolling with him, when it ain't looking great don't try to be a part of it later. He already sees the end. He don't want you with him, when the shit gets rolling. That ain't him. That ain't who he is."

Dennis Thurman and Michael Pollock received similar phone calls and pledged to follow him.

"You go. I go. We go. That's kind of his deal," tight ends coach Tim Brewster said. "He's got some guys on this staff who have been with him for fifteen years through the little flag football leagues. You talking about love. You talking about loyalty and you talking about respect."

When schools began considering Coach Prime for Power 5 jobs, athletic directors wondered whether he could create a quality staff. Most head coaches have friends on their staff because coaching is a relationship-based business. Coach Prime is no different, yet the questions persisted. Among African-American candidates, the story is common. It's the same reason coaches didn't let Black players play quarterback, center, or middle linebacker for years. Those were positions that required high intellect, mental toughness, and leadership and too many folks in power didn't think Black athletes could handle those jobs.

For an icon like Coach Prime, relationships should never have been a question. He played in the league for fourteen years and worked for the NFL Network for another fourteen. His list of contacts is limitless.

"You can see he's on a mission. He knows the goal for this team and he's on a mission to make sure everyone is on board," Mathis said. "He's talking about it every day. Every day. Every day. If something is out of line he's quick to correct it."

At the end of the 2021 season, Coach Prime called Mississippi State coach Mike Leach for offensive coordinator recommendations. In 1989, Hal Mumme and Leach created a one-back, four-receiver scheme—the Air Raid—at Iowa Wesleyan.

Brett Bartolone, who played receiver for Leach at Washington State before shoulder injuries ruined his career, is one of three coaches Leach recommended.

"When I first met him, we were on the whiteboard talking about schemes," said Shedeur. "He helped me look at the game with a different eye, a different view, a different light."

Coach Prime hired him and shifted T. C. Taylor to receivers coach. Mike Markuson, who had spent nearly twenty years in the SEC at Arkansas and Ole Miss, coached the offensive line.

Gary Harrell, nicknamed Flea, was the assistant head coach and running backs coach. Coach Prime believed Brewster elevated JSU's staff.

"He's tough. He's disciplined," Coach Prime said. "He can coach his butt off, and he has a lot of energy."

Brewster, among the staff fired at Florida, wasn't thrilled with his options.

Mo Sims, who was interviewing for JSU's strength and conditioning coach job, called Brewster. They had worked together at North Carolina, and Sims wanted to know if Brewster had heard about any openings. They wound up discussing a potential opportunity at JSU.

"Insecurity is a disease that permeates our profession," Brewster said. "This guy is a very secure man. He may be the realest cat I've ever been around. A lot of coaches wouldn't want his assistants talking to the team because they don't want to be outshined."

Coach Prime loved his offensive staff but believed his defensive staff was the nation's best.

It started with Thurman, who spent four years as defensive coordinator with the New York Jets and the Buffalo Bills. Jeff Weeks, who worked for Thurman at both places, coached the defensive tackles.

Trevor Reilly, drafted by the Jets when Thurman was the coordinator, coached the defensive ends. He did it for free because he wanted an opportunity, and JSU couldn't afford to pay him.

Mathis coached the secondary and Hart coached the linebackers.

Coach Prime met Mathis in 1997, when Mathis joined the Cowboys as a 5'9", 175-pound undrafted free agent cornerback from East Texas State.

Coach Prime quickly bonded with the rookie cornerback. Coach Prime started calling Mathis "Lil Fella" a few weeks into training camp. Coaching for TRUTH, Coach Prime's youth football and baseball organization, let Mathis, who had a nine-year NFL career, and Hart stay close to the game. Mathis enjoyed teaching kids fundamentals the way he had been taught growing up in Gainesville, a town of about 16,000 an hour north of Dallas.

Hart grew up in Arlington, a Dallas suburb, and played linebacker at Kansas State. When his career ended, he spent ten years as a business analyst making six figures before the lure of coaching snatched him, and he started volunteering at TRUTH.

Hart never met his daddy. His father's absence inspired him to become one of the state's top high school linebackers.

"If he wasn't going to come see me for who I was, he would come see me for what I did," Hart said. "I'm going to get some accolades and he'll come find me since I can't find him. When it didn't happen, I had to find another why because I was playing to find my dad."

For this staff, it's about showing young men how to receive love or be disciplined by another man. Those who didn't grow up with fathers in the home are often given the title of "man of the house" and treated accordingly by their mothers. That can make it hard to take orders from another man because they see it as a challenge to their manhood. After all, nobody tells the man of the house what to do. Sometimes they must be humbled or put their pride aside so the coaching staff can help them maximize their skill set.

"A coach is a leader of men, and I've been leading men since 1985," Coach Prime said. "I think God truly blessed me with the gift of connectivity to touch them in their chest and their hearts, reach them and try to build them up."

Growing up in a single-parent home in Knoxville, Tennessee, Sims's father figures were coaches. Sims, the strength and conditioning coach, wore No. 2 and a bandana just like Coach Prime as a high school safety.

"[Deion] is somebody I looked up to and somebody who did a lot for my life," Sims said. "He was like a father figure to me, even though I didn't know him. I never told him that."

Pollock, who filled in where needed and handled administrative duties, said, "I used to wear a headband around my neck 'cause he did. Anybody that played in that time wanted to be like Prime Time."

Alan Ricard played fullback for the Baltimore Ravens. When the University of Louisiana Monroe fired Ricard, his old teammate gave him a job coaching special teams.

Coach Prime is an old-school coach like those who taught him the game. He's demanding and blunt. He's economical with words, but doesn't mince them. He demands accountability.

Coach Prime gives his coaches, especially the coordinators, autonomy and latitude. Position coaches can start who they want—even if he disagrees. Coach Prime, who prefers independent thinkers, has no use for "yes men."

"There are days I don't even see him. Obviously, he makes suggestions but he gives you an opportunity to do your job," Bartolone said. "He wants certain guys in the game either to take advantage of someone or because they have the ability to make plays."

Coach Prime coaches to a standard—not an opponent. He demands maximum effort every play.

"He demands greatness. That's why I call him a hard-ass. If we win by fifty or win by ten he's going to be the same way every day," Taylor said. "He's going to be on coaches, players, and the cleaning crew. Everybody.

"Coach loves to win. All he knows is winning. If you don't have that appetite for winning you're not going to make it with him. We have to dominate. It has been preached. It's not just coaches and players. It's everybody."

Craig Campanozzi, nicknamed Campo, met Coach Prime at Florida State, when he was a team manager. Campo normally had the practice video ready for the coaches an hour after practice. The defense typically met first, then the offense. The meetings lasted about an hour.

Coach Prime rarely spoke, though he might ask about the scheme.

"Who has the tight end, if he goes down the seam? I don't want to be vulnerable there," he'd say.

Or he'd issue a reminder.

"Make sure you have the personnel in the game to do what you want to do. It's on you, if you don't," he'd say.

Coach Prime built this team to dominate and win a championship. To do so, he needed a strong staff.

PART II

CHAPTER 6

I want to send love to Jackson, Mississippi.
—Coach Prime

About six minutes remained in the fourth quarter of the Orange Blossom Classic at Hard Rock Stadium in Miami Gardens, Florida, and it was celebration time.

You can do that with a 59–3 lead.

First, T. C. Taylor and Michael Pollock walked toward Coach Prime.

"You called it," said Pollock, fist-bumping Coach Prime, who sat on a portable stool because his left foot throbbed when he stood too long.

Shedeur walked over to his famous father and knelt on one knee beside his dad, his right elbow resting on his father's left knee. They exchanged knowing smiles and an intimate conversation, while backup quarterback J. P. Andrade tried to lead yet another scoring drive against Florida A&M.

Robinson walked over followed by Associate Vice President for Athletics Alyse Wells-Kilbert.

"You told us this would happen!" she yelled. "You told us!"

She was talking about obliterating Florida A&M. The Rattlers' fan base had insinuated that its 7–6 loss in the 2021 Orange Blossom Classic was a fluke.

It wasn't.

In that game, JSU scored one touchdown in five trips to the red zone, committed three turnovers, and surrendered the ball on downs once. This game was about dominating FAMU and delivering a message about JSU's superiority.

"You've seen us win," Coach Prime said every time he spoke about the Tigers. "Now we want to dominate. That's how you get to the next level. You dominate where you're at."

Before JSU could dominate opponents, Coach Prime needed to teach his coaches and players how to dominate life. He spent countless hours teaching his staff and players the importance of consistency and discipline.

He wanted players to dominate fatherhood. And business. And life.

Consistency, he'd tell them, is about attacking practice and life with the same vigor every day. It's about creating habits that lead to success. Discipline teaches players and coaches how to fight through the adversity on and off the field. Discipline is doing what must be done, with passion, regardless of whether you feel like it.

Focus is about eliminating distractions and winning the moment. Do that enough times, he told them, and you'll win the day.

You can find this information in a hundred different self-help books. But Coach Prime delivered the message eloquently and consistently and it eventually seeped into his players' souls.

Coach Prime is direct and confrontational without cursing. The strongest words he ever uses are "durn" and "bull junk." Occasionally, he says "pissed off."

The lessons Coach Prime taught his players and staff became even more meaningful during a water crisis that forced the team to live away from its dorms, apartments, and homes during the season's first two weeks.

Two days of heavy rain in Jackson the week before the Orange Blossom Classic led to flash flooding, overwhelming the city's antiquated water system and breaking it.

Five days before the Orange Blossom Classic, Coach Prime arrived on campus at 5 a.m. to discover low water pressure and no air-conditioning. He immediately canceled the daily team meeting, which begins about 7:15 a.m., and began working as a crisis manager.

"How in the hell you ain't figured out the water problem? It's been thirty years," a frustrated Taylor said between phone calls to each of his seventeen receivers on the roster.

When the annoyed coaches weren't complaining, they fed their roster information about who needed housing to Bartolone, who wrote it on the bottom right corner of the whiteboard in the team meeting room with a black marker.

QB = 3
TE = 2
RB = 5
WR = 17
DLine = 16
LB = 6
DB = 10
ST = 5

Campus shut down. Students took classes online. The team relocated to the Sheraton Flowood, where JSU houses its players before home games.

"The world would see it as a challenge as we deal with the water situation in Jackson," said Coach Prime, "but since I've been here we've dealt with the pandemic, we've dealt with ice storms, and now we're dealing with the water crisis.

"We're good. This city, this town is resilient. This is who they are. All you have to do is instill hope."

In early 2021, a winter storm created a similar issue and residents didn't have water for more than a week. The water issue has been created by years of neglect in a city that's 82 percent black. Jackson has a low tax base because the state of Mississippi is the city's largest employer.

"Growing up in Jackson is rough. I've had a lifetime of boil-water alerts. But honestly it literally prepares you for the worst. So when the worst happens you can still keep rolling," said Demarcus Leflore, a volunteer member of the JSU's video film crew who played the tenor drum in 2013 for the Sonic Boom.

"I love Jackson from the bottom of my heart. There's a sense of pride because when you come from the bottom you can't go any lower."

A boil advisory had been in place since July, meaning residents boiled water before using it for cooking, drinking, or bathing. One local restaurant spent about $10,000 a month just on water to cook.

Mayor Chokwe Antar Lumumba spoke with President Joe Biden and Vice President Kamala Harris about the situation. Governor Tate Reeves declared a state of emergency and President Biden signed paperwork that freed up federal funds to help Jackson's residents.

"Until it is fixed, it means we do not have reliable running water at scale," Reeves said in a statement. "It means the city cannot produce enough water to reliably flush toilets, fight fire, and meet other critical needs."

During times like this, football matters more than usual. Mississippi doesn't have a professional sports team, so Jackson State's football team belongs to the city. Those who didn't go to JSU have friends or family who did.

Jackson is among the country's poorest cities and Mississippi is one of the least-educated states. The city's vibe is better when JSU wins because it provides hope to a city devoid of it.

There's a lot of pain in the city, and folks use whatever they can find as a salve. Some use drugs, while others walk up and down Martin Luther King Drive with brown paper bags hiding bottles of brown or clear elixirs. Folks work hard, but escaping poverty without education and opportunity is like trying to get out of a labyrinth without a map.

A victory over FAMU would provide Jackson with the briefest of respites, but it would be better than nothing. Coach Prime had his own issues before the game, when he learned his mom's mother, Hattie Mae Mims, had died.

"Grandma had a good run. Grandma was well into her nineties. Grandma was the matriarch of our family. Grandma was the one who took me to church. Grandma was the one who taught me about the lord," Coach Prime said after the game. "Grandma was the one I stayed with when I was ignorant. Grandma was the one who whipped my butt. . . .

"Grandma was a God-fearing woman until the day she left. Grandma was everything. So, I lost a real, a real woman. We're all going through something, but I had to do what needed to be done."

While Coach Prime worked through his grief, he also needed to decide whether Travis would make his college debut against FAMU.

Three days before the game, Travis was eating with Forsett, Mathis, and Rashad Davis, a grad assistant who worked with the receivers.

"You let the dude run right past you today," Mathis said. "You 7-Eleven. They were open all day."

Travis laughed.

"But did you see my catch-up speed? That was the only time they got past me all day," he said. "I didn't give up one catch."

Davis suggested he play offense, if he wasn't ready for defense. All eyes turned toward Bartolone, who was sitting at an adjacent table.

"Fuck yeah," he said. "You can run the post and the slot fade."

Defensive coordinator Dennis Thurman wanted Travis to play, but he was fine letting others make the decision.

"You know you ain't getting no shot," Forsett said. "I know you got a bunch of crazy stuff rolling around in your head, so I'm just telling you what's not happening."

Travis said, "What's crazy is I was thinking about that, but I know you can't shoot into the bone."

The ballroom where Jackson State's players ate dinner less than forty-eight hours before the season opener was just about empty. The players, after a lively team meeting, had been dismissed to their position-group meetings followed by a late-night snack and then bed at 10 p.m.

Coach Prime, sitting alone at a round banquet table, scooped out a plate full of yellow rice and shredded chicken from a large rectangular Tupperware bowl. He had eaten a few spoonfuls when Mathis sauntered up to him and leaned on a chair.

"You know he thinks he can just turn it on in a game but it don't work that way," Mathis said.

"Who?" asked Coach Prime.

"Twelve," Mathis said.

Travis practiced for the first time since the spring six days before the Orange Blossom Classic. He did individual drills and rehab work on Monday and participated fully on Wednesday and Friday.

"He's a warrior. He's tough. He's wanted to fight through it but this man is going to have a career—not just a moment. I feel like his name is going to be set in stone one day," Coach Prime said during a zoom call with ESPN announcers Tiffany Greene and Jay Walker.

"He's a workaholic and he's in good shape, but when people see Travis they want to see Travis. That's on me. I can't selfishly throw him out there. I have to give him the best possibility to be who he is."

Five hours before the game, Travis sat in a banquet hall at the Hilton Aventura hotel with his right foot elevated by two pillows. Ninety minutes before the game, the same scene played out in front of his locker.

The locker room scene before the Orange Blossom Classic would've given most coaches heart palpitations. DJ Jamie—turntables and all—set up in the locker room and played NBA YoungBoy, Finesse2tymes, and Young Dolph, among others.

Amazon Prime Video's camera crew shot video, while showrunner Anthony Smith wondered how much it was going to cost to use the video that contained the various artists' music in the background.

"They're probably gonna make us pay out the ass," he said with a wry grin. "The only good thing is Coach Prime is close with a lot of these guys, so a few of them might cut us a break."

In addition to Amazon's crew, Bucky and Neely and Charles Bishop from *Thee Pregame Show* shot footage for use on their various platforms. Gillie da King and Wallo, who host the *Million Dollaz Worth of Game* podcast on Barstool, were getting the players hyped by going live on Instagram.

The locker room scene is straight out of Miami's Club LIV, South Beach's hottest night club.

"If you had your phone out playing music at Alabama, they'd kick you out of the locker room," said punter Sam Johnson, who played two years at Alabama. "I get here and there's a DJ and everybody is dancing in the locker room. It gives you a little energy before the game."

Jan Patterson, Miss Jan to most folks, the unofficial team photographer, walked around snapping pictures. Her identical twin sons—Josh and Jake—played for Coach Prime's TRUTH organization in 2010.

Jan, a single parent, immersed herself in the program.

"I was really trying to give back because of my sobriety and when I found TRUTH it just connected with me," she said. "It connected with my AA where I found my higher power, which is God and it just all connected with me."

Jan, an alcoholic, said she's been sober since Valentine's Day 2007, when a judge threatened to take her sons away and sentence her to 120 days in jail if she failed another Breathalyzer test. At the time, she had been arrested for driving while intoxicated multiple times, and twice failed the Breathalyzer installed on her vehicle.

"I haven't had a drink since," she said. "I loved my kids more than I loved alcohol, and I wanted to change."

Once her kids were too old to play for TRUTH, she volunteered to take photos of Coach Prime's various athletic teams at Prime Prep, Trinity Christian, and Jackson State. Miss Jan pays for her own lodging and flights to Jackson and the road games.

Coach Prime provides love and a sideline pass.

"Jan has a powerful story," Coach Prime said.

Ten minutes before kickoff, Travis met in Coach Prime's office with Forsett and the cameramen for the Amazon Prime Video documentary to discuss whether he'd make his much anticipated debut.

The meeting lasted two minutes, thirteen seconds.

On the field just before kickoff, Travis pulled in Coach Prime for a long embrace. He wept as he thanked Coach Prime for the chance to play.

"It was so emotional for me and Coach Prime because I wasn't with the team during the summer having surgery," he said. "It was very emotional because I hadn't seen him that much since I got back with the team.

"When I walked in the meeting, I didn't think I was going to play. But he told me I could and I was so happy."

It was an easy decision for Coach Prime because he asked himself what Florida State coach Bobby Bowden would've done for him in that situation.

All of that is why Coach Prime enjoyed JSU's near-flawless performance over FAMU so much.

Shedeur passed for 323 yards and a school-record five touchdowns. The defense recorded four sacks, forced three turnovers, and scored two touchdowns.

After Ke'Vric Wiggins returned a third-quarter interception 35 yards for a touchdown, Coach Prime walked over to the group of players celebrating and yelled, "Is this fun? Is this fun?"

Tight end Hayden Hagler extended the lead to 45–3 when he slipped out of the backfield and caught a two-yard touchdown pass with 2:02 left in the third quarter. Aubrey Miller Jr.'s 19-yard fumble return made it 52–3 early in the fourth quarter.

"I want to send love to Jackson, Mississippi. I know throughout the game it was like an escape for a lot of people who are dealing with this consistent water situation that we're dealing with as well," Coach Prime said. "If we can give them the escape we did today, their resilience and their mental toughness will show. I'm just thankful we can do it."

After the trophy presentation, Shedeur made sure the fans who made the trip had an opportunity to take cell phone pictures and videos of him and his teammates celebrating with the trophy. Then the players took a group photo.

"We do this for the city—Jackson, Mississippi, first and foremost. My pops taught me this. When you're in life and you have everything, you still need people around you," Shedeur said. "You could have everything in the world and still be lonely. To share this moment with all my guys—the people we work with every day—was beautiful."

CHAPTER 7

I'm loyal to winning.
—Coach Prime

Soon after Alejandro Mata arrived on campus, Coach Prime nicknamed him Squiggy, after a sitcom character from a TV show that ended twenty years before he was born.

Squiggy, just so you know, was the obnoxious but lovable character from *Laverne & Shirley*, which ran on ABC from 1976 to 1983 and starred Penny Marshall and Cindy Williams. The show was about a pair of roommates and their escapades in Milwaukee, set in the 1950s. Squiggy and his best friend, Lenny, were Laverne and Shirley's upstairs neighbors.

Mata, the 5'9", 190-pound kicker with jet-black hair, a round face, a wisp of facial hair, and a slight paunch, was thrilled Coach Prime noticed him.

"He saw me and said, 'You look like Squiggy, so I'm gonna call you Squiggy from now on,'" Mata remembered. "I didn't know who that was, but a nickname from Coach Prime? I'd take that any day. Neely showed me a picture of Squiggy and I saw the resemblance."

On one of the country's most talented FCS teams, it's fair to say no one figured a freshman kicker from Buford, Georgia, an hour north of Atlanta, would receive the crystal egg-shaped trophy for being named MVP of the 33rd Southern Heritage Classic in Memphis.

But that's what happened after Mata kicked field goals of 28, 27, and 30 yards in a 19–3 win over Tennessee State at the Liberty Bowl.

Traditionally, Buford has one of the state's top programs, so Riddley inquired about a few players.

"In my conversation with the coach, he doesn't even mention Mata but I came across an article where, as a junior he kicked the game-winning field goal in the 6A state championship over [teammate] Baron Hopson's team," he said. "So I called the coach back and asked, 'Where is the kicker? I need more info.' I sent Mata to our kicking consultant and he loved him."

Longtime NFL punter Louie Aguilar is JSU's kicking consultant.

Riddley found Mata, Ricard found Gerardo Baeza, and each plays a valuable role on the Tigers. Mata handles extra points and field goals, while Baeza kicks off.

Until Riddley phoned, Mata didn't have any scholarship offers. Riddley figured the championship game experiences would make him more prepared to help JSU win championships.

Coach Prime wanted players competing at every position, every practice, whether they're kickers, receivers, or linemen. The best players play.

"I'm loyal to winning," he told his staff during one personnel meeting. It didn't matter who the player was or how big their natural talent.

At Thursday's practice, Pollock had grown weary of Tony Gray complaining about being on the scout team. The scout team prepares the starters for the game by running the opponents' plays. The coaching staff had to play Tony their first two seasons at JSU because they didn't have anyone better. That was no longer the case.

"He's been given several opportunities at several schools to display his talent," said Pollock, who coached him in high school. "It's disappointing for him not to realize his God-given ability. All the kid had to do was work and do what he's supposed to do and he could be an NFL player. There's no doubt he has that kind of talent.

"I've known him for a long time, so I'm disappointed for him. We have standards. He's a young adult, he's not a kid."

Well, Gray wasn't going to get to display his talent against Tennessee State in Week 2 at the Southern Heritage Classic in Memphis, because Coach Prime suspended him for three games.

Just before the start of the season, Coach Prime tried one more tactic to motivate Tony. During an offensive line meeting, Coach Prime walked in and asked every offensive lineman to give their thoughts on Tony—good or bad—as he listened.

"I went to the bathroom and I came back and walked in on that," Willis Patrick said. "I said, 'I'm not partaking in this, man.' He knows his talent level. He knows what he could be. He knows he has NFL potential.

"He sitting there smiling, happy as one-two-three. I don't have to tell him how good he is. I didn't say a word. I want to see him work. I want to see him do it. He's one of the most gifted offensive linemen I've ever seen in my life."

Talent alone wouldn't get Tony into the NFL. Or even back into JSU's starting lineup. He needed to work.

When it was time for Coach Prime to speak during Friday's team meeting, the plan was for the team to watch Bucky's highlight video from the FAMU win.

When Coach Prime called for the video, Quonte Salley, nicknamed Q, couldn't get the laptop attached to the white projector to work. The Bluetooth speaker in the ballroom connected to Trevor Reilly's cell phone instead of his.

Coach Prime lacks patience. He didn't want to hear about any computer, Bluetooth, or internet issues.

"He should've had a couple practice runs way before Prime asked for it," Taylor said the next morning. "You know how the man is."

For Q, it was bitter moment.

After all, he left a job as an assistant student coach at McPherson College, an NAIA school, in Kansas because he wanted to work for Coach Prime, even though he didn't know him, didn't have a job, and wasn't enrolled at Jackson State.

In January, his parents dropped him off with nothing but faith that God would make a way.

"It was really intriguing for a Hall of Fame football coach at an HBCU around the time of the George Floyd death," said Q, "and I wanted to be a part of that."

Persistence created an opportunity.

Q worked out each morning about the same time as some of the coaches, so they would get used to seeing him. Once he enrolled in school, Q found a job at a liquor store. He didn't have a car, so it required three different buses and an hour to get to his job and two buses to travel from his apartment to campus.

Finally, Dennis Driscoll, then in charge of media relations, agreed to help Q connect with the football team, if he worked in the media relations department. His break occurred when JSU made Q part of its video team.

After Q's mistake, Coach Prime continued with Part 2 of his presentation.

"There's something about this song DT is gonna love," he said. "Coach Markuson is gonna love it. Everybody who's my age, like Coach Brewster, is gonna love it. It's in my spirit and I can't get it out. Come on, Bucky, help me out. Some of y'all were probably conceived from this song."

Seconds passed and the music hadn't started.

"You should've went over this stuff before we got in here. We talk about the players doing their jobs and y'all ain't doing your durn job," Coach Prime said. "Y'all want to walk around and take every picture and be in every durn thing like you part of the team and you can't do your durn job.

"Five. Four. Three."

Suddenly "Let's Do It Again" by the Staples Singers blared from a large floor speaker in the back of the room. Thurman started two-stepping with an imaginary woman, who's clearly the finest woman in the club. Then Brewster boogied to the front of the room.

An impromptu *Soul Train* line began with Shane Hooks followed by Caleb Jolivette. Several others joined before the music faded out.

All week, JSU's coaching staff harped on Tennessee State's running game. Eddie George, the former Ohio State and Tennessee Titan running back, coached Tennessee State, and he was building a team in his own image.

George punished anyone bold enough to try to tackle him in a nine-year career that saw him gain 10,442 yards and score 76 touchdowns.

A game that JSU's players and coaches expected to win handily was a struggle from the start because the Tigers played an awful first quarter.

The Tigers fumbled twice, had a field goal blocked, and went 0-2 in the red zone but only trailed 3–0 after the first quarter.

"They soft as fuck!" Nyles Gaddy screamed to his teammates after TSU took a 3–0 lead on an 11-play, 58-yard drive. "They soft as fuck! This should be a highlight game. They shouldn't get shit. It should be a long game for them."

Jackson State led 6–3 at halftime.

Thurman stood in a corner of the coach's section holding his flip card, seething. He noticed Nyles and Devonta Davis and called them over.

"Hey, Gaddy, you're one of those dudes," Thurman said. "Get your guys going."

Then he turned to Weeks.

"They're not scoring in the second half. We took the best they've got," Thurman said. "Fuck them. We can't lose if they don't score. They're not scoring."

Coach Prime spent most of halftime in his office.

"We feel terrible that we're only winning by a small margin. You know why? Because we're not dominating," Coach Prime said. "Let's get your head out of your butt, go out there and dominate."

A 30-yard field goal by Mata pushed the lead to 9–3 and Shedeur's 27-yard touchdown pass to Willie Gaines clinched the win.

"Willie might take one to the house," Taylor had said on the bus ride to the game. "We got some dawgs on this team but he's a dawg's dawg. He ain't scared of nothing."

While Willie was ascending on the roster, Malachi was still searching for a role. Taylor wanted to start building Malachi's confidence, so he devised a plan to position him for success.

"We gave him a wristband with ten slots and all of them say 'fade,'" Taylor said laughing. "He doesn't have to think, just play.

"I think he'll score. I'm going to put him in position to score and we'll see what happens."

Malachi played one snap.

"I put him out there to run his play and the corner throat-slammed him. I've been telling him that he comes out of his release too high," Taylor said a few days later. "Well, the corner grabbed him by the throat and then he tried to get loose inside and by the time he got back outside No. 2 had already thrown the ball.

"It was embarrassing. I had to get him out of there. I wasn't going to let him embarrass himself or me. He actually went up to Prime to plead his case during the game but he saw the same thing I did."

The Tigers won without Malachi, but needed him to be dynamic for this offense to reach its apex.

Mata, Shedeur, and Nyles, who had four sacks, accompanied Coach Prime to the postgame news conference.

Last season, Nyles was supposed to do what James Houston did. Gaddy was supposed to be that dude. Houston had 16.5 sacks and 24.5 tackles for loss. Nyles played well early and was designated a "leader," but Coach Prime eventually stripped him of that title.

"When I was watching film, I saw the left tackle every three steps, he's going to punch and the right tackle gives up the inside as soon as he turns his shoulders," Nyles said. "I used power with the left tackle and ripped inside with the right tackle."

Coach Prime liked his approach.

"He's causing havoc. We thought he had a few sacks last week, so we checked and that wasn't the case and it upset him because he thought he had them," Coach Prime said. "He didn't want to leave with the same feeling he had last week. He left a lot of meat on the bone last season and someone else ate and he's not happy about it.

"He's not happy seeing somebody get all the accolades and all the attaboys. He's not happy with that. He wants that. He's hungry. He practices at that level and he prepares. Those intricate things he just told you that should let you know how detailed he is about his game and getting to the next level."

For Nyles, the sacks validated his offseason work. The former walk-on at Tennessee transferred to JSU and was Coach Prime's second recruit. Shedeur was his first.

"We have an expectation. We expect to be dominant. People who came to the game expect us to be dominant. Even the opposing team pretty much expects us to be dominant and we have to fulfill those expectations to our teammates and ourselves first," Coach Prime said. "The standard is a new standard. We won 16–3 with a decent defensive game and we're pissed-off.

"Do you understand how we think? That's the level where we are. We expect to be dominant. We're going to get back on the practice field tomorrow and we're going to work."

In the locker room, the players spoke in hushed tones after showering and dressed quickly. The lucky ones grabbed a couple of Chick-fil-A sandwiches on a table as they left the locker room.

A few members of the support staff had grabbed sandwiches, which meant some players made the three-hour bus ride home on empty stomachs. This is life at HBCUs, where nothing can be taken for granted—not even a postgame sandwich.

CHAPTER 8

If I don't blitz on ten of the first fifteen plays,
I'll give somebody else the script.
—defensive coordinator Dennis Thurman

The boil-water notice ended on September 14, 2022—forty-four days after it began in late July. Demarcus Leflore, nicknamed Filmanati, rejoiced. Filmanati shoots and creates videos for JSU's football program to use on its various social media pages.

He works for free.

"I had to understand I was going to be out here every day working and not getting paid," he said, "but the opportunities that would come up in the next six months or year would make up for all of the time I was out here."

A workout video he created for JSU cornerback De'Jahn "Nugget" Warren in the spring of 2022 led to the opportunity.

During the season, he arrived around 7 a.m. and spent the next eight hours or so shooting and editing. With the ban lifted, Filmanati no longer had to make the daily drive down Interstate 20 West each morning to Bolton for clean water.

"I have to drive forty-five minutes to my mom's house just to shower and be back in time for practice," he said. "You just have to roll with the punches in Jackson."

A 2023–24 *U.S. News & World Report* analysis of the top 150 most populous metropolitan areas showed Jackson ranked 120. Mississippi, which has a higher percentage of Black residents than any other state (38.8 percent), has a poverty rate of 19.6 percent. The median household income is $45,081, about $17,000 less than the national average.

Mississippi has one of the country's highest rates for diabetes. Obesity and premature death rates are high, too. It's a state where only 22 percent of folks twenty-five or older have college degrees, about 10 percent lower than the national average.

Jackson, Mississippi's largest city, has seen its population plummet from 202,895 in 1980 to 149,761 in 2022 because locals see it as a place without hope. In 1980, Jackson was the country's 71st largest city. These days, it ranks 177. The number of students in Jackson public schools has dipped from 28,780 to 18,874 from the 2014–15 school year until now, according to the *Jackson Clarion-Ledger*.

The system, locals believe, works against them.

"People stay here because it's all they've ever known," Riddley said. "Or they don't have enough money to leave."

Tysha Stewart, a corporate event guru based in Jackson, orchestrated Coach Prime's events. She also designed his office space from the plush fire-engine-red carpet to the custom-designed desk.

"I'm really only here because my family is here. That's the truth," she said. "We're looked down on here in Mississippi. People feel like there's no talent here. They feel like you're just looking to eat watermelon and go home."

Ashton Johnson's mom and several relatives graduated from Jackson State. Like most kids who grew up around JSU football, Johnson imitated the Sonic Boom drum majors when he wasn't pretending to be a football player.

"There are a lot of things that go in Jackson that are messed up," said Johnson, who grew up fifteen minutes north of the city. "We don't have the infrastructure to keep things going.

"Being from Jackson is harder than being from a lot of other places. After one game we played, there were no shootings that night and that was a big deal. It was incredible."

Jackson had 138 murders in 2022, which was 22 fewer than the 160 that occurred in 2021, according to a WLBT-TV analysis. Jackson led the nation with murders per capita at 92.1. New Orleans ranked second at 74.3.

Coach Prime understood all of this. It's the primary reason he wanted home games to start at 1 p.m.

He arrived at his office each morning, making the forty-minute drive down Interstate 55 South from his home in Canton. An elliptical and an ab machine were to the left of his desk. He spent thirty minutes on the elliptical, while he watched the local news to better understand the city's vibe.

Coach Prime spent time in the city. When he found a restaurant he liked—whether it was a chain like Waffle House or Cracker Barrel or a local joint like Iron Horse Grill or Johnny T's Bistro & Blues—he visited frequently.

He preferred a corner booth or a table in the back where he drew little attention. It was a bonus when the staff remembered his order. He frequently visited mom-and-pop spots and shouted them out on Instagram. Coach Prime occasionally ate Sunday dinner at the home of strangers, who promised a delicious meal.

He made Jackson his home. He embraced the community and it loved him. They shouted "Coach Prime! Coach Prime!" wherever he went, hoping for a glance, a nod, or a wave.

Coach Prime enjoyed feeling part of the community and, selfishly, he liked to be seen around town so often that his presence no longer created a stir.

As part of the community, Coach Prime met with city leaders, pastors, and gang leaders to understand from different perspectives how Jackson operates.

"It's unusual for someone of his stature to have that level of humility and wisdom to make that important to him," said Chokwe Lumumba, Jackson's mayor since 2017. "He pops up at local restaurants. He wants to be more than a football coach. He wants to lift up the community."

When the mood was right, Coach Prime took selfies with fans. Each time, he flashed a perfect smile. He hated mediocrity, so if he's posing for a picture, he did it well.

He also visits nursing homes because he likes bringing joy to elderly people.

Lumumba moved to Jackson in 1988 from New York via Detroit as a youngster because his father was doing human rights and social justice work to make America better.

"Jackson State football is one of the things that gives the city of Jackson a sense of place," Lumumba said. "We didn't see Black college football. We didn't see the Sonic Boom. It's a different event. It's a different occasion.

"A good portion of the people in [The Vet] never went to Jackson State or spent significant time on campus. They love it because they're from Jackson—not because it's their alma mater."

When he entered the team meeting the night before the Grambling game, the city of Jackson was on his mind. He knows the people here are hurting. Despair hangs in the air like fog. Jackson State football provides a beacon.

All of that was on his mind when he addressed his players before their first home game. It was going to be Jackson's first look at the only thing in the city Black folks can brag about.

"We're putting on for the city tomorrow and that's a little different," Coach Prime told them. "The city has been through a lot since we've been here.

"We had the ice storm, then the tribulations with the water, and we've all persevered and the city has as well. They're looking for you to give them hope and give them love and give them an escape and satisfaction—and I think we're going to do that."

The coaching staff respected Hue Jackson, the former Oakland Raiders and Cleveland Browns coach, and knew he'd have Grambling ready to play its best football. They also knew that Grambling, which lost its first two games, didn't have the personnel to compete with JSU.

Jackson wouldn't be coaching Grambling if Coach Prime weren't coaching JSU. His success at JSU and the publicity he brought the university are among the reasons Grambling hired Jackson.

Coach Prime wanted Jackson to succeed just like he wanted Tennessee State's Eddie George, Alabama State's Eddie Robinson Jr., and Prairie View's Bubba McDowell to succeed.

The more good coaches with NFL backgrounds coaching at HBCUs, the more the standard will rise because they know how quality organizations are run. Better coaches should lead to better staffs and better players, which eventually leads to more exposure and more players getting drafted.

Last year, 19 different NFL organizations sent scouts to JSU. In the 2022 season, all 32 teams had sent representatives by September 22.

Coach Prime believed HBCU programs should be run like scaled-down Power 5 programs, not glorified high school programs. They're not because they lack resources.

Jackson State is an exception. So is Prairie View, which has excellent facilities, and a few others. Coach Prime used his resources and connections to upgrade the locker room and players' lounge, provide dining services, and get a new practice field installed. Robinson excelled at raising money so Prairie View could have several new facilities built.

Too many other schools lag, though they're trying to catch up quickly.

"I'm very transparent. There's nothing to hide. We ask them to come join us and do things necessary to make that happen," Jackson said. "We don't need to have long bus rides. There are certain things from a resource standpoint we struggle with and we gotta have those things now. We should've had them yesterday."

No matter how much Coach Prime wanted his former NFL colleagues to do well, he didn't want them to have success against him. Neither did Thurman.

So he prepared a game plan designed to attack from start to finish.

"If I don't blitz on ten of the first fifteen plays I'll give somebody else the script. We're going to come out firing. Whether you guys are hot or I have to get you hot. We're going to come out and open up on this football team.

"I love Hue Jackson. We coached together for five years, but we're gonna kick his ass."

The Vet also had to be prepared for the opener, which was going to be televised on ESPN3. The Tigers' win over Tennessee State was its only game not nationally televised on one of ESPN's platforms.

The stadium situation was a mess in 2020, so Robinson hired Terence Johnson from Alabama State to fix it. Johnson, a former marine, is the kind of make-it-happen person Robinson and Coach Prime respect.

He provides solutions to problems and he doesn't accept excuses or make them. Johnson is 5'7" with close-cropped hair, usually hidden with a baseball cap, and a goatee. He wears glasses with a thick plastic frame.

Johnson's biggest concerns before the season were crowd flow and concession lines. In 2021, fans could only enter the stadium through one of two gates. Fans who arrived just before kickoff might not make it into the stadium and find their seat until halftime.

Johnson opened up all of the stadium gates for fans to enter and it was a much better, faster-moving process. In the past, concession lines had been notoriously long and slow. A second-quarter trip to Sha's Grill, where you can order fried catfish ($14), chicken livers and gizzards ($8), or fried green tomatoes ($10), might result in missing a part of the Sonic Boom of the South's halftime performance.

The lines moved faster but were still too long and too slow, and on a steamy day in Jackson they ran out of water and Gatorade in the second half.

"That was totally unacceptable," Johnson recalled. "I made sure they ordered twice as much this week."

New speakers were added outside the stadium and inside the locker room. The secondary scoreboard was operational for the first time in years and a fresh coat of blue paint was slapped on a backdrop to the end zone so it would pop on the television broadcast.

Then Coach Prime, the marketing genius, had nineteen red theater seats placed on a red stage around the twenty-yard line for his VIP guests.

On this day rapper Young Dolph's family and friends, like Key Glock, occupied the seats. Young Dolph, a good friend of Shedeur, was killed in 2021. Coach Prime and JSU honored his family before the game with a ribbon-cutting ceremony.

The television news program *60 Minutes* conducted a pregame interview with Robinson for a thirteen-minute segment that would be televised the day after they played Bethune-Cookman.

Then it was time to blow out Grambling. Or so they thought.

Cam'Ron Silmon-Craig recovered a fumble on the game's third play—Aubrey forced it—and the turnover set up Shedeur's one-yard touchdown run and a 7–0 lead. The defense forced a punt and Sy'Veon Wilkerson's three-yard touchdown run made it 14–0.

Just like that, JSU was on the verge of blowing out Grambling.

Anthony Balancier, A.B. to friends and family, had figured out a tendency during the week that gave one of the best FCS defenses an advantage.

Balancier, a graduate assistant, noticed that Grambling quarterback Quaterius Hawkins kept his feet together on running plays before the snap. On passing plays he moved his right foot about six inches in front of his left foot.

"I went to the film and it was one hundred percent. I looked at the next game and it was one hundred percent, too," he said. "I told the other coaches to check it out to make sure I wasn't tripping."

The staff shared the information with the players during their position meetings.

"During the game," Balancier said, "I'll say 'rabbit' if it's a run and 'bird' if it's a pass."

The one element of JSU's defense that concerned the coaching staff was busted assignments that led to big plays. In the first two games, neither opponent had driven the ball and scored without help from JSU in the form of penalties, turnovers, or mental mistakes.

"Fitting in the right gap. Staying in the right gap. Trust. Communication," Hart said. "There is no trust. We have a bunch of motherfuckers who fly around right now and they make plays with a scheme that is pretty simple. It doesn't require much thinking."

Well, Maurice Washington went 78 yards up the middle for a touchdown because someone didn't maintain their gap integrity and suddenly it was 14–7. Eleven seconds later, Shedeur fumbled and Bryan Powell returned it 17 yards for a touchdown, tying the score at 14–14.

JSU led 21–17 at halftime.

"You don't want to dominate. You just want to win. You don't want to go pro, you just want to be good," Coach Prime said. "We got a few people who want to dominate but that's it. We don't have any leaders; we have a bunch of followers.

"Someone take it upon themselves and lead. What we just did out there was pathetic. Pathetic."

The tirade lasted forty-one seconds.

"This is what's wrong with y'all," Thurman yelled at a group of defensive players who moved too slowly for his liking. "Half of you are asleep and half of you are pouting."

Thurman rarely raises his voice. He prefers to reason with players, though his words can be as sharp as a Ginsu knife.

"They're the worst fucking team we've played, but we're in a game because we didn't come out ready to go. We're everybody in the SWAC's championship game," he said. "Anybody loafing, your ass is coming out. This is the worst fucking team we've played and you're not running to the ball or getting off blocks.

"You better run to the football like your life depended on it or you're coming out and you will not come back in the game."

As the Sonic Boom wrapped up its performance, Tupac's "All Eyez on Me" blared from the locker room speakers. Coach Prime reappeared just before the end of halftime.

"Fellas, I don't need to scream at y'all no more. I don't need to yell," he said softly. "Let's fix those errors. Let's make all the plays we missed and go dominate the second half. It's not too late to dominate."

Shedeur hit Dallas Daniels in stride on a crossing route they failed to execute in the first half for a 26-yard touchdown and a 28–17 lead on the first drive of the second half.

"We had it in the first half, we just needed Shedeur to see it and throw it," Bartolone recalled. "Sometimes, you just need that one throw and then everything else opens up."

Andrade, the backup quarterback, entered the game with 4:35 left and a 59–24 lead, but JSU throws the ball no matter who's playing quarterback or the score.

This was also an opportunity for Taylor to get a forgotten member of the team on the field. Enter Malachi, who had played one snap in the first two games.

On third-and-seven from the Grambling 46, Andrade found Malachi down the right sideline. Malachi leaped high, made a contested catch, shrugged off a defender, and cut inside before being dragged down at the 17. On the next play, Andrade hit Malachi, who broke a tackle and stumbled into the end zone for his first touchdown of the season.

Jackson State 66, Grambling 24.

His teammates were ecstatic. They hugged, high-fived, and slapped his shoulder pads as he walked down the sideline after exiting the end zone. When he saw Coach Prime talking to Thurman, he waited patiently behind him before he tapped him on the right shoulder.

They exchanged a quick hug and a few words. As Malachi walked away, his biggest supporter yelled at him.

"Malachi!" Trevor Reilly shouted.

The receiver turned to see Reilly with his arms outstretched.

"Come give me some love," he said with a laugh.

Malachi hugged his coach, big brother, and mentor. Then he celebrated some more.

"Hey, fellas, I'm proud of you," Coach Prime told his players in the locker room. "We overcame adversity and then we came out in the second half and did what we're capable of doing."

Before dismissing them, Coach Prime reminded the players to make good decisions as they celebrated the win.

"What do I always say?"

A cacophony of unintelligible sound filled the room. Finally, one voice rose above the others.

"Don't let a moment of satisfaction," Malachi said clearly, "leave you with a life of regret."

CHAPTER 9

My daddy was always there for me, so I know daddy love.
—offensive lineman Tre'von Riggins

Tyler Brown's chest felt tight. His mind raced. Flulike symptoms consumed his body.

No way he could practice. Not this Tuesday in September five days before Jackson State played Grambling.

Anxiety overwhelmed him. He couldn't focus. And the kid Coach Prime nicknamed Rock knew he'd be useless on the field. He texted trainer Lauren Askevold that he needed a mental health day. Later, he met with a guidance counselor.

He hadn't taken his anxiety medicine and he thought it contributed to subpar performances in the first two games. The medicine, he said, made him sweat profusely and led to cramps.

He stopped taking it to play better, but the anxiety made him play worse. He took it again, but he took too much—a dose before bed and another about 5 a.m.—and it wrecked his body.

"I was truly embarrassed," said Tyler. "I didn't really want anybody to know what I dealt with."

When he met with Coach Prime later, the conversation didn't go the way Tyler anticipated.

"I love you for you," he told him. "Just be the best Tyler you can be."

"For him to do that, it was a powerful moment," Tyler said. "My barriers were fully down, and that's why I could go out and play my game. Coach Prime said you have to speak victory into yourself. That's when I started getting better.

"I still struggle with it but I'm at a place where I'm happy, playing the game I love."

It was an equally powerful moment for Coach Prime.

Tyler was a good student and a better kid. He wanted to be a speech pathologist like his mom and he practiced hard. On the outside, Tyler looked fine. Inside, anxiety and depression tormented him.

In a way, Tyler reminded Coach Prime of himself when he was a young man.

In 1994, Coach Prime played baseball for the Cincinnati Reds and football for the San Francisco 49ers. He was having a great season on the way to being named NFL Defensive Player of the Year, but he wasn't happy.

Nothing filled the emptiness he felt, and he spent the next three years trying to find the peace he craved.

Nothing helped. Not the seven-digit salary. Not the mansion. Not the fame. And he couldn't figure out why.

In the spring of 1997, his marriage to his first wife, Carolyn, ended.

Coach Prime, then playing football for the Dallas Cowboys and baseball for the Cincinnati Reds, contemplated suicide. He drove his black Mercedes over an embankment with a thirty- to forty-foot drop in Cincinnati but emerged uninjured. A few weeks later, at 4 a.m., Coach Prime's life changed forever.

"I was awakened by these awesome lights in my room. In my testimony, I say it was like a 747 had landed beside my bed, and there was this incredible rush of wind that felt like a helicopter had come in with it," he wrote in his 1999 book, *Power, Money & Sex: How Success Almost Ruined My Life*.

"I remember opening my eyes the slightest bit and saying, 'God if that's you, take me Lord!'"

That night he opened his Bible and read Romans 10:9–10, which talks about eternal life. Since that day, Coach Prime has been praising God. Coach Prime has a strong faith and an intimate relationship with God. He's been answering the phone with "Praise the Lord" for more than twenty years and he's the kind of man who tells his friends, "I love you to life."

This has undoubtedly affected the way he connects with his players, who he knows might be from different religious backgrounds.

A few weeks into the season, he walked into the morning meeting and asked if any players weren't Christians. Two players raised their hands.

Kevin May, a red-shirt freshman from Jackson, said he believed in Hinduism, the world's third-largest religion. Donald Turley, a twenty-nine-year-old former marine, said he was agnostic. Coach Prime requested a definition.

"I didn't take it as hostile or he was attacking me," Turley told me. "Not a lot of people believe that way and I know he's very strong in his faith. I don't think he judged me or saw me any differently. He knows I believe in something else and he was open to it."

Coach Prime said he wanted a deeper understanding of Turley's beliefs.

"I don't want anyone to feel awkward. I'm a different religion. I pray to such-and-such. Then pray to him. I want you to do your thing. We're going to support you," Coach Prime said. "I don't condemn other religions—some Christians are different—because I'm not one to think this is all God would see.

"There are some people who don't know anything about Jesus. They've never been introduced to it and never saw a Bible in their life. You want me to believe they're going to hell? I can't do that in my heavenly mind. My God is too kind for that. As long as they're not cursing God. However you pray, do it. We're here for you."

If a kid like Tyler had emotional issues, then other kids probably had them, too. Coach Prime decided to have a weekly conversation with several players who had dealt with anxiety, depression, anger management, and other emotional issues.

"Certain people were always getting into stuff whether it was here or outside the building," said Rashad Davis, a graduate assistant who's known Coach Prime since high school. "He was like, 'Let me talk to them as a group and see if I can connect with them.'"

He scheduled the conversations for Thursdays at 3 p.m. Coach Prime will tell you how much he respects psychologists and guidance counselors, but he also believes some folks need spiritual healing more than mental healing.

"I use the Bible and relate it to them and football and life," he said. "But we just don't talk about the Bible. We get naked. We talk about everything and I tell them about my trials and tribulations.

"I bring it practically. I use terminology they can understand. I give it to them so they see what I'm talking about. They're rich in talent and they have influence with friends and teammates and family.

"You can't call something good unless you've seen bad. Then you know the difference. I talk to them like that and they get it."

Coach Prime's faith is the epicenter of his life. He asks someone to "pray us up" at the start of every team gathering, but he doesn't spend time trying to save souls. He uses parables as an entry point to talk about life with his players.

On another team, this approach might not work. But the players on this team see the way he conducts his life and they want to know his secret to success. He'll tell them his power comes from Jesus, who provided a peace he never had.

These players respect his consistency and lack of condemnation. He tells them not to smoke weed, but he doesn't condemn them for doing it. He doesn't curse, but he doesn't judge those who do. Nor does he demand his sons don't curse. Every man, he believes, must make his own life choices.

Coach Prime had the position coaches text the players he wanted to attend the meetings.

Understand, this is not typical of most college head coaches. They might see a need and ask an assistant to run the meeting. But this is what's required when you've promised moms and dads that you're going to mold their boys into men.

"I got a text that said Coach Prime wanted to meet with me at three o'clock," Aubrey said. "I was like, 'Oh shit. What did I do? Am I in trouble?'"

Tyler thought the same thing.

Coach Prime invited twelve players to the meeting. He sat in the right corner at the front of the room, so he made eye contact with everyone.

"We have good back-and-forth. I let everybody have an opportunity to speak and some guys I've never heard speak—like Andre Hunt—are vocal in there," he said. "I had never heard him talk outside of practice.

"I don't want them to think I'm perfect. That's why I try to be transparent in front of them. Everyone has something. I'm human just like y'all. The more I open up about me, the more they open up about them."

The discussions were often biblically based, but not always. Sometimes the players broached the topic. Once they discussed Matthew 19:16–30, about how a man becomes rich.

Coach Prime wanted his players to think, because in today's world they don't always have to think. Siri does it for them. Google, too. Kids don't converse like they did twenty and thirty years ago.

They believe texting and commenting on Instagram stories equals communicating.

In one session, Coach Prime asked the players how their position applied to their everyday life.

"I play corner, so I'm put in a lot of uncomfortable and awkward positions," De'Jahn Warren, nicknamed Nugget, said, "but it's all about how you get out of trouble."

Tyler said, "My job is to protect the quarterback. In life, I feel like I'm a protector for my friends and family."

After listening to several answers, Coach Prime answered his own question.

"I'm a corner and on the corner you have to make decisions every day about whether to turn left or right," he said. "So I study and prepare and look both ways, so I can make the best decision about whether to turn left or right or keep straight."

No topic was off-limits.

Sex. Family. Finances. Love. Grief.

One player discussed his feelings after a breakup. Another wanted to know how to handle family members who wanted money because they believed he was headed to the NFL. Grief consumed another.

"It's a safe haven. We can keep our peace and keep people from going crazy and that's why he has the selected few he got," said linebacker King Mwikuta, a transfer from Alabama via Arkansas State.

Tyler said the raw nature of the Thursday sessions makes them powerful. Tears flowed. Hugs were exchanged. Growth occurred. The players learned there's power in vulnerability.

"He's telling us about his life. He's not Prime Time. He's Deion Sanders, the guy who had to deal with a crazy home life," Tyler said. "The guy is human. He made mistakes. He told us about his trials and tribulations. He told us about his suicidal thoughts. That's real.

"That's when I stopped being starstruck. He talked about the things he went through mentally and emotionally. He was at the top of his game, and he didn't feel complete."

In the first meeting, as expected, apprehension filled the room. Everybody waited for everybody else to speak. Coach Prime opened the conversation with a discussion of his own frailties to earn their trust.

"When they see he can relate his life to it, it opens them up. If he's just citing stuff out the Bible or off a piece of paper, they're not going to listen to him," Rashad said. "Coach ain't perfect and he showed them he wasn't perfect.

"They see him as this perfect person, but for them to get an inside glimpse that my coach wasn't perfect but he made it work. And if he made it work then I have the ability to make it work."

Nugget and Coach Prime share a special bond. In the first meeting, Nugget told the group he needed to regain his confidence.

"You never know what somebody is going through or how much they're going through until they tell you," he said. "It might be more teammates going through what you're going through, but you'll never know because everyone is hiding behind a smile. I was one of them people.

"I was letting my mental get the best of me. I found myself in a dark hole that I put myself in. Now that I accepted that, I'm feeling better and moving better.

"Coach Prime's Bible study really be helping. I get a chance to express myself and I don't really get a chance to do that when I'm by myself."

Nugget's words gave Tyler the power to broach his own anxiety.

"I was like, this guy is amazing. I didn't know this about him. That's why I felt comfortable saying I get nervous because I want to be perfect," Tyler said. "I don't want to make mistakes. I want to be the best. I don't want my guy to make the tackle."

Tyler empathized with Nugget because he had to rebuild his confidence after two seasons at the University of Louisiana at Lafayette.

Offensive line assistant coach D. J. Looney is the reason Tyler wound up at Louisiana–Lafayette. Looney was Tyler's primary recruiter.

"He was our guy," said Angelia Mikel Brown, Tyler's mother. "If they did something to piss me off, I'd call D. J. He loved Tyler and we loved him."

Tyler struggled at Louisiana–Lafayette as he adjusted to better competition and tougher coaching. The self-induced pressure combined with offensive line coach Rob Sale's in-your-face, profanity-laced coaching style contributed to Tyler's anxiety.

"He never had anxiety before he went to college," Angelia said. "Never had it. Not one day."

Tyler and Looney were so close, teammates referred to Tyler as Little Looney. On the first day of fall practice in 2020 at a team workout, the thirty-one-year-old Looney died doing what he loved.

Looney had been working with Tyler on his footwork during practice when the horn sounded ending that portion of practice. As they sprinted to the next station, Looney fell to the ground.

"Coach Looney is always joking," Tyler said. "He fell down and we were like, 'Ha! Ha! Get up.' When we looked at him we were like, 'Oh my God.'"

The trainers tried resuscitating him. A couple of hours later, the players were told Looney had died.

"I cried for a week straight. That was really, really hard," Tyler said. "He was like my other dad."

After Looney's death, Tyler and Sale became closer.

"I knew Tyler would be vulnerable when D. J. passed away. We both loved him. We cried together and we hugged each other," said Sale, "and I just made sure I had a watchful eye on Tyler."

At the end of the season, the New York Giants hired Sale as offensive line coach. Tyler felt abandoned.

Again.

"I was just devastated. I cried," Rock said of Sale's departure. "It went from a place where I'm happy and I can thrive to a place I wanted to leave."

Tyler, a Jackson native, spurned offers from Indiana and Boston College to play at Jackson State. He chose Jackson State to provide a pathway to the NFL; the Thursday meetings were an unexpected bonus.

"[Coach Prime] has pushed me to be better as a player and as a man and as a person," Rock said. "I deal with really bad anxiety and depression, and he tells me it's OK to be me. He helped me fall in love with football again."

See, the Thursday meetings are all about helping each player understand what made him tick, so he can be the best version of himself. It's about teaching them how to avoid triggers, and it's about teaching them how to properly channel their emotions.

It's about teaching them to be men.

"It's like counseling. It has a lot of benefits," Aubrey said. "I'm not going to call it a Bible study, but it's more like a come-together meeting but it's major."

Fatherhood was a recurring theme.

In one meeting, backup lineman Tre'von Riggins asked Coach Prime why he walked the length of the field with Shedeur just before kickoff every game.

"My daddy was always there for me, so I know daddy love," said Tre'von, whose father, Thomas, died from complications of a stroke in 2019.

A couple of minutes before each game, father and son walk from about the fifty-yard line to the end zone. Then the coach turned to Shedeur and looked him in the eyes. At that moment, Coach Prime said he knew exactly what Shedeur thought or felt and what he needed to tell him before the game.

It was their private moment.

Jacob Humphrey had a connection with his father, who died when he was eight.

"I didn't really have a father in my life. I had father figures," he said. "In football all these coaches are your father figures."

He played football, even though he preferred baseball, to honor his father. As Jacob spoke, tears rolled down his cheeks.

"Somebody give Jacob a hug," the coach said softly.

Quay Davis, an African-American father of four, from one of Dallas's roughest neighborhoods, quickly stood and embraced his white teammate from Lake Charles, Louisiana.

Nugget, now a father, spoke about the frustration of building a relationship with his father, who had been more absent than present in his life. Coach Prime told him he needed to make peace with the relationship.

Coach Prime told them about his flawed fathers.

Nugget said Coach Prime is part coach, part mentor, and part father figure. He understood players, said Nugget, because he wasn't always rich. Remember, he said, Coach Prime was just another Black kid from a single-parent home.

"Coming here, I've been able to grow as a person, as a man, and as an athlete," Nugget said. "Where I'm from, you don't even have a father figure. People we're used to looking up to are the people in the streets and that usually leads you in the wrong direction."

Anthony Petty grew up with his father in his house, but he never attended his games. His father's absence motivated him to play as well as he could, hoping newspaper articles might entice his father to watch him play one Friday night.

"He was always working," Petty said. "My parents are not those people to have genuine connections and genuine conversation and give your child genuine hugs so you'll feel loved."

Coach Prime connected with the players on several levels because of his life experience. What he respected most was players who worked hard without complaint, especially if they weren't playing much.

Andre Hunt fit that category.

Andre transferred from Nebraska after getting expelled in April 2020. He was accused of sexual assault and later accepted a plea to two misdemeanor counts: accessory to attempted false imprisonment and giving false information. He paid a $1,000 fine.

Coach Prime said he was nearly brought to tears when Andre caught two passes for 18 yards against Texas Southern. Part of the reason was a story Andre shared with the group one day about his grandfather, who had died of cancer.

"Three months before he got cancer, we were supposed to come down here and talk to the coaches at Jackson State," Andre said. "Once he passed, a week later, Coach Brett hit me up."

Coach Prime interrupted.

"The man who gave him hope, the man who gave him love, the man who has protected him and guided him and held his whole life has died," he said. "So what did God do? He found [Bartolone]. How does that happen?

"So while y'all bull-jiving on the sideline when I saw this man on the field making catches, you don't know his story so you don't understand the joy, compassion, and love I have for what I just witnessed.

"When I saw him get that opportunity I had tears inside of me. This is a durn miracle. I'm proud of you, man."

Tre'von was one of Coach Prime's favorite players. It wasn't always like that.

"Before he knew I was funny, before he knew anything about me," he said, "the first image in his head was that I'm a quitter."

Tre'von, a Florida native, spent a season playing at IMG Academy in Bradenton, one of the best prep football programs in the county. He signed with Illinois and transferred after a coaching change.

He committed to Jackson State but didn't realize just how big the chasm was between a Big 10 football program and one in the SWAC.

"I was just looking at penthouse in the seventeenth floor now they got me in a dorm staying with somebody," he thought to himself. "I'm a grown man fam. I ain't about to be staying with nobody."

He had been on campus two days when Tre'von packed his belongings and left. He hadn't even practiced yet when he drove home.

Hart, the linebackers coach, called to ask why he missed Friday's practice.

"I'm gone," Tre'von said. "I can't stay here."

Tre'von spent a couple of days playing *Madden* and relaxing at home. He quickly discovered the streets don't change. If he didn't leave, it was only a matter of time until he found trouble or it found him.

"I didn't even know how to break it to her that I can't go back," he said of his mother.

On Sunday after church, they prayed about the situation. Kateka Riggins told her son to ask JSU for another chance. When Hart said he wasn't sure Coach Prime wanted Tre'von back, Kateka offered one solution.

"My mama said, 'Get in the car, put on your suit, and wait for Coach Prime to see you.'"

Tre'von loaded up his silver Infiniti with 150,000 miles on its odometer and made the twelve-hour drive to Jackson. He pulled into the players' parking lot wearing a white dress shirt and khakis with brown dress shoes. When he saw the coach's black Escalade pull into the lot, Tre'von slipped on a blue blazer with gold buttons and asked the coach for a meeting.

He told Coach Prime about getting cut by Illinois, his father's death, and the other issues that convinced him to return home.

"I don't even know you, dawg. I can see that you want it," Coach Prime told him. "I can tell you were going through something."

Then he welcomed Tre'von back to the program because sometimes humbling yourself and admitting a mistake is what being a man is all about.

"For a coach to truly have insight into what's going on in a player's life is really big," Malachi said. "To have a conversation weekly speaks volumes about how Coach Prime likes to roll. He's a real family-oriented guy so he treats it like a family."

For Nugget, Coach Prime represents family. The guys in the Thursday sessions have become his brothers and they've helped him gain a greater understanding of who he is.

"Ever since we first started it, it was another way to feel more comfortable and get things off my chest and express myself," he said. "Changing certain habits. Changing my lifestyle. Trying to interact with people more instead of locking myself in my room. I wouldn't speak to people for days. That was just my coping mechanism."

That's the kind of growth Coach Prime wanted. The meetings worked. The emotional outbursts and incidents decreased. They didn't have a meeting during the bye week and a couple of issues popped up.

"They need that meeting to get through the week," Rashad said. "Literally."

Rashad can relate to the players in the room because he used to be just like them. He was a kid who fought because he didn't know how to channel his emotions.

He could've wound up in jail like most of his crew, but he became friends with a kid named Bucky, whose dad happened to be an NFL star. Rashad and three others spent the weekends hanging out with Bucky. During the summer, they'd spend weeks at a time at his daddy's mansion.

Only Bucky and Rashad avoided prison. Now each works for Coach Prime.

"The man been helping me my whole life," Rashad said. "If not for that man, I'd probably be dead."

CHAPTER 10

I want to strike the fear of God into
our opponents at halftime.
—assistant coach Michael Pollock

Mississippi Valley State ain't been good in forever.

Valley has never won more than nine football games, and the last time it happened Jerry Rice was wearing a green, red, and white Delta Devils uniform, Willie Totten was throwing him passes, and Archie "Gunslinger" Cooley was calling plays.

That, of course, was in the mid-1980s.

Coach Vincent Dancy has made Valley respectable. He won four games in 2021, the most Valley had won since 2012. Valley made JSU work hard for its 28–19 road win last year, while Coach Prime was hospitalized.

Jackson State's coaching staff knew Valley would be physical and play hard, but it couldn't hang if the Tigers played well.

The players? Well, they had been loved on and praised all week after blowing out Grambling. They had been on social media, seen all the blowout predictions, and practiced accordingly.

They're still kids.

Yes, they have beards, they can vote, and some of them can buy alcohol. Technically, they're adults but they're still maturing. Over-looking Valley would be easy.

Coach Prime, as he often does, started the week with a parable.

He talked about Adam and Eve, the forbidden fruit, and how it relates to football. Frankly, Bishop T. D. Jakes couldn't have preached a better sermon. Coach Prime challenged his players and coaches to rid themselves from distractions (forbidden fruit) and focus on football.

"You showed us a snippet of domination. Now, you're not showing us the same thing, and it leads me to believe you're touching that forbidden fruit," Coach Prime said. "You're touching that one thing that God is saying, 'I got you, but if you do that you're on your own.'

"How bad do you want this that you're willing to sacrifice for that? Whatever it is, you need to stop. Whatever it is, you need to relinquish it. Whatever it is, you need to stop."

The players didn't practice to Coach Prime's standard on Tuesday, either, so he increased the intensity. To understand Coach Prime is to understand his love of practice. He learned as a kid that the harder he practiced, the easier the game seemed.

"You have to practice at a certain level and with a certain intensity. You practice and you work. This ain't no psychology thing," he said. "That's how our parents did. If you didn't work, you didn't get paid. If you don't work at practice, the game is the pay.

"That comes from me as a kid. That's how it has always been. I don't know no other way. Maybe I was blessed with some wonderful coaches that were honest, ahead of their time, and rewarded people for work. All I knew was work. That comes from the coach. He was a worker."

Really, what he wanted his players, guys like Malachi, to understand is that life is about a process, not a result. He wanted them to understand winning and dominating came with mastering the process.

It was about a daily journey that started with getting enough sleep, eating healthy, practicing hard, studying video, and doing well academically. If any of that was subpar, it showed up on the field.

He hoped Malachi could build upon his touchdown against Grambling and start being a difference-maker.

"Malachi can play. He just has to stay focused as a man. I'm trying to keep him locked in as a man and football player," Coach Prime said. "He's a great kid. If you have him in a room, he's going to win it because he's a great kid. He's more detrimental to himself than he is to others."

Coach Prime spent Wednesday's team meeting reviewing video of Tuesday's practice.

Play one.

"Any linemen getting down the field? Nothing. Play over. Everybody just standing there," he said.

Play two.

"Straight chilling. Play still going on. Anybody getting to the ball? No," he said. "They only do what we tolerate."

Play three.

"Linebacker comes right through the hole," he said. "We have a play where nobody blocks the linebacker?"

Play four.

"Get downfield? No. No. No. No. No. None of them," an exasperated Coach Prime said of the offensive line. "They only do what we tolerate. I guess that's what we're teaching over there.

"Anybody running to the ball on defense? DT, that what you teaching over there?"

"No sir," Thurman said.

Suddenly Coach Prime raised his voice.

"Seventeen plays, and fifteen of them are garbage right now. Is this what you're coaching?" He yelled at Markuson, the offensive line coach, who stood along the left wall like he did every morning.

"Is this what you're coaching?" he yelled. "Yes or no?"

"No," Markuson said.

"Gunnar, where you at? Is this what he's coaching? Is that what you're coaching?"

"No, sir," grad assistant Gunnar White said.

Coach Prime stared long enough to make the players uncomfortable.

"We gonna put up with this? I'm sick of this. I'm sick of y'all. We're better than this," he yelled. "You're setting yourself up for a durn fall this weekend. You're setting yourself up for an upset.

"Let's clean this up today. I'm sick of this. Mediocrity is not who I am. It's not who we are. It's ridiculous."

This game, it seemed, was going to be all about the offensive line, which had been completely rebuilt after its embarrassing performance in the Celebration Bowl.

The Tigers had managed just 194 yards on 65 plays in that game. They rushed 29 times for 19 yards.

Tony, a preseason All-American and one of Shedeur's best friends, had been demoted to third team after his suspension. Demetri Jordan started at left tackle and Tyler started at left guard. Center Zack Breaux and right guard Evan Henry had each transferred from Louisiana–Monroe.

Right tackle Willis Patrick arrived as a Division II All-American from Angelo State. At 6'3" and 310 pounds, he was better suited for guard because of his size, but the Tigers needed him at right tackle.

"Patrick is the leader. He's a dog. He's nasty," Coach Prime said. "He's the leader of that bunch."

Patrick earned Coach Prime's respect by dominating the offseason workouts.

"I won every sprint. I was trying to lift the most weight," he said. "I wanted to be the strongest and when we got on that field I wanted to be the fastest. It was a pride thing."

The backups were also solid with Tony, Kirk Ford, Devin Hayes, Trace Shumans, and Deontae Graham.

Coach Prime had enough competition to keep players practicing at a high level and enough depth to withstand injuries. Coach Prime wanted to be physical enough at the line of scrimmage to run whenever he wanted, which wasn't often, and to protect Shedeur.

"Did he get his point across?" Markuson asked the linemen at their morning meeting.

"Yes, sir," they said glumly.

"I tried to tell you about this team we're about to play," Markuson said. "If you're saying, 'FU' in your minds, then it's a bad, bad deal because they're coming. This is their homecoming."

Forty-five minutes later, when the players gathered around the midfield block before practice, Pollock delivered some truth. Ten days earlier, Appalachian State had upset No. 6 Texas A&M, 17–14, at Kyle Field.

"Every coach and every player in this circle needs to step it up. That's how you prevent being Texas A&M and getting your ass whipped by Appalachian State," he said. "The difference between the talent level at Texas A&M and App State is the same as Jackson State and Mississippi Valley.

"If you think it can't happen, your ass will be on national TV and ESPN for the wrong reasons. Great teams prepare for inferior opponents just like it's the Super Bowl. If you wonder why we're on edge or why we're getting on you a little bit more this week it's because we're not embarrassing ourselves on Saturday.

"I want to strike the fear of God into our opponents at halftime. I want them picking up the phone at halftime and calling their friends saying, 'Do you see what Jackson State is doing to them?' We got that kind of team, if we don't accept mediocrity."

At Friday's night's team dinner, Brewster asked players to dedicate their performance against Valley to someone they love via a phone call or text.

"I'm coaching for my mom, dad, and brother in heaven," he said. "I will never let them down because of the pride I have in my name."

When Coach Prime spoke, he spoke about his friendship with Dancy.

"The head coach for the opposing team is my friend until we kick off," he said. "I don't give a durn about none of them. I promise you we're going to try to make sure that every light on that scoreboard works tomorrow."

Coach Prime and Dancy met at SWAC Media Day before the COVID spring season in 2020 and quickly connected over conversations about life and football. The coach admired Dancy's work ethic and Dancy, who grew up a San Francisco 49ers fan, appreciated Coach Prime's willingness to mentor him.

"All the other coaches were so jealous and upset about his presence. I admired him, so I was excited to meet him and he was coaching my alma mater," Dancy said. "We sat down and had a conversation and it was amazing.

"When somebody can look at you and tell you that they want you to be successful and they want greatness for you, it makes you want to go harder because you know the level and status he's achieved. It makes you more determined to be successful."

Dancy, an All-SWAC linebacker/safety, played for JSU from 2002 to 2005. He coached at JSU from 2009 to 2013. The thirty-three-year-old Dancy replaced his college coach, Rick Comegy, at Valley.

Three weeks after they met, Coach Prime FaceTimed Dancy and connected him with executives from the New York Jets and Miami Dolphins. Coach Prime implored them to send everything they weren't using, from shoulder pads to cleats, to Valley.

"I got boxes of stuff," Dancy said, "I would've never had if it wasn't for him."

A few months later, Coach Prime pulled up at Valley, toured the facilities, and told Dancy he would help get him a new practice field. Later, he posted a video on Instagram about his visit.

The next day, Valley's administration admonished Dancy.

"The first thing I did was call coach and tell him what happened to me," Dancy said. "It was some bull crap. He said, 'Don't worry about it, I won't help them get nothing.'"

Well, JSU started slowly again.

Jamari Jones's 25-yard touchdown pass to Jacob Rankin gave Valley a 7–0 lead just 1:02 into the game.

"That's on me," safety Cam'Ron Silmon-Craig said walking off the field.

A 42-yard touchdown pass to Willie Gaines and a sensational tackle-breaking 30-yard touchdown run by Sy'Veon Wilkerson made it 14–7 JSU. Slowly, Sy'Veon was taking control of the running back position because Santee Marshall and J. D. Martin didn't have his combination of speed, power, and vision.

Sy'Veon, though, fumbled into the end zone midway through the second quarter and Valley recovered. He carried only twice more.

"He's a grown man. He's a thumper. He hits it. He's relentless," Coach Prime said. "But he fumbled and he had to go through the process that all the other backs had to go through. You fumble in the end zone, you're out.

"Next man up. So Santee got his opportunity and he did his thing."

Santee's entire career has revolved around taking advantage of opportunity. We're talking about a dude who transferred from Division II Miles College in Fairfield, Alabama, after his sophomore season to play for JSU.

Coach Prime let Santee try out for a roster spot as a walk-on player. Instead of quitting when he didn't make it, Santee started harassing Riddley for any tasks that would allow the new coaching staff to get to know him.

Eventually, Santee became a member of the video team that filmed practice.

"It was real hard knowing that I could be on the field being productive, but I was determined," Santee said. "My whole focus was getting back on the field no matter what I had to do."

A few weeks later, injuries and poor performances created an opportunity for Santee to rejoin the team as a walk-on. He practiced hard and Coach Prime rewarded him.

"I'll appreciate [Coach Prime] forever for what he did for me because he didn't have to do it," Santee said. "When I was on the scout team, he told me he was going to try to get me an opportunity in the game because he liked the way I worked—and he kept his word."

In 2020, Santee gained 126 yards against Alabama A&M in the only game he played. In 2021, Santee gained 87 yards on 28 carries in the first four games.

Then he gained 122 yards against Alabama A&M and followed it up with a 96-yard performance against Alabama State on homecoming. When he heard his mom's voice in the locker room after the Alabama State game, he thought she was about to get him in trouble.

"I heard her voice talking to coach Prime," Santee said, "and I ran to the front of the locker room as fast as I could."

Coach Prime and Anita Marshall had worked out a skit worthy of *Chappelle's Show*.

"They say you got a problem with me, Mama," he said.

"Yeah, I got a problem with you," she replied.

Coach Prime turned to Santee.

"Your mama said I got problems," he said. "Don't I take care of you?"

A stunned Santee said, "Yeah, you've been taking care of me. I don't know what she's talking about."

A smiling Coach Prime said, "I don't want no problems with Mama, so you know what that means . . . You're on full scholarship."

His teammates mobbed him.

"I'll remember that moment forever because of how happy my teammates and everybody was for me," Santee said. "It was a special moment."

Santee started against Florida A&M, gaining 63 yards on 12 carries. He fumbled in each of the first two games and carried just nine times in the next two games.

"I was supposed to be the starter," he said, "but I had fumbled and that set me back. I could never get back into a starting role."

Sy'Veon's fumble, though, had created an opportunity for Santee and Martin, whose five-yard touchdown catch gave JSU a 21–7 halftime lead.

"If you're not pissed-off right now, something is fucking wrong with you," strength coach Mo Sims yelled from the middle of the locker room. "Who dedicated this game to somebody yesterday? Raise your hand.

"It's OK if you didn't, but if you did and this is the effort you're going to give them, you should be ashamed of yourself. Your last name is on the back for a reason. That's what you represent. A lot of people are depending on you and that's what you're going to give them? Come on."

Santee had dedicated his performance to his mom.

Whatever opportunity I get, he texted her Friday night, *I'm going to do it for you.*

The first half hadn't created many chances for him; the second half did. JSU started at its own five-yard line. Santee burst through the middle on an inside zone behind blocks from Patrick and Evan.

He cut left when he hit the secondary, and Shane Hooks delivered a nice block. Santee cut inside Shane's block and shrugged off a safety at the 20.

"Oh Lord!" he thought. "There's nothing but grass in front of me."

A defender with an angle dragged Santee down at the four after a 91-yard run.

"I was tore up, man. I was tired," he said. "I hadn't been in a game in like three weeks. I was mad. I wanted to score so bad. Nobody was even talking about the run because I didn't score."

The lead swelled to 28–7 on Shedeur's 4-yard touchdown pass to Shane and his 8-yard touchdown pass to Cam Buckley provided the game's final points in a 49–7 win.

The coaches shared a long hug at midfield.

"He's a friend, somebody special who means something to me," Dancy said. "He's genuine."

In the locker room, Coach Prime asked a familiar question.

"Did we dominate?"

"No, sir," they replied.

CHAPTER 11

It's nice to be mentioned.
—Coach Prime on *The Rich Eisen Show*

Nebraska fired Scott Frost in September after a 1-2 start that included a 45–42 home loss to Georgia Southern on September 11, and Coach Prime's name appeared all over social media as a potential candidate.

The same scenario played out when Arizona State fired Herm Edwards a week later after a 30–21 home loss to Eastern Michigan on September 18, and when Georgia Tech fired Geoff Collins after a 27–10 loss to Central Florida that left the Yellow Jackets 1-3.

"It's nice to be mentioned . . ." Sanders said October 1 on *The Rich Eisen Show*.

A few days later, sitting in his office, Coach Prime said, "This could be divisive to somebody else but I've been in the light all my life. This ain't nothing new to me. My main thing is to make sure everybody around me is steady and stable and they're not looking and thinking and listening to these conversations and talking about this and that.

"They have to stay focused. I've always had something going on in my life. We're in a good position. We just have to wait."

Coach Prime was open to leaving JSU, in part because his relationship with President Hudson had deteriorated.

Coach Prime, sitting at his desk, wearing a gray Jackson State sweatshirt and a red baseball cap, stared into the camera in late July and let it rip on Instagram.

"I spoke about this several months ago and still to no avail and it's bothering me," Coach Prime said. "Governor Reeves, can you help me with this issue? How is it fathomable that our refund checks for our kids are consistently late but the checks for administrators are consistently on time?"

Coach Prime said the refund checks his players were supposed to receive during the summer arrived just as summer workouts ended.

The day after his comments, which received nearly ninety thousand views, President Hudson's office contacted Coach Prime and scheduled a meeting for July 26. Ashley Robinson, the athletic director, came off vacation to moderate the meeting.

"I don't like to be chastised under any circumstances," Coach Prime told Robinson.

"We'll see how it goes."

Hudson asked Coach Prime why he aired his grievances publicly instead of coming to him.

"We don't have that kind of relationship," said Coach Prime, "and you know that."

The meeting ended without a resolution but showed the contentious relationship between Coach Prime and Hudson.

"I thought it was funny that nobody reached out when I said I was paying for the locker rooms, but I ask why the checks are late and everybody's upset. That makes no sense to me," Coach Prime said. "I gave the president a list of every player on the team and how much their fall check is supposed to be, and we'll just see how long they take to arrive."

The relationship between Coach Prime and President Hudson took an awkward turn between the end of the 2021 season and the start of the 2022 season.

"You have success when the president, the AD [athletics director], and coach are all aligned. Were the president and head coach on the same page here? No," defensive line coach Jeff Weeks said. "Who's going to end up losing that battle at the end of the day? Prime, if you can't keep winning.

"Even if you do, you get frustrated. It happens a lot of places. I don't dislike Prime. I don't dislike the president. Those are just facts."

The disconnect began when Hudson turned down Tracey Edmonds's request to shoot a weekly TV show on Black Entertainment Television. *College Hill: Celebrity Edition* is an eight-episode series that follows eight celebrities as they're immersed in an HBCU experience. The cast included NeNe Leakes, Ray J, Lamar Odom, Big Freedia, Stacey Dash, India Love, DreamDoll, and Slim Thug.

For Edmonds, Sanders's longtime girlfriend, shooting the show on JSU's campus made sense because she'd be near Coach Prime and it would bring additional publicity to JSU. Edmonds, an award-winning executive producer, wound up shooting the show at Texas Southern, a SWAC school located in Houston.

"We talked about it," Hudson said. "There were a lot of negotiations but in the end, it wasn't the project for us."

How come?

"There's a time and a place for everything," he said. "This wasn't the time or the space to do that type of show."

Why not?

"Based on what we know about the show, there's no ill will. I think it went to Texas Southern and it was a positive experience for them," Hudson said. "It just wasn't for us.

"Here, we're getting a lot of publicity. We aren't really seeking out more cameras at Jackson State. What's in it for the university? Is this something you should do at this time?"

Coach Prime, as expected, fumed. When Texas Southern accepted the show, Edmonds tweeted about it.

"I took one of her posts," said Chris Neely, who creates content for his social media pages as well as Coach Prime's pages, "and said, 'So happy that a SWAC school got this. Missed opportunity for JSU.'"

The next morning, Hudson and Neely exchanged texts. Then Hudson phoned. Their conversation lasted ten minutes.

"Hey man, I saw your post. You have the right to post what you want to post, but I wish people would have all of the facts before they went out there," Neely remembered President Hudson saying.

"We weren't getting any money."

According to Neely, JSU wanted financial compensation for being allowed to produce the show on campus, which is their right. Still, Hudson should've understood Coach Prime's mentality and that he would take Hudson's decision personally. It wouldn't be just business.

Neely had a close relationship with former JSU president William Bynum but not with President Hudson.

"It's ego, immaturity, and insecurity," Neely said. "This president is not secure enough to have someone else in his proximity that is bigger, so there is always a concern to prove that you're just as powerful."

Talk to enough people about HBCU presidents and football coaches and you'll hear about many contentious relationships. Folks say HBCU presidents become envious when the head football coach gets too much attention, much like when a pastor at an African-American church believes the music director is getting too much shine.

"The future of HBCUs lies in the hands of the presidents of those universities," said Wayne State coach Tyrone Wheatley in a December 2022 article on Andscape. "If they want HBCU athletics to survive, they have to get off their butts, stop being so pompous and righteous, eat some crow, and admit they don't know what the hell they're doing when it comes to athletics.

"If HBCUs want to grow and want to survive, and they want to flourish, you got to come out of the Stone Ages."

The president outranks the football coach on any organizational flowchart. At most universities, students and alums can name the football coach, usually the highest-paid employee, but not the president. At HBCUs, it's the reverse. University presidents typically earn more than the coaches. Coach Prime's presence at JSU upended that dynamic.

The much-anticipated football wing of the Walter Payton Recreation & Wellness Center required much more of Coach Prime's offseason attention than he figured.

One July morning, Coach Prime and Constance Schwartz-Morini, the cofounder and chief executive officer of SMAC Entertainment, rode from the practice field to the Walter Payton complex. As he approached the building, Coach Prime pointed out the various tasks he had paid to have completed.

"We cut the gates down. We put the grass down. We're putting more picnic benches out there," he said, referring to a grassy area where players can catch their breath and remove their cleats after practice.

"We pressure-washed the building and cut all the trees down."

Then Coach Prime and Schwartz-Morini toured inside the building, which was cluttered with boxes, furniture, and debris. Oh, and the actual locker room still needed to be finished.

Coach Prime wanted it completed by August 4 so the players could use it on the first day of fall camp in two weeks. During the Instagram video, Schwartz-Morini suggested Coach Prime donate a quarter of his salary to complete the project; he suggested half.

"You do know, I know how much all this costs," he said. "I'll donate half. You gotta make it back."

"Don't we always," she said laughing.

The next week at SWAC Media Day, ESPN's Tiffany Greene asked Coach Prime why he paid to have the locker room completed.

"They deserve it. A lot of folks talk about it. I'm truly about it. A lot of people talk about bringing solvency to problems, I'm truly about it," he said. "A lot of people talk about what they're going to do. I actually do it. A lotta folks talk about where they're going, I actually go. . . .

"I'm sick and tired of us trying to say, well, other Power 5s do this or do that and we can't even do the little things we can control doing. I'll do it. I don't worry about the money, the financial part. I don't even worry about that. God got that. I got them."

The locker room and the TV show were huge issues, but there were also small annoyances, like when Evis McGee, a member of Coach Prime's two-man security team, had the veracity of his hours questioned, and when Coach Prime learned two undergrad classes would be held in the football facility.

Coaches, players, and support staff need an ID with a bar code to enter their section of the building. Having non–football players in the football wing meant twice a week, the security staff had to cordon off parts of the facility to prevent students from wandering.

"There is a ton of available space with real classrooms. Tons," one member of the coaching staff said. "Their director came over and told me, 'We don't have to come here.' [Hudson] catches wind of it and says, 'You go back over there because that's where I want you to be.' That's unbelievable."

In October, Coach Prime met with President Hudson about a variety of topics, including their relationship. Coach Prime said Hudson came for support; Hudson said he came to clear the air.

"Sometimes it's necessary to sit down. He and I never got a chance to sit down a whole lot. Coach Prime is here to do a job," Hudson said. "I just kind of wanted to reset some things. Sometimes people are in your ear about, 'I think this or I think that about you.'

"I'm good at blocking out noise and going to the source and saying, 'Hey, this is where I am. This is where you are. As far as I'm concerned you're doing a hell of a job as coach and you're doing what we brought you here to do.'"

Coach Prime said the meeting didn't last all that long.

"He came in here, when all hell was breaking loose and he was putting classrooms in here and all that stupid stuff," Coach Prime said. "He knew I was fuming."

Coach Prime said Hudson asked for his support.

"What does that mean?" Coach Prime asked.

"With all of the things we're trying to do around here I need your support," Hudson replied.

"So, this is like a political thing," Coach Prime said.

"No, I just want to be on the same page. You've always had an open dialogue with me," Hudson said.

The men also discussed the locker room situation. Coach Prime said Hudson told him that he shouldn't have used his own money on the project because it was a state-sponsored project that began in 2019, and certain protocols needed to be followed, slowing the process.

"If I wouldn't have expedited it, we wouldn't have been in here and we would've been a laughingstock," said Coach Prime, "because we showed the world half of it and we're still not finished."

Coach Prime didn't think much of the meeting.

"It was a bunch of bull junk," he said. "He came to me like a politician."

Hudson supported the program on social media, often tweeting about the program's success and tagging Coach Prime.

Coach Prime had made enough money in his lifetime that dollars no longer motivated him, so he wouldn't leave JSU just because another university offered him considerably more. The reality was that any Power 5 job he took would probably increase his salary by a minimum of ten times the amount JSU was paying him. Purpose— not money—made him rise each morning at 3:45 and arrive at the office by 4:30 to prepare for the day.

"Any type of money don't change my life. I'm good. God got me," he said. "Remember, I gave half my salary to the complex. Money doesn't enhance me, so that's not what would it take. It has to be something that whispers in my ear and tells me this is what you need to do."

The work Coach Prime did at Jackson State in 2021, when the Tigers won a school-record 11 games, and the publicity he generated for his program made him one of college football's darlings.

It certainly helped that JSU won its first four games by a combined score of 188–40.

Whether his name was being bandied about for openings at Nebraska, Arizona State, Georgia Tech, Wisconsin, and Colorado or potential openings such as Auburn and Louisville, it became clear Coach Prime's availability was being discussed over country club lunches and at covert meetings all over the country.

All of those programs needed someone who would make their football programs relevant and winners.

"We have a footprint in college football. People aren't saying 'where is Jackson State?' anymore. They say we have to see them play," he said. "I want to see their highlights. That's a blessing."

When asked if he might visit Auburn, a forty-five-minute drive from Montgomery since JSU was playing Alabama State, Coach Prime decided to have some fun.

"How far is Auburn from Montgomery? How far is Atlanta? What about Louisville? Colorado and Wisconsin? All of them are jumping. Let's keep going."

Then he turned serious and recounted a story from earlier in the week about Colorado.

"The guy is a great guy and he wants to interview you," one Power 5 athletic director told Coach Prime. "I don't know if it'll work out, but he's the kind of guy who will let you do whatever you want. I know it's not an ideal place to live . . ."

Coach Prime promised to do the interview, with one caveat.

"I gotta win, man. I got a sensation for winning. If a program just wants to compete, that's not the program for me," he said, "because I attract too many kids that want to win. I can't do that."

At that point, JSU had shown no inclination to sign him to a contract extension.

"Once the chatter came up and it felt like it was getting strong and you started to get calls and see some things," Hudson said, "I did talk to the AD and say, 'Do you think it would be worth it to even offer him, or is what he's going to be offered more than we could even pay anyway?'

"There was never a point where it was like, 'Hey, this is a number that will keep him here.' That never came up."

Even if Hudson and Robinson expected him to leave, offering a deal should've been their way of ensuring the public understood they had done everything in their power to keep him if Coach Prime left.

"Deion isn't signing an extension," one member of the athletic department said.

Jackson State discussed what an offer might look like, but never formally offered him one, so we'll never know.

In college football, coaches get extensions when they have the kind of success Coach Prime had at JSU. It's the cost of doing business, which is why in the span of twelve weeks, Georgia's Kirby Smart ($112 million), Clemson's Dabo Swinney ($115 million), and Alabama's Nick Saban ($90 million) signed contract extensions.

Jackson State officials did discuss a deal that would've taken Coach Prime's salary to $1 million, while creating a pool of $500,000 he could spend on his assistants.

What might have made sense is for JSU and the city to find a way to generate income for Coach Prime, the coaching staff, and the program by partnering with the city, the state, or both. Perhaps Coach Prime could've been the voice for tourism in Jackson or Mississippi as a whole.

"They're supposed to take a shot," said Coach Prime. "If you don't take a shot you look like a fool."

In December 2021, Visit Jackson, the city's marketing organization, calculated an economic impact of more than $30 million for the Tigers' 2021 season. That's double what it was in 2019.

"You're not supposed to let me get to the end," Coach Prime said. "You saying I'm gonna stay here for $1 million after I have given you 150K for a project you still haven't finished and for some of these coaches that you're pimping because they're making 60K or 55K."

Other fan bases and athletic directors noticed, too. They wanted Coach Prime and his unique ability to serve as a catalyst for change wherever he went to make their football teams elite.

Texas Christian University interviewed Coach Prime in 2021, while he was in the hospital recovering from the surgery. He thought he had interviewed well enough to earn the job, but TCU had some boosters—the money people—who weren't ready to commit to Coach Prime.

TCU settled on Sonny Dykes, who's a quality coach. But he's not the kind of big-name coach who's going to provide any kind of national buzz—and he didn't until the Frogs won a series of heart-stopping regular season games and played Georgia in the BCS championship game.

The Frogs lost 65–7.

Coach Prime is not for everyone. He knows that and he's good with it. Coach Prime wasn't looking for a contract to create generational wealth. He already had that, but he wanted to take care of his assistant coaches.

"The way I live is the way I live," he said. "It helps my guys because most of them ain't never had it like that."

Coach Prime is demanding and impatient. If you're not a high achiever, he's going to be difficult to work with because your job is whatever it takes to help the program win—not your official job title.

If that means picking up trash off the floor or making copies or hanging TVs, then that's what it takes.

None of the jobs, for now, made sense. The one job that did make sense hadn't come open yet. Auburn.

Questions about Bryan Harsin's future at Auburn began from the start of the season. They intensified after a 41–14 loss to Penn State.

A 21–17 loss to LSU led to a front-page story about various buyout possibilities.

"I can't believe we have this coach doing the things he's doing for the program and we're not going to be able to keep him," said Greg Manogin, who founded the 1400 Klub. "There are too many egos involved. We have to try to get Hudson to understand what we have. Once [Coach Prime] leaves, it's never going to be like this again."

As of the first week of October, Auburn seemed like the best potential Power 5 fit among the jobs available or those thought to become available.

Auburn, an Under Armour school, was in Alabama, which meant there was plenty of talent. Plus, he'd love to compete with Alabama coach Nick Saban. A picture with Saban from an Aflac commercial sits in a four-by-six frame on his desk.

Coach Prime, though, has never worried about the future.

"If you dominate your moment, you will elevate," he often says. "You don't have to seek them, so I don't ever worry about tomorrow. I'm too busy trying to dominate today."

Back in the day, Coach Prime gave off the impression that swag was all he cared about. He wore more necklaces than Mr. T, but that was to show the fellas back in Fort Myers that they didn't have to sell drugs to flex. The Rolex and custom suits were part of Prime Time's image.

As a coach, he's old-school, which should come as no surprise when you consider those who influenced him the most. Ron Hoover, his high school coach, once suspended Coach Prime for the last few games of his junior season because he broke a team rule.

That moment taught Coach Prime about being a man. It taught him about decisions and consequences and how his actions affected others. North Fort Myers was competing for a playoff spot. Without him, it missed the playoffs.

Coach Prime worked the entire offseason to regain Hoover's trust after letting him down. It didn't matter that he was an innocent bystander in the fight: Coach Prime had positioned himself to be wrongfully accused.

"Coaches lead men. Coaches influence men. Coaches excite men. Coaches motivate men," he said. "They can durn sure teach Xs and Os. That's the easiest thing for me on a daily basis.

"I love it. I love the coach moniker. I really do."

Earrings were prohibited in the football facility because of that time, years ago, when Coach Prime's dad told him that earrings and football players just don't go together. The players arrived to team meetings ten to fifteen minutes early because they began when Coach Prime entered the room. The offense wore red practice jerseys—the quarterbacks wore green—and sat on the left side of the room by position.

Quarterbacks sat in the front row, followed by two rows of receivers and tight ends, two rows of running backs, and two rows of offensive linemen. The defensive players, wearing blue jerseys, sat on the right side of the room. The defensive linemen sat in the first two rows, followed by the linebackers, specialists, and defensive backs.

The offensive and defensive coaches either sat with their position groups or stood along the wall near their unit. Players must wear black socks and no-show socks weren't allowed. Neither were T-shirts that exposed the armpits or gear from other programs.

On game days, players must look uniform because he wants them to get used to how it's going to be in the NFL, where players get fined thousands for uniform violations. Plus, he saw his stepfather put on a uniform every day whether he felt like going to work or not, because that's what was required of him to earn a paycheck. So he respects the uniform and those who wear them every day.

What most folks don't realize is that Coach Prime was always among the hardest workers on any team he played. The practice battles between Jerry Rice and Coach Prime in San Francisco and Michael Irvin in Dallas were legendary.

"Practice with him was always so intense and competitive with us going one-on-one and it made everybody better," Rice said. "It made all of the receivers better and all of the defensive backs better because we raised everybody's level."

After the position coaches delivered their scouting reports on Alabama State, Brewster asked for some extra time. He talked about a time when he coached tight ends at Florida State (2013–17) and ate lunch with former defensive coordinator Mickey Andrews a couple of times a week.

"One time I asked Mickey who the best player he ever coached was and he said without hesitation, 'Coach Prime,'" Brewster said. "Later on, I asked him who the hardest-working player he ever had was and he said, 'Coach Prime.'

"Think about that. The best player he ever had was Coach Prime and the hardest worker he ever had was Coach Prime. If you'll marry a great work ethic with the blessings you've been given then you can accomplish great things."

He's a classic CEO head coach.

"I love it. He's a true CEO coach and he lets you do your job and holds you accountable for the results," said Gunnar White, the assistant offensive line coach. "I've worked for a guy who spent all his time on one side of the ball and it didn't work out all that well."

Coach Prime often makes suggestions, like when he wanted Dallas moved to the right slot instead of the left slot, so he would be the first or second read in Shedeur's progression of where to throw the football. Or when he wanted Thurman to use a specific coverage behind a certain blitz or to make sure a specific player had an opportunity to touch the ball in a game.

One week, he told defensive ends coach Trevor Reilly to bench Nyles Gaddy and Jeremiah Brown for lack of production. A couple of days later, Coach Prime said he wanted Justin Ragin benched, too, which meant Reilly didn't have enough defensive ends to start.

After the staff meeting, Reilly asked Thurman, Hart, and Mathis—the men who knew Coach Prime the best—for advice in executing Coach Prime's plan.

"I told him to start Gaddy and Brown and if he says something I told him to get the sorriest guy we have out there because one thing I know about Prime is he's loyal to winning," Hart said. "If he has to make the decision for you, then why does he need you around? He wants you to be every bit the person he hired you to be.

"You can't spend all your time figuring out what he wants you to do. If you're damned if you do and damned if you don't, then I'm always gonna say fuck it and bet on myself and the decision I made."

As much as Coach Prime values an old-school coaching approach, he's also unconventional.

He has DJs at practice and spends as much time talking to his players about winning in life as he does winning on Saturdays.

"I love that my guy does it his way. He's unconventional in everything we do but there's a method to what he does," special teams coach Alan Ricard said. "It shows the rest of us that we don't have to act in a certain way that others think we should and we can still get the job done."

When he met with the coaches the week of the opener, Coach Prime explained his approach to the staff, but it was primarily for the newcomers. What Coach Prime demanded is single-minded focus, discipline, and accountability.

The first point Coach Prime made to the staff was to separate their personal and private lives. Two coaches were contemplating divorce, and another had recently gone through one.

"Coaches, I need the best version of you, not a tattered version. Not a broken-down version. Not a damaged version but the best version of you on a daily basis," he said. "Now, this is very profound: don't allow home to interfere with your work and don't allow work to interfere with your home. Wherever your feet are, that's where I need you to be at that moment.

"I don't need you to be at work thinking about an argument you had last night with your [spouse] and your kids. I don't need you at home playing with your kids thinking about a player who cussed you out and got ignorant with you on the field and you're taking it out on your spouse or your loved one. Don't do that."

Then he encouraged his coaches to know their players intimately, so they understood how to motivate them.

At a place like JSU or any HBCU, resources are tight, so something always needs to be done. Coach Prime is the kind of dude who sees something that needs to be done and does it—even mowing the grass at the football facility.

He expects his staff to do the same.

"A title doesn't justify who you are. It just tells us where your office is and what position you have," he said. "If all you do around here is what your title says, then I'm wrong for letting you be here. Then I'm wrong for hiring you because we have to go beyond the call of duty."

Coaches spend about seventy hours a week together in a high-stress business. Emotions can run high on the practice field and in meetings among highly competitive people.

"We will have conflicts. That's the nature of our business. I need you to resolve it before we leave the building," he said. "Offense and defense, we about to go at it. I don't need that conflict and chaos. Leave that for the kids. We compete at everything and anything, so when defense starts talking junk, don't act like you didn't know.

"When DT starts sending all kind of blitzes, 'cause I'm gonna act like you shoulda known it was coming. You think he's going to let you embarrass him and dial 911 on him every day? He's coming. And he's not gonna tell you everything he's doing. It's a competition."

Coach Prime believed in second and third chances, but he also believed in decisions and consequences. Legal trouble meant removal from the team.

Period.

"Everyone loves a winner, so the goal is to win on the field, in the classroom, the community, and at home," Coach Prime said. "We have to develop these young men who can handle adversity. Finances. Relationships. We have to develop men. I don't want to see you babying them."

CHAPTER 12

It's a new day and age, and we aren't losing.
—quarterback Shedeur Sanders

Coach Prime wanted to rip JSU at halftime of its 49–7 win over Mississippi Valley State. The Tigers led by only 14 points at halftime.

Then he looked at the stat sheet.

Shedeur had completed 21 of 24 passes for nearly 300 yards and two touchdowns in the first half.

Wow.

It's pretty silly, he said to himself, to complain after a half like that.

Shedeur finished with 438 yards passing and five touchdowns, which is why the next day Coach Prime decided his son was worthy of Heisman consideration.

Yes, the Heisman Trophy, college football's most prestigious award, presented annually to the sport's best player. After all, Shedeur was the face of HBCU football as the star quarterback on the highest-profile team in FCS.

Through four games, Shedeur had completed 75.5 percent of his passes for 1,381 yards with 14 touchdowns and one interception as the Tigers outscored their opponents 190–37.

It was hard to imagine Shedeur winning the Heisman, since, realistically, he'd be competing against quarterbacks such as Alabama's

Bryce Young, Ohio State's C. J. Stroud, USC's Caleb Williams, and Georgia's Stetson Bennett IV.

None of that concerned Coach Prime, because he never worried about stuff like that. Neither did it concern him that only three FCS players had ever been seriously considered for the Heisman in the last sixty years, and only one of them played for an HBCU. Cornell running back Ed Marinaro finished second in 1971 and Holy Cross's Gordie Lockbaum finished third in 1988. Alcorn State quarterback Steve McNair finished third in 1994 after accounting for 5,799 yards—4,863 passing and 936 rushing—and throwing 47 touchdown passes.

"Forget that he's my son, and his last name is Sanders," Coach Prime said Monday during the SWAC's weekly teleconference. "Any other man doing what he's doing and accomplishing what he's accomplishing thus far deserves recognition. That's all. Thank you for allowing me to have a 'dad moment.'"

Through four games, Young had 1,029 yards passing with 13 touchdowns and two interceptions, Stroud had 1,222 yards with 16 touchdowns and one interception, Williams had 1,054 yards with 9 touchdowns and no interceptions, and Bennett had 1,224 yards with 5 touchdowns and an interception.

Coach Prime's proclamation created headlines all over the country and provided plenty of fodder for sports talk radio nationally. Locally, each of Jackson's TV stations did stories on the topic.

Shedeur embraced his father's words. Growing up the son of an athletic icon meant that being mentioned for the Heisman wasn't going to put additional pressure on him.

"I don't picture it as playing around, hype, or just throwing around a name," Shedeur told Michael Strahan on *Big Noon Kickoff.* "I like to picture real things. All I can focus on, week in and week out, is going out there and dominating."

As a freshman, he passed for 3,231 yards with 30 touchdowns and eight interceptions to win the Jerry Rice Award, presented annually to college football's best freshman.

Part of the reason he joined his father at Jackson State was to change the narrative that HBCU players couldn't sign lucrative name, image, likeness (NIL) deals or get to the NFL.

Shedeur, nicknamed Grown as a child because he was mature for his age, wanted to be a quarterback for as long as he can remember. He loved the position's complexity, and he showed an aptitude for diagnosing coverages at an early age, prompting Coach Prime to move Shilo, his other son and a safety on the team, to receiver and safety and use Shedeur at quarterback.

"I always wanted to be a quarterback. There's a certain level of intensity and respect and trust that they're going to have," he said. "I don't use those words because I'm trying to be a leader or anything else. I'm just doing what I do.

"I'm not a big fan of putting things in categories. I feel I'm the most levelheaded person. I'm the most realistic. I know what it's going to take to accomplish what we're trying to do in a realistic sense."

Shedeur started working with former NFL quarterback Jeff Blake in middle school to correct an elongated delivery. Blake lived in Houston, so they'd meet in Waco, about one hundred miles south of Dallas.

A year later, Blake had fixed Shedeur's delivery. As a high school freshman, Shedeur began working with Darrell Colbert Jr., a former quarterback at SMU and Lamar University.

Colbert received several scholarship offers, but most wanted the 5'11" 185-pounder to play receiver or safety. He committed to SMU and coach June Jones to play quarterback, which is where he met Bucky, Coach Prime's eldest son.

Bucky eventually introduced Darrell to his younger brothers, Shilo and Shedeur. One day, Shedeur was hanging with his mom, Carolyn, in Houston, when he called Darrell.

"I'm out here for a couple days and I want to work out," he said.

For the next few days, Darrell scooped the eighth grader each morning and they worked on Shedeur's game.

"There's a reason his nickname is Grown. He's always been mature," Darrell said. "It's amazing the stuff you could see him doing from the sideline. You could see him running the offense, and changing plays at line. When your knowledge of the game is above others at high school, you can do that."

Darrell has nearly 120 players in his program, from seven-year-olds to NFL players such as Kyle Trask. He works with many of Houston's top high school quarterbacks.

"Darrell understands me as a person," Shedeur said. "He understands the overall picture that everyone can't understand."

On game days, Colbert oversees Shedeur's pregame warm-up, which includes tossing a weighted ball the size of a tennis ball to activate his shoulder muscles. He'll make sure the correct game balls are selected and he'll take care of anything Shedeur needs, so he can focus on the game.

"He's comfortable with Darrell, and I don't like to send him to a lot of people because everybody has different philosophies," Coach Prime said. "You have to be careful who you let get in their heads."

Shedeur led Trinity Christian High School to three consecutive Texas Association of Private and Parochial Schools Division II state championships.

Shedeur, a four-star recruit, ranked 61st on the ESPN 300 list. He had a multitude of offers, but wanted to play as a freshman. Shedeur committed to Florida Atlantic University and coach Willie Taggart, a longtime friend of Coach Prime. A couple of weeks after Coach Prime became JSU's coach, Shedeur asked for a meeting.

Thirty minutes later, he decommitted from FAU and committed to Jackson State.

"Whenever you are deciding on your life and who you want to put your life in the hands of, I'd rather go with someone who understands me," Shedeur said. "I'm so happy it's my pops. We were used to winning; coming here, we wouldn't expect anything else. It's a new day and age, and we aren't losing."

Shedeur was everything JSU alums and fans hoped he would be as a freshman. Three times he passed for more than 300 yards and twice he threw four touchdown passes in a game.

"I was like, this is cool, but I have to take it up a big notch. I had a decent year but my sophomore year I have to do something different," Shedeur said. "I'm watching the games and it don't look flawless. I see reads I missed and throws I missed. I could've done a lot more."

Like any teenager, Shedeur likes to have fun. He can do all the latest dances and knows the words to the hottest rap songs. He has a taste for expensive clothes, sneakers, and jewelry, and a plethora of NIL deals worth about $1.7 million allowed him to afford it.

He has a logo and wore custom-painted cleats every game. His YouTube channel had 54,500 subscribers, his Instagram page had more than one million followers, and his girlfriend is an actress.

But he's committed to being a number-one draft choice and an NFL quarterback.

"Every distraction in my life, I cut off," Shedeur said. "All the distractions are gone."

This is why he's all about business on the field. Every practice. Every day.

Mistakes weren't tolerated, and he confronted repeat offenders without hesitation. While his dad doesn't curse, Shedeur believes a well-placed "fuck" or "motherfucker" motivated teammates into performing better.

"Now, it's about disciplinary actions. If a receiver busts, now you're not gonna be with the first group for the next two days," he said. "If a tight end busts, now you not gonna get back with the first group until you prove yourself. We have to make guys prove themselves and show they're worthy of being with the first group and executing on every play."

Shedeur's occasionally colorful language isn't for show, which is why he didn't want ESPN to put a microphone on him during the 2021 spring game. He didn't want to censor himself during the heat of the moment.

"Daddy, you know how I am on the field," Shedeur told his father. "I go off."

"Son, that's going to endear you to coaches and everybody," said Coach Prime, "if they know how you actually get down."

Shedeur didn't change his mind. In 2022, he made himself more of a leader.

He worked hard to develop relationships with his teammates, so they understood that any criticism came from a place of love. They partied hard and trained harder.

"I tell them about themselves. A receiver shows up late, I'm gonna really tell him about himself, 'C'mon, bruh, you tripping. I ain't out here doing this just to do it. You think I wanted to get out of my bed? No, I didn't but we're here. Quit wasting my time.' Now, they know I'm serious but I don't do it in a disrespectful way.

"The words I use to them, to somebody else it sounds like I'm tripping, but we have a relationship. You know this is how I talk. You know what I'm getting at. So you can't even feel some kind of way. They know what I'm getting at."

The respect came because he worked hard at practice and being a good teammate.

He's been a coach's kid his entire life, so he understood the scrutiny that came from teammates.

"He ain't always cussed folks out but he's always been a leader. Always," Coach Prime said. "He's older. He's more mature and he understands the expectations at Jackson State, what I expect from him and what HBCUs expect.

"He's the face of HBCU football."

He played like it during the first month of the season. None of it excited Shedeur, though. He wanted a championship. Nothing else mattered.

"Last year he was going off raw ability. This year he took the field like he knew he was that guy," T. C. Taylor, the receivers coach, said. "This year he surpassed the speed of the game. It slowed down for him."

No one should be surprised. After all, Shedeur was supposed to thrive in this scheme.

Bartolone, a slot receiver, played for Mississippi State coach Mike Leach at Washington State. As a freshman, he caught 53 passes for 435 yards and 4 touchdowns. Labrum injuries to both shoulders limited him to five games and 10 catches for 53 yards as a sophomore.

"Every other day it was popping out," he said. "It was just kind of ridiculous. I wasn't playing nearly as well as I had and we had other guys passing me up on the depth chart. I knew, physically, I couldn't do what I wanted to do."

The medical redshirt jump-started his coaching career. Coach Prime wanted an up-tempo passing offense that averaged about 40 points a game, but also had a physical element. Bartolone studied every throw Shedeur made in 2021.

"The arm talent is ridiculous. Mechanically he's very sound," Bartolone said. "I give him the framework and the tools and he makes the plays."

Shedeur liked what he heard.

"Coach Bartolone challenges me almost every day to get better and just learning from him and the tree he came from. There's a lot of creative things that you can do each week," Shedeur said. "He just broke the game down in a way I could understand. He made it easy."

The nation had noticed Shedeur and Jackson State, with some urging from Coach Prime. For now, an invite to New York for the Heisman Trophy presentation was a possibility.

CHAPTER 13

I can actually do whatever I put my mind to.
—receiver/cornerback Travis Hunter

Travis Hunter played in Jackson State's first game. Then he missed the next five games because he needed another ankle surgery.

"It was either play and get the surgery or don't play and still get the surgery," Travis said. "That's why I wanted to play because I was going to have to get [another surgery] anyway."

To understand how Travis became one of the country's best high school football players, you have to go back more than a decade to the games of Throw It Up, Bust 'Em Up that he played with his older cousins: Fela, Jet, and T.J.

"I started playing when I was four years old with my cousins who were a lot older than me," Travis said. "They'd make me cry and go in the house when we played Throw It Up, Bust 'Em Up. They were busting me up, so I went in the house a lot, but I always came back out."

A couple of years of getting his butt kicked and Travis started coming in the house less frequently.

"They're kids. They're gonna play rough," said Ferrante Edmonds, Travis's mother. "He had to learn. He got knocked down, but he kept getting up."

He learned to contort his body to avoid tacklers and use his speed to escape the older boys.

"I love football. The game means a lot to me. Once I stepped on the field with my cousins, I started to believe that I could dominate," he said. "I want to win. I don't want to walk off a loser. My cousins and my dad always wanted to beat me when I was little. I don't like losing. Crying and going in the house all the time built me so I want to win."

Travis planned to play at Florida State just like his idol. The kid grew up a Florida State fan—his dad loved Coach Prime as a player— and committed to the Seminoles in March 2020.

Then JSU hired his idol. Less than two months later, Travis signed with JSU.

It's like Travis dropped an anvil on college football, because his signing sounded a warning that Coach Prime and JSU were going to be a force in recruiting.

Coach Prime, without any previous college coaching experience, swooped in at the last minute and flipped the nation's top player from his own alma mater. No, JSU didn't promise him any NIL money—so what if they did—even though University of Alabama coach Nick Saban claimed they did.

No football player has marketed himself better than Coach Prime. Michael Jordan, if you think about it, is the only professional athlete whose brand is bigger than Coach Prime's.

Today's athletes don't want to just play for a school. They want to know how the program will brand them, whether they've created a logo or a marketing plan for them.

"Jackson State paid a guy one million dollars last year that was a really good Division I player to come to school," Saban said on May 18 while talking to local business leaders in Birmingham. "It was in the paper. They bragged about it. Nobody did anything about it."

A day later, the Southeastern Conference publicly reprimanded Saban, who also made allegations against Texas A&M. Saban's comments disappointed Coach Prime, who considers Saban a friend and college football's best coach.

"I don't make a million. Travis ain't built like that. Travis ain't chasing a dollar. Travis is chasing greatness. Travis and his family don't get down like that," Coach Prime said at the time. "They never came to us in search of the bag. They're not built like that. This kid wants to be great.

"He wants my hands on him. He wants me to mold him. He wants me to be his navigational system through life. He wants to be that dude."

When Coach Prime spoke with parents and players, they saw and heard a different side of him, which resonated with Travis and his parents. Travis's mom liked the idea of Coach Prime taking her son and returning a man to her, and she liked God's role in Coach Prime's life. She trusted he would keep her baby safe.

Travis loved the idea of playing cornerback and receiver just like Coach Prime did with the Dallas Cowboys in 1996. Coach Prime pledged to coach Travis hard and prepare him for the NFL.

In Collins's 24–8 win over Milton in the 2021 Class 7A state championship game, Travis caught 10 passes for 153 yards and forced a fumble.

"I think he's a better receiver than cornerback," Taylor said. "Just watch him play, but it's harder to find cornerbacks with his skill set than receivers."

The 6'1" 165-pounder has elite athleticism. He has excellent speed and changes direction quickly. His long arms allow him to deflect passes others can't, and he attacks jump balls at their apex.

"You can see when he plays receiver that he has great vision," Thurman said. "He has the ability to see the bigger picture. He can see the safety and the linebacker. It starts with the eyes."

Travis's competitiveness sets him apart. Whether it's fishing, football, or video games, winning matters to him.

"Deion had great vision but his preparation allowed him to lock in. Nothing would distract him. He's a big vision guy and that's a gift. He chose to play a position that took advantage of his strength,"

Thurman said. "The matchups that challenged him were what he desired and that's why he was so great at it.

"He didn't care about what the other ten guys did. It was all about that one-on-one matchup play after play after play after play, and you have to want that."

Travis occasionally searches the internet for footage of Coach Prime getting beat.

"It's rare video, but it shows he's human," he said.

Travis will also tell you that he didn't just talk football with Coach Prime. They talked fishing, bass fishing to be exact. "In Georgia, if you have a fishing pole, you can find a creek or a park to fish," said Edmonds.

Travis's cousin T.J. taught him everything he knows about a rod and reel. Travis and Coach Prime regularly exchanged fish photos.

They fished at a private lake in the spring. Asked about the experience, Travis showed his competitiveness.

"I caught more fish than he did," he said with a loud laugh.

For one of few times, Coach Prime had nothing to say.

"I spent a lot of time talking to Coach Prime and Pretty Tony and Coach Mathis," Travis said. "It was never really about football. We know it's about football, but we didn't keep that the main focus."

The day before he committed, Coach Prime hinted on his Barstool podcast that he was about to shake up the college football world.

"I'm going on record to tell you guys we're going to shock the country," he said. "I'm telling you right now. You've heard it from me. We're going to shock the country."

No doubt.

Travis knew his decision was about more than football. He wanted to change the perception of HBCU football. If Travis, who could play anywhere, chose to play at an HBCU, then other elite players could do the same.

Guys like four-star receiver Kevin Coleman, who joined his friend at JSU, could be a conduit for change. After Travis made his decision, he released a two paragraph, 159-word statement on his Instagram account.

Florida State fans and others flooded social media and message boards with vitriol toward Travis and Coach Prime.

"I don't pay attention to it and I don't listen to it," Travis said. "People come and tell me about it but nobody can distract me. Nobody is going to get me out of my game and my mindset."

His mom was more direct.

"It doesn't matter where you go," she said. "It matters what you do when you get there."

Travis enrolled at JSU in January. Quickly, he began living up to the hype associated with one of the nation's top recruits joining a personality like Coach Prime in a place like Jackson that moved at a turtle's pace.

"It wasn't real until I got here. I knew I had to lock in because he's my coach—not my friend. He's driving me to be great," Travis said. "He's straightforward. He don't mess around. He caught me loafing one time and told me not to loaf no more or I wouldn't see the field. It didn't feel like I was loafing, but if he says I'm loafing then I'm loafing."

He's used to it. His dad has always pushed and prodded.

"He used to cuss me out in the middle of games and tell me I gotta do better," Travis said. "He'd tell me what I need to fix and if I do better, he say didn't I tell you."

Whenever a player like Travis arrived on any campus, his new teammates challenged him to see if he was real or hype.

JSU was no different.

Once spring practice started, JSU's best receivers challenged him. They called him out in one-on-one and seven-on-seven drills. Travis avoided no one.

"He took them all on and shut them all down," Thurman said laughing. "Travis is competitive. He's never going to back down."

Travis laughed as he remembered that day, "I proved myself."

In the spring game, televised nationally on ESPN, Travis inter-cepted two passes. On offense, he gained 25 yards on a reverse and scored on touchdown receptions of 9 and 80 yards.

"In the spring game, I showed I could play with any competition. It felt normal. It showed that I can actually do whatever I put my mind to," he said. "I don't know what pressure is. I ain't never felt pressure. I block out negative. It's always going to be a lot of haters, so I don't even listen to it."

PART III

PART II

CHAPTER 14

Who is SWAC if I ain't SWAC?
—Coach Prime

A week's worth of perceived disrespect had first-year Alabama State football coach Eddie Robinson Jr. seething.

When backup quarterback J. P. Andrade misfired on a hitch-and-go down the left sideline with 1:04 left, Robinson viewed it as one more disrespectful act from a coach he believed had been disrespectful all week.

When the game ended, the coaches met at midfield and Coach Prime extended his right hand.

"Hey, man, you had them ready to play. Good game," he said.

Coach Prime attempted to pull Robinson close for a half hug, but the Alabama State coach shoved him hard with his left hand. Coach Prime swatted his hand away.

"What was that?" Coach Prime said loudly, raising his arms and showing his palms.

Ashley Robinson, who prefers watching from the sideline, sidled up to Coach Prime with 1:27 left and suggested the players leave without shaking hands after the game.

"I learned from last year," Ashley Robinson said a few hours later as his phone vibrated constantly with texts about Coach Prime, Robinson, and "the shove."

"I should've done it at Southern [last year]. I didn't and we had an incident. I wasn't going to let that happen again."

Getting to Alabama State from Jackson requires a four-hour journey through the South's racist past. The route takes travelers through Philadelphia, Mississippi, and Marion and Selma, Alabama, before ending in Montgomery. Each of those cities is synonymous with the civil rights movement, just like Birmingham, where JSU stayed the night before the game.

An hour down I-20 East from Jackson is Philadelphia and Exit 152, James Chaney Road.

James Chaney, born and raised in Meridian, about forty miles east of Philadelphia, was one of three civil rights workers killed by the Ku Klux Klan in June 1964. Chaney, Michael Schwerner, and Andrew Goodman were investigating the burning of Mt. Zion Methodist Church, a site for a CORE Freedom School.

All three men were shot, killed, and then buried in a dam that hid their bodies for forty-four days. The movie *Mississippi Burning*, starring Gene Hackman and Willem Dafoe, depicted the search for their bodies. Their disappearance became a national story, and media flocked to Mississippi to cover it.

Doing so exposed Mississippi's harsh treatment of African Americans. It's not like America didn't know about Mississippi, but the media coverage meant it could no longer lie to itself or ignore the truth about folks like Fannie Lou Hamer, who received a hysterectomy without her consent in 1961.

Doctors performed this kind of forced sterilization to limit the African-American population so often it was nicknamed a "Mississippi appendectomy." We're talking about a state that lynched 539 African Americans between 1882 and 1968. No state had more.

Two hours down Highway 80 is Marion, Alabama.

The Civil Rights Act of 1964 ended segregation in public places and banned employment discrimination on the basis of race, religion, sex, color, or national origin. But it wasn't really impacting everyday life in the South, where time seemingly stood still.

Voting was the best way to create change and the South's power brokers weren't letting that happen without a fight.

In February 1965, three weeks before the march on Montgomery, Alabama state troopers shot and killed twenty-six-year-old Jimmie Lee Jackson, a deacon at St. James Baptist Church in Marion who had tried to register to vote for four years. He was participating in a peaceful voting rights march when state troopers beat and shot him while he protected his mother. She was attempting to stop her eighty-two-year-old father from being beaten.

Eight days later, Jackson died.

Twenty-seven miles down Highway 80 from Marion is Selma, where Bloody Sunday occurred on March 7, 1965.

Activist John Lewis led more than six hundred men, women, and children across the Edmund Pettus Bridge, where they hoped to march fifty-four miles to the capital city of Montgomery and protest Alabama's voting inequities.

Billy club–carrying state troopers wearing gas masks attacked Lewis and the protestors as they crossed the county line. The incident became known as Bloody Sunday, and it was the first of three voting rights protest marches that contributed to the passage of the Voting Rights Act of 1965.

An hour down Highway 80 sits Montgomery, made famous by Rosa Parks and the bus boycott that lasted from December 5, 1955, to December 20, 1956. It's considered the first large-scale fight against segregation.

Coach Prime was often the only Black player on the youth football and baseball teams he played on growing up in Fort Myers, and if he wasn't the only Black player, he was one of only a handful.

He integrated at least one youth baseball league.

Those experiences are why he goes out of his way to make sure the white and Hispanic players on his team don't feel like minorities on a campus and team that's predominantly Black.

One morning in late August as players trudged wearily toward the locker room after practice, Sanders stepped out of his red golf cart and said in a loud voice, "Everybody who's not Black come over."

Then he proceeded to tell the program's twenty-eight non-Black players, coaches, and support staff that he appreciated their efforts and he never wanted them to feel uncomfortable in their environment.

The Tigers had thirteen white players and three Hispanic players.

"One day they're going to write a story or a movie about what we're accomplishing," Coach Prime told them as they gathered around his golf cart. "I want to know how you feel. I want to know what's the mood. I want to know how you make it because this is probably the first time you've been the minority.

"Why is a white player reluctant to come to an HBCU? I want to know. I want honesty. This is why I came. This is how it is. This is what I think about it. Black folks are always asking for equality but we don't give it.

"We want equality at HBCUs but do we give it at HBCUs? When you watch Jackson State play, you see equality. You see it all over. I don't give a durn what color you are. As long as you do your job, I'm happy with you."

Sam Johnson, who's white, picked Jackson State over the University of Alabama at Birmingham because it provided the best opportunity to kick.

"See, I grew up playing AAU basketball and I was the only white guy in the league, and I wasn't a shooter," he said. "I've been around Black people and Black culture forever. It makes me not see the HBCU side of it because I'm so used to being the minority."

Lane McGregor, JSU's holder, came to Jackson State because he wanted to learn more about the history of African Americans and figured it would be better to do it an HBCU than a predominantly white institution.

"I grew up in government housing. I grew up in the trenches," said McGregor, who was raised a couple of hours north of Jackson. "I've just learned so much about African-American people and I know that wouldn't have happened anywhere else. Everybody is the same. That's what I was taught from birth."

Coach Prime and his players weren't thinking about history when they arrived at Alabama State because kickoff was only an hour away.

The buses carrying players, coaches, and support staff usually arrive at the stadium three hours early, giving the players plenty of time to get taped and go through their pregame rituals before preparing as a team.

Jackson State stayed in Birmingham, ninety minutes north of Montgomery. The team left with a police escort at 10:15 a.m. but a fiery one-car accident on Interstate 65 South at Exit 254 stopped traffic.

As he did every game, Coach Prime prepared to take a lap around the field. It's a routine he started in the NFL to clear his mind and focus. He headed left out of the tunnel and walked right into Alabama State's team.

The Hornets, who were warming up, spilled out of the end zone, giving Coach Prime no choice but to walk through them. One player, wearing No. 88, could clearly be seen looking at Coach Prime and saying, "Fuck Jackson State. Fuck Jackson State."

He wasn't the only player who used expletives.

"I've never seen players talk to a coach that way. Some of the stuff those dudes were saying to Prime, I was blown away," Taylor said. "That let me know it was echoed all week. As a player you never talk to a coach that way."

Coach Prime gathered his team on the field before the game and reinforced the importance of focus and discipline because of the language and hostile environment.

"No talking. No talking. No talking. We're really just going to come out here and play some football. We ain't doing no talking," he said. "We're not going to do anything stupid. No penalties, no nothing.

"We're not talking. There's been too much disrespect. We're going to show them."

Jackson State had outscored its first four opponents 190–38, including 118–7 in the second half.

Coach Prime used ASU's selection of the Tigers as their home-coming opponent as a motivational tool. He mentioned it during Monday's SWAC teleconference as well as Tuesday during his weekly availability with the local media.

"He kept talking about disrespect, but the only thing I said close to that was, 'Why would you schedule us for homecoming?' That's a real question. Why would you? We were undefeated. We're the SWAC champions. Who schedules the SWAC champions for home-coming? That's an insult. That's the truth," Coach Prime said. "That's the way we felt here. So I went with that. The disrespect. We played Aretha Franklin's 'Respect' all week, and I'll be durned if the second we walked out on the field the disrespect started.

"They cussed me out. They cussed the coaches out. They cussed the equipment girls out. I've never been so disrespected in my life."

Once again, JSU started slowly.

A 19-yard touchdown pass from Dematrius Davis to Kisean John-son gave ASU a 6–0 lead. Alabama State gained 120 yards on 40 plays the rest of the game.

Twice on JSU's first three drives, Alabama State stopped the Ti-gers on downs. The Tigers finally put together an eight-play, 80-yard scoring drive, but it required a four-leaf clover, a horseshoe, and a rabbit's foot to get it done.

Middle linebacker Colton Adams dropped a pass he should've in-tercepted on second-and-15 from the JSU 15. The drive ended with a 35-yard touchdown to Willie Gaines on a go route. Mata's extra point made it a 7–6 lead.

A 34-yard field goal by Mata with 25 seconds left in the first half pushed the lead to 10–6, and it swelled to 17–6 on a beautiful 25-yard touchdown pass to Kevin Coleman, the first of his career. Shedeur threw off his back foot just as a defender drilled him.

"When I saw the corner backing up, he was so far inside the outside receiver I knew I had a chance to get the ball," Kevin said. "[Shedeur] always told me if safety shoots down, you have a chance to get it even if the outside receiver is primary.

"In high school, I learned if the ball slows you down, attack it high. I had the corner beat, but I felt him catching up so I attacked the ball."

When ASU pulled within 17–12, Coach Prime spoke briefly to Shedeur.

"It's time for you to take us home," he said above the roar of the crowd.

And that's just what he did.

Shedeur's 16-yard touchdown pass to J. D. Martin made it 23–12, and Gerardo Baeza's 30-yard field goal extended the lead to 26–12. Shedeur, who finished with 332 passing with 3 touchdowns and an interception, did not take the field for the final drive after ASU turned the ball over on downs.

Between the end of the JSU twelfth consecutive SWAC victory and the postgame news conferences, several members of JSU's support and coaching staff watched video of the incident between Coach Prime and Robinson multiple times.

In his postgame news conference, Robinson, who is not related to the legendary Grambling coach with the same name, made an opening statement and answered one question about Alabama State's defense before describing what happened during the post-game handshake.

"I was just pulling away. We had a handshake and that was it. It ain't no need for an embrace. He's a great player. Goddamn. Everybody wanted to be Prime Time when they were a little kid. We ain't friends. I never called him and he ain't never called me," Robinson said. "I got a lot of respect for him as a coach, but you can't do that stuff all week, put your backup quarterback in the game and run a hitch-and-go to put more points on the board. The shit is disrespectful. The game was out of line. It was 26–12. Forty seconds left. We don't have no timeouts. Take a damn knee.

"We ain't friends. You didn't shake my hand before the game. Why are you trying to shake my hand now? I'm not about to give you the Obama bro hug. I'm going to shake your hand and go on."

The more Robinson talked, the more agitated he became. The perceived disrespect angered him, especially when Coach Prime walked through his team during warm-ups.

"I'm going to always be respectful and respect the game. You've got the great [coaches], W. C. Gordon, Eddie Robinson, those guys, Marino Casem, I'm living on the shoulders of the SWAC. He ain't SWAC. I'm SWAC, he ain't SWAC.

"He got the W, great job. I hope he comes back next year. I pray he don't get a Power 5 job," Robinson said. "We can play them next year in Jackson, and I pray they put us for their damn homecoming."

Coach Prime, surrounded by Robinson, Lewis, Forsett, personal assistant Sam Morini, and Tracey, Coach Prime's girlfriend, listened to a tape of Robinson's comments before he spoke to the media. Lewis and Morini weren't sure whether Coach Prime wanted to have a postgame news conference. As soon as he heard Robinson's first comment, it was clear Coach Prime would talk.

The problem for Robinson is that he entered a war of words with Coach Prime, a battle he could never win.

"I'm not one to come back the next day and you're going to pick up the phone and you're going to apologize and we straight," he said. "No, not whatsoever. You meant that mess.

"And one of the comments that kind of disturbed me out of all the comments, that I'm not SWAC. Who is? I got time today. Who is SWAC if I ain't SWAC? Who is SWAC if I ain't SWAC?"

Taylor played and coached in the SWAC. He took offense to Robinson's comments.

"He's not SWAC. What does that mean? There are three or four other coaches in this league that didn't play in the SWAC, so what does that mean?" Taylor wondered. "You have to play in this conference when you coach in this conference to be SWAC. Some of the greats didn't go to SWAC schools."

Coach Prime said he doesn't always greet opposing coaches before a game. He didn't speak to Dancy, one of his best friends in the SWAC, before their game.

"I'm not one to go find a coach," Coach Prime said.

ASU announced the game as a sellout during the week. They had not drawn more than 17,000 in their previous five homecoming games at their 26,500-seat stadium.

"I was a durn good salesman leading up to the week," Coach Prime said. "Did we sell the game out? Did we sell the game out? Yes or no? Had they ever been sold out here? So I thought I did my job. I thought I should be applauded, really."

If Robinson thought a new day would end the controversy, he was sadly mistaken. While Robinson issued a statement apologizing for his language at the news conference, Coach Prime's social media team showed videos of Alabama State's players cursing Coach Prime as he started his pregame walk.

Coach Prime walked into Monday's team meeting wearing a navy blue hoodie that read "Who is SWAC?" on the front and "I Am SWAC" on the back.

JSU's players and coaches went crazy. At the end of practice as they gathered around the block, the players started chanting, "Who is SWAC? Who is SWAC? Who is SWAC?"

In two days, the video had 1.4 million views on Instagram. Snoop Dogg phoned Coach Prime on Wednesday afternoon and asked him to send him a hoodie. Tank, the R&B singer, put out a video in which he asked the question, "Who is R&B? Who is R&B?"

While Coach Prime and his friends had fun at Robinson's expense, the Alabama State coach turned off his comments on Instagram.

CHAPTER 15

Who is 36?
He's toting that thang.
—Coach Prime

Sy'Veon Wilkerson's freshman season at Delaware State left him unfulfilled.

Sure, he finished second in the Mid-Eastern Athletic Conference in rushing with 848 yards and 8 touchdowns. He earned first-team All-Conference honors and was a finalist for the Jerry Rice Award.

He wanted more.

"I wanted to play on a bigger stage. I wanted to play in front of larger crowds and get more exposure," he said. "I wanted to play for Coach Prime. Once he came to Jackson State, I was like, 'Yeah, this is it.' This was the place to be."

Sy'Veon entered the transfer portal after the season and committed to West Virginia. He stayed one semester.

"It was too many white folks," he said. "I'm just being honest."

He contacted Riddley, who told him the Tigers didn't have any scholarships available for running backs. Riddley offered Sy'Veon priority walk-on status and promised him the best players play at Jackson State.

That's all Sy'Veon needed to hear.

"I got confidence in myself. I can get a scholarship. That's not a problem," Sy'Veon said. "If I had to take out a loan for a semester, that's nothing. I felt like I could come here right away and play."

In 2021, Jackson State ranked ninth in the SWAC in rushing with 111.8 yards per game and tied for ninth at three and a half yards per carry.

"I was watching everything they did and I thought it would be a perfect fit. I thought I could go there and be the difference," he said. "I knew a running game would put them over the top because the passing game was already there."

Sy'Veon didn't make much of an impact in the summer because he has an abnormally large heart—a warrior's heart—and doctors wanted to make sure it wasn't diseased. He worked out three times with the team during the summer. Doctors didn't clear him for physical activity until fall practice.

Coach Flea, who coached the running backs, didn't like Sy'Veon's hands or his route running. He didn't think he'd crack the two-deep depth chart, which lists the starter and backup at each position, and the travel team wasn't guaranteed, either.

"I'm going to be honest with you, I was figuring out how to help the kid," Riddley said. "I told him to see if there were some other places he wanted to go. I told him I didn't want him spending any money on school, if he wasn't going to play."

Sy'Veon appreciated the conversation, but he wanted to bet on himself.

"Coach," he said, "I'm going to stay."

After a few pile-moving, leg-churning inside runs, Coach Prime asked, "Who is 36? He's toting that thang."

Coach Prime told Coach Flea to give No. 36 more opportunities in practice.

"I thought Santee and J.D. [Martin] did a great job, so I was going to give them an opportunity to solidify their spots," Coach

Flea said. "But Sy'Veon opened some eyes with the physical runs and some of the cuts.

"The other two guys saw what he could do. They saw what he went through and they saw when he got his opportunity and they saw the performance he put on and now the respect level is there and it creates a good environment in your room."

Five games into the season, Sy'Veon had gained 470 yards. He averaged 5.0 per carry and shared the position with Martin and Santee.

"If we don't have Sy'Veon," said Riddley, "we're in fucking trouble."

At 5'8" and 205 pounds, Sy'Veon was a compact, thickly built runner who was rarely tackled by the first defender and powered through arm tackles. He did most of his damage between the tackles, but he became a special player when he hit the second level and linebackers and safeties were forced to tackle him.

"He's a gritty runner. He doesn't stop his feet in the hole, and he has good knee drive," said graduate assistant Brandon Morton, who works with the running backs. "He's twitchy and makes good cuts. He's not easy to tackle. He studies. He watches the most film. He's always the first on the practice from the running back group. He has a lot of passion. He loves it."

Credit his mom, ShaQuida Haywood, who introduced him to football as a two-year-old and taught him to root for the Chicago Bears. Watching YouTube made him a Walter Payton fan and partial to Jackson State.

"Walter Payton is the best to ever do it. People argue Barry Sanders and Emmitt Smith are better, but I like Walter Payton," Sy'Veon said. "I try to model my game after him, but I really try to be myself. I like to be my own person."

As a child, Sy'Veon had anger management issues. A fight in second grade when another student snatched a paper towel out of his hands forced him to change.

"My mom got tired of it and sent me to jail one time," he said laughing. "When I got home, my mom said, 'Get your stuff, we're leaving.' I didn't know where we were going. She gave me a picture of us, dropped me off at the police station, and said, 'Y'all can do whatever you want with him now.'"

He sat there for hours until she returned.

"This was some beyond scared-straight stuff," he said.

Now Sy'Veon focuses that rage on the field. You can see it in the way he attacks the hole and punishes linebackers.

"When you give him the ball," said tight ends coach Tim Brewster, "his personality comes out and you see the person he really is."

Jackson State's scholarship players occupy the new locker room. The nonscholarship players use the old one, which has wooden stalls, tight corridors, and a stale smell.

Coach Prime believed in rewarding hard work.

As a kid, Coach Prime often skipped school to hang out at the Kansas City Royals spring training, a few blocks from his home. He'd shag balls hit over the fence and persuade players to sign them. He'd sell some balls and play with others. Sometimes he gave an autographed ball to the teacher who let him skip.

Coach Prime discovered the connection between work and reward early in life and it's been a constant motivation.

"He wants everyone to work as hard he does," said Campo, who told some great stories about Coach Prime in his college days, "and that's impossible."

Coach Prime devised a plan to reward walk-on players by moving them from the old locker room into the new one.

"The only way a walk-on can get on this side is you nominate him. Now he needs another one of you guys to validate it. You guys make that pitch to me," Coach Prime told his staff. "You got one vote, the other coach got one vote, and I got two votes. If I say no, we're even. The tiebreaker is Pretty Tony.

"That's how it's going down. Nominate who you want. We already got a theme song. It's gonna be a good time. We're going play the song, they're going to pack their little plastic bag, Dominique is going to have their travel bag packed and they're gonna move on up."

Coach Prime chose "Moving On Up," the theme song for the sit-com *The Jeffersons*, which aired on CBS from 1975 to 1985. The show was about an African-American family that used its dry-cleaning business to move from Queens to Manhattan.

Players could be banished from the new digs to the old digs for missing treatment sessions or weight room sessions or being dis-respectful to coaches or women.

"You do have an opportunity to move up. All you have to do is work your butt off, make a difference, and ball out," he said. "Now, it's going to be a ceremony because you achieved something tremendous."

Then he asked Campo to play "Moving On Up." The players quickly found the beat. They clapped and laughed.

"There's another song when you get demoted. You get your butt kicked. You're not doing your job. Coaches gotta yell at you, they gotta get on your butt. You're late for meetings," Coach Prime said. "Coach Mo says you ain't lifting worth a durn. Miss Lauren says you're missing treatment and you got an attitude around here. You gonna get up out of here and go to the other locker room. I don't care if you're on scholarship or not."

On a picturesque fall morning, Coach Prime decided today was the day to see if any players were worthy of a locker room promotion.

After a few announcements, he opened the floor for nominations. Brewster nominated tight end D. J. Stevens, who stood while he received a second.

"I agree with it one hundred percent," he said. "I thought he was already over there. My bad."

As the song played and the players and Coach Prime clapped, Markuson nominated offensive lineman Josiah Laban, who arrived just before the season started but quickly became one of Coach Prime's favorites because of his consistent effort.

Then Coach Flea nominated Sy'Veon.

While Sy'Veon stood, his teammates pounded their hands to-gether and Coach Prime danced.

Coach Prime didn't even cosign on Sy'Veon.

Sy'Veon moved into the starting lineup in Week 2 against Tennessee State and produced 109 yards of total offense and plenty of attitude. Two weeks later, against Alabama State, he produced 136 yards of total offense and converted a third-and-15 in the second quarter that changed the game.

On Friday, when the assistant coaches addressed the team, Pollock asked Sy'Veon to stand after the players dined on pans of steak, grilled chicken, garlic mashed potatoes, steamed broccoli, and Caesar salad.

"He started in the old locker room and you know what he did? He didn't say shit. He ain't say nothing. I respect you. I look at how you go to work every day. He's never said a word," Pollock said. "If I'm All-Conference and I go to another school and they put me in the old locker room, how many guys do you know are going to take that as a slap in the face?

"He was fifth team and scout team for a long time until we ran power in practice and said, 'Dang, who is that guy?'"

Coach Prime shared with his staff the importance of developing boys into men.

The vast majority of college football players will enter the workforce, not the NFL, after their college football careers end. Those are the men who will become the pillars of their neighborhoods and significant contributors to society. They will coach youth teams, raise families, and make a difference in their communities.

"I'm focused on the ninety-five, when most coaches are focused on the five. The five are going to the pros. The ninety-five ain't. My main focus has to be on the ninety-five because I have to build men," he said. "When you pull up to the grocery store in your car and he pulls up in his, I don't want you to lock your doors."

Coach Prime spent a chunk of his adult life showing boys how to become men.

It's important because so many players on his team grew up without fathers in their homes or without strong role models. For many, the first time someone they respect challenges them occurs on campus.

"We have some more maturing to do as a team. You have to be able to take that feedback from your brother. They're trying to look out for you," Sims said. "They want the best for you. If we can't accept constructive criticism from somebody who loves us and is on the same team with us, then how are you going to handle yourself in the real world when somebody who don't care about you gives you the same type of criticism?

"Accountability feels like an attack when you're not ready to take responsibility for your behavior."

When discussing what's required to be a man, Coach Prime started with the basics: personal hygiene.

He wanted every player to shower after practice, which hasn't always been the case. The equipment staff placed a towel and washcloth in every player's locker.

"If they don't shower, they're going over there to the locker room. All the showers work, they got curtains, so you don't have to worry about anybody seeing what you got," Coach Prime said. "They're going to have towels so they can wrap up on the way to the shower. Ain't no funkiness and no nastiness in the locker room."

Given the tenor of the week, it made sense that Coach Flea shared a story that's more about God's grace than anything he did. But when you're part of a coaching staff determined to mold boys into men, Coach Flea wanted to earn their trust. Exposing his flaws did that.

"You have to go to class. You have to go to study hall. You have to come to practice. You have to bust your ass," Coach Flea said. "Your focus. Your plan. Your purpose. That helps you understand why you're here.

"Why are you here? Why do you wake up every morning dealing with Coach Mo in the weight room? Why do you get up at six a.m. for meetings with Coach Ricard, who's cussing you out? You're doing it because you have a plan and you have a focus."

Coach Flea grew up in Liberty City, a poor section of Miami rife with drugs and crime. For Liberty City kids, the world held two options: sell drugs or play sports.

In an idealistic world, those kids would be told to get an education or find a job. The reality is that the schools in places like Liberty City are typically subpar and the students often lack family support. Besides, they don't usually have money for college or the grades for scholarships.

"I had to play football. Understand I had to be good at football or I wasn't going to college. I had to be good at football or I couldn't support my family," Coach Flea said, his voice rising as he smacked his hands together. "Those were my have-tos. What's your have-to?

"See, where I grew up—I know some of you guys can attest to it—you only had two things: play ball or slang dope. And those guys who slang dope never let you cross that line. They wanted you to stay focused. Stay in your plan and stay in your purpose."

Coach Flea, who held school records for receptions (13) and yards in a game (184), graduated from Howard University.

He played two seasons with the New York Giants and a year in the Canadian Football League with the Montreal Alouettes. When Montreal released him, he returned home with no plan, no focus, and no purpose.

"It was tough at first when it came to an end. I knew what I could do, but I could never just get that opportunity to do it," Coach Flea said. "I always felt like I had to prove something. That's been my whole life. I couldn't watch football for a long time. I couldn't talk about it."

Coach Flea found himself in Liberty City hanging around guys who chose the streets as their occupation.

"Life is a circle. I found myself right back on Twenty-Second and Seventy-First in Liberty City with those same guys I grew up with," he said. "But there was a time in my life I went back to that corner after I got through playing pro ball.

"I felt good about that money and I wanted to sustain that lifestyle. I had a college degree and played pro ball, but I went right back to the same spot hanging with the guys I grew up with."

For weeks, he waged a war within himself. Finally, Coach Flea entered a game he literally knew nothing about. He didn't know the cost of a pound of weed or a kilo of cocaine.

"One guy, the last guy on the corner, I went to him and said, 'I got this money. I don't know about the dope game, but I want to continue to make money and have this lifestyle. I'm just going to give you this amount of money and you do what you gotta do and bring me back what you wanna bring.'

"I had no focus. I had a poor plan. I had no purpose. That's where I was in my life. It took that guy—that's all he did in his life—that's all he knew how to do. He looked me in my eyes and said, 'Flea, I have to do this. You don't have to do this.'

"See, his have-to was different than my have-to, but it set me on a path to go focus and continue my plan and my purpose. I still see him when I go home and I thank him every time. Understand, you go through things, but we have a focus, we have a plan, and we have a purpose."

The plan and the purpose this week was to destroy Bethune-Cookman University at TIAA Bank Field in Jacksonville, Florida.

Coach Prime didn't want to play in an NFL stadium (Jaguars) that seated 67,164 because the optics on TV were going to be awful. Bethune-Cookman, located about ninety minutes from Jacksonville in Daytona Beach, averaged 5,323 per game in 2021.

"I want it to look good on TV and a half-empty stadium looks bad," Coach Prime told ESPN's broadcasting team.

Coach Prime addressed the potentially small crowd with his players. The Tigers usually play in packed stadiums, so Coach Prime wondered whether his team would be infected by lethargy.

"All across the nation they're talking about the Jackson State Tigers. They're talking about Jackson State just like they are Alabama and all these other Power 5 teams," Brewster said. "You know what you are, men? You know what you've done? You know what you've accomplished? Jackson State University is relevant again. You mean something."

Jackson State had trailed three times in the first quarter, and the slow starts perplexed Coach Prime.

Bethune-Cookman was 1-4 and had been destroyed by Miami (70–13), South Carolina State (33–9), and Tennessee State (41–17).

"One thing about losing football teams is they know how to lose. Once they start losing, what do they do? They want to make the people beating them losers, too," Taylor told the team at their Friday team dinner.

"You can't fall into that trap as a football team. Once we go up twenty-one points, the first thing that's going to happen is one of them is going to swing. When it happens, walk away."

A couple of minutes before kickoff, Weeks, the defensive tackles coach, used a purple marker to write "Start Fast" on a small whiteboard he placed in front of the bench.

Isaiah Bolden made sure it happened with a 55-yard kick return. The drive ended with Shedeur throwing a 5-yard touchdown pass to Rico Powers for a 7–0 lead.

A 4-yard touchdown pass to Dallas Daniels and a 13-yard touchdown pass to Shane Hooks, who caught the ball at the eight and ran past three defenders who didn't even attempt to tackle him, made it 21–0 with 4:10 left in the first quarter.

"The number one thing I'm looking for right now is a lazy motherfucker," Ricard said. "If you don't run your ass down the field on this kickoff, you're coming out."

Understand, "motherfucker" was Ricard's favorite word on the football field. He used it liberally as a noun, verb, adjective, and adverb. He used it so much, the players chuckled when they heard it—at the appropriate time—even when it was directed at them.

"It's a country cuss word," Ricard said sheepishly. "It's versatile. You can use it in a lot of different ways."

It was 30–0 at halftime, but Coach Prime didn't like the second quarter's intensity level. Plus, something was wrong with Shedeur's right arm.

"In the first quarter everyone was tapping out. They were falling down and getting hurt—not in the second quarter," Coach Prime yelled as he entered the locker room. "We got complacent. Don't get complacent. Let's do this, fellas."

Shedeur's arm problem was a bigger issue. In the second quarter, Shane was open by five yards down the right sideline, but Shedeur underthrew him by five yards and the pass was intercepted.

Shedeur had sprained his right shoulder a week earlier against Alabama State. He didn't miss any practice time, but he had been compromised. None of the other four quarterbacks on the roster would be an adequate replacement, which didn't matter against Bethune-Cookman, but a lot of the season remained.

JSU pushed its lead to 39–0 after three quarters with their second safety and a 9-yard touchdown by Santee. A third safety, tying an NCAA record, and a 7-yard touchdown pass to Shane made the final score 48–8.

Sy'Veon rushed nine times for 66 yards and JSU finished with 234 yards rushing on 34 carries. Shedeur passed for 272 yards with 5 touchdowns and two interceptions.

Not bad for a dude with a sprained shoulder.

The next day Jackson State became the talk of the college football universe because Coach Prime was featured in a *60 Minutes* segment.

He spoke about the importance of having elite players like Travis compete at HBCU programs. He also made it abundantly clear that if any Power 5 programs reached out, he would listen. What he left unsaid was that his relationship with Hudson made him more open to leaving.

CHAPTER 16

He'll make you want to reach a certain level of greatness.
—safety Cam'Ron Silmon-Craig

Coach Prime loves the moment when dawn shifts slowly into day. It's quiet and peaceful, allowing thoughts to flow freely, because no one wants anything from him.

"The morning shapes your day," he said. "However your morning goes is usually how your day goes most of the time."

JSU practices in the morning. The Tigers usually hit the field by 8:30 a.m. and they're done at 10:30 a.m. Coach Prime wants short practices with a fast tempo.

"I want the best out of them. If we practice in the afternoon they're gonna get high, be lazy from school, have an attitude because they had a fight with their girlfriend or be mad with their parents 'cause they ain't sent them no money," he said. "That's just what happens in a day. A day brings trials and tribulations."

He's committed to learning his players and their personal stories, which helps him figure out whether a hug, a lecture, or an ass-chewing will motivate them the most.

"As arrogant as he probably comes off in the media, his heart is gold. He really does mean well," trainer Lauren Askevold said. "Hart, Mathis. All the guys he brings with him really do care about their players and they really do care what they're trying to do in terms of changing lives, changing the program, and changing the culture.

"He's given chance after chance after chance to some kids. I don't want to even say 'coach.' He's a great coach, but he's genuinely a good human."

Every day after practice, Askevold massages Coach Prime's amputated foot as part of his continued therapy. He spends that time engaging with players and support staff, which is how he wound up helping Darshena Marion, a student trainer, with an assignment.

"I was writing a poem about my brother and my cousin because they didn't go down the right path," said Darshena, a junior from Chicago, "and I asked him to read over it, and he pretty much helped me with it."

Coach Prime made players check in for breakfast. Most days, the players had a choice of scrambled eggs, boiled eggs, grits, turkey sausage, bacon, hash browns, and biscuits. Occasionally, breakfast burritos wrapped in aluminum foil and waffles were served.

"Let me catch one of you taking breakfast out of the cafeteria and it's going to be a problem," he said. "I want you guys to sit down and have a great breakfast with your teammates. Talk and get to know somebody and be charming and hospitable. Breakfast should not happen on the run.

"Coaches included. Get your butts there early, sit down, and eat breakfast with your players and get to know them. That's how we're gonna get down."

Lunch and dinner could be consumed elsewhere.

Most players lived off campus. They had classes in the middle of the day, so they were scattered all over campus. Sure, they had position meetings and weight-lifting sessions, but when you think about it, they didn't really spend much time together as a team.

Breakfast, their daily ten-minute team meeting, and their Friday night team meetings were the only times the players gathered as a unit.

"If we don't have that cafeteria, we're fucked," Riddley said. "I don't care what nobody says. Seventy percent of our players stay off campus. When would they ever sit down together and have the kind of conversation they have in that cafeteria?

"Those dudes are in there breaking bread every day. You have O-linemen with DBs. Sometimes they clique up but they mix and match."

Coach Prime started each team meeting with a prayer. He'd walk into the meeting room, remove his hat, usually a baseball cap, and say, "Somebody pray us up." Normally a player immediately stood and led the team in a brief prayer.

Sometimes a coach did it. Coach Prime never did it. It's important to him that his players do it.

After several weeks of the same few players leading the prayer each morning, Coach Prime asked different players to do it. Toward the end of the season, he asked two or three players each morning to pray, ensuring each player did it at least once.

"It's important because these guys are going to have families one day," he said, "and they're going to have to lead their families. Sometimes, they're going to have to pray about something and they need to know how to do it."

He also wanted to show players there's no right way to speak to God. You can call him father, man, or almighty, depending on your relationship. Coach Prime wanted them to know they didn't have to use religious language like "thee" and "thou." They could speak to God the way they talk to their friends.

Granted, these skills might not apply to all of Coach Prime's players, depending on their religion. But he knows the type of young men he attracts. He has strong beliefs about what those young men must learn to succeed and live the life they claim they want. And he's determined to give it to them.

Donald Turley played Marine Corps football for two years. Before he wanted to be a football player, and an agnostic, Turley wanted to be a preacher.

He grew up in Chillicothe, Ohio, about fifty miles south of Columbus, and spent his Sundays listening to the word at Chillicothe

Baptist Church. Entering middle school, Turley studied the Bible because he planned to preach the gospel one day.

More study led to questions that those in leadership couldn't or wouldn't answer.

"I brought up the question, if God is so almighty and powerful and sends his only son to die for everybody, why are there are so many different faiths in Christianity?" Turley wondered. "It ranges from Judaism to Christianity to Zionism. Where do we differentiate what is the Word and how to be saved or how to get to heaven?

"I wouldn't say I was challenging anyone, but I was questioning which one of these is the way. Why do Baptists follow it this way and Catholics follow it that way? Anytime I would bring something up they would just attack me, attack me, attack me."

Since he couldn't get the answers he sought, Turley studied other religions.

"I see [Christianity] as a discipline and a way to live life with morals and good values and stuff like that," he said. "Christianity contradicts itself a lot. No man is perfect, so how can a man say this is the way you should live, when we have so many branches of Christianity?"

A few weeks later, Coach Prime noticed Tyler, JSU's starting left guard, crossing himself after he prayed and inquired about the gesture's significance.

"I thought it was kind of funny. I love my religion. I love my faith. I went to Catholic schools my entire life so the sign of the cross is something I do," Tyler said. "I love informing people and I love being informed about other people's religions. I always want to learn. I'm always willing to share."

Coach Prime is receptive to learning, even if his own belief system is fixed. Discussing God and relating it to life and football was only a portion of his daily message. The idea was to give JSU's players something bigger than themselves to hold on to when life starts kicking their butt. Good coaches share what has enabled them to win in life with their players and coaches. Those players and coaches can accept it or reject it.

"As a young man, you have to learn how to win to keep winning," right guard Evan Henry said. "Coach Prime has won at everything. He doesn't know how to lose."

Coaching is teaching. He enjoyed teaching his players and coaches how he won in life because he wanted them to experience their best life. This comes from a man who often says, "I don't have bad days."

"I never told him this, but he impacted my life like no other. When he speaks words there's a wisdom about it," Taylor said. "I get my workout in and my word from him and I'm ready to go. I needed to be around him."

Cam'Ron Silmon-Craig said playing for Coach Prime is life-changing because the only standard he's ever accepted is greatness. Weeks, the defensive tackles coach, said Coach Prime's daily message helped him work through a child custody battle and his eighty-nine-year-old mother's death.

"He helped me find my way and get my purpose back after my mom died. He gets up every single day and walks in the light," Weeks said. "Regardless of if he pisses me off or I get mad at him or he's yelling at me, I respect him.

"He got me back to being a positive person. It's been a brutal time in my life with my ex-wife and my mom. I look forward to coming here at seven a.m. and hearing him every single day."

Turley said Coach Prime's daily message is a consistent soundtrack of how to succeed in football and life.

"He talks about God consistently, but he doesn't pound it down your throat. He means it in a metaphorical way of how to live life as a man," Turley said. "It's a way to be a better human being because not everything is about football. It's about going through life.

"A lot of these young men come from fatherless backgrounds and he's providing structure and a guide on how to live."

Sometimes, Coach Prime gave the players a word for the day or words for the week, like "complacency," "satisfaction," or "adversity." One morning, the word of the day was "investment."

First Coach Prime read the definition, then he used a handful of players who dabbled in stocks, bitcoin, or cryptocurrency to lead a conversation about assets and liabilities.

Once they understood, he shifted the topic to football.

"Liabilities are friends, family members, girls, drugs, alcohol, and the way you spend your time. What's constantly on your mind becomes a liability and you don't have a lot to invest in," he said. "You are your own investment. I'm trying to help you get a good return on your investment."

Then Coach Prime asked the group, "How much time do you sleep?"

"Seven hours," they replied.

"How long do we practice?"

"Four hours," they said.

"How much do you dedicate to schoolwork?"

"Three hours," they said.

"This is where it gets tricky," he said. "What are you doing with your ten? I got time today. Let's talk about it."

Studying film, talking to women, playing video games, eating, and lifting weights, they decided, consumed the rest of the day.

"That's your investment in your dream so you can live the life-style you want. That's what you put in this game, when this game has been known to retire people for generations," Coach Prime said. "That's your investment, not mine. That's your investment, not the coaches'.

"Not Trevor, not Weeks, not Coach Mathis, not any coach in here. That's what you're putting in this thing to become successful and you wonder why we look at you the way we look at you."

Those words resonated with receiver Rico Powers.

"Honestly, he taught me how to become a better man and person than football player," Rico said.

A few weeks later, Coach Prime talked to the team about their love of the game. They say they love it, but do they really?

What will they sacrifice? It's different for everyone—and that's OK. Each player must determine whether he wants to be average, good, or great because the commitment for each level is different.

"One thing a coach really wants to have is a team full of men who love the game, but we're not foolish enough to think everyone in these seats loves the game," he said. "Some of y'all are in lust with the game. Some of you are dating the game, but you're not in love with the game.

"Some of you are having intercourse with the game, but you don't love the game. So how do you signify that you love the game?"

"By your actions," one player said.

"Time spent," said another.

"Doing work that's not required," a third chimed in.

Again, it's about using relatable examples to inspire his players to be better men and better players. Conversations like this aren't for guys like Shedeur and Travis because they're expected to play in the NFL. Most players aren't going to the NFL, so they must thrive in the real world.

"I'm not a guy who needs motivation. I motivate myself. If I want to go to the NFL and see I haven't been playing the way I need to get to the NFL then I need to do more," Shilo Sanders said. "I'm not a player who seeks external motivation.

"I do listen to what he says, but if you need him to tell you to practice hard, that's a problem."

Discipline was always at the forefront of every team function.

"I give Prime credit. The way the team is constructed—even though ninety-nine percent of the time it's about him—in house he does a good job of making it about the boys," Riddley said. "The ability to be loose and allow them to be themselves is good. He ain't got a lot of rules, but he has his rules."

Any violation of those in a team meeting was met with a glare, followed by a guttural "Get out." Rarely was an explanation provided.

The player simply left. One morning, Charlie Goodell dozed off in a meeting.

"Get out!" Coach Prime yelled.

Goodell's eyes instantly popped open. He grabbed his belongings and left. Later, he apologized to Coach Prime and explained he has narcolepsy, a neurological disorder that affected the brain's ability to control sleep and wakefulness cycles.

It affects approximately one in two thousand people.

"I already knew I was going to get caught. Usually, I try to stand up when I'm getting sleepy because I can feel it," Charlie said. "That time I didn't make it. I just wanted to apologize. I didn't think he knew I had a sleep issue. I wanted him to know it wasn't out of disrespect.

"I just deduced that from falling asleep every day meeting after meeting for three years. It feels like a thousand pounds on your eyelids. It's like my brain shuts down and it's impossible to stay awake. I have to do something to get active."

The next day, midway through the team meeting, Coach Prime and Goodell locked eyes.

"You all right today? You good?" Coach Prime said with a smile. "He came and apologized yesterday. He said he had a condition called narcolepsy. That means you sleep everywhere?"

"Yes," Charlie replied with a grin.

"What's the craziest place you ever fell asleep?" Coach Prime asked.

"I almost fell asleep while I was driving," Charlie said.

"Everybody has done that," Coach Prime said.

"No, we were in a convertible going about a hundred miles an hour," he said as his teammates laughed.

"Yeah," said Coach Prime. "You got a problem."

Coach Prime created an environment that doesn't exist anywhere else in college football, which should surprise no one. There's not another coach with his combination of effervescent personality and marketing genius.

"It's unique playing for Prime because your coach sets the vibe and atmosphere for the team. This is unparalleled," said reserve quarterback Matt Ricciardi-Vitale. "A lot of people will try replicate it, but you can't replicate what Coach Prime does.

"The spiritual side, not religious, but how you have to act, feel, walk, and talk. The 'I believe' mantra is all very different. We're original. We're authentic and that's cool. We're different. You can't copy that."

CHAPTER 17

There's a spirit of complacency in here, fellas.
—Coach Prime

A phone rang on the left side of the ballroom at the Embassy Suites hotel the night before their seventh game of the season. Coach Prime, in the midst of making a point, glared in that direction.

He was pissed. And disappointed. And exasperated.

And it wasn't just that he was perturbed about being at the Embassy Suites in north Jackson instead of the Sheraton Flowood, where JSU normally stays the night before home games.

All week, Coach Prime had preached about the danger of complacency infecting the team because JSU had blown out every opponent. He had told them about the importance of practicing hard, watching video, and getting enough sleep.

"Fellas, we gotta not be complacent. We gotta be consistent and we gotta dominate. Do not take this team for granted. Do not take this game for granted. Do not take this stage for granted," Coach Prime told them. "This is the largest stage they've ever played on.

"We're winning and we're being dominant, but I don't think you understand you have an opportunity to do something that has never been done in the history of JSU, but you're becoming complacent.

"I need you consistent. I need you to know your job and do your job. I need you to play with passion, purpose, and love. I need you to empty yourself."

He continued a season-long emphasis on domination because he understood that the number of distractions for the players was multiplied by 100 during homecoming week.

That's why Coach Prime removed any ambiguity about what would happen to any player who snuck out of the hotel.

"You decide to sneak out of this hotel tonight and go celebrate and party with everybody else on that campus and everybody in town, I want you to enjoy yourself, because you'll never play here again," Coach Prime said. "Pretty Tony put everybody at the spots. Put everybody around. Put all the dogs out and let me know if we catch somebody."

Homecoming at Jackson State bears no resemblance to homecoming at predominantly white institutions. Homecoming at an HBCU is a weeklong celebration filled with parties, step shows, block parties, and a battle of the bands.

The game? An afterthought.

"Once the school schedule comes out, people start booking hotel rooms and scheduling vacation at their jobs," said Duane Lewis, who was in charge of JSU's public relations and sports media. "The hope of alums is that they can book a room before hotels can jack the rates up."

Lewis, a Southern graduate, began his career in the St. Louis Rams media department in 1997. Three years later the Rams ushered in a new era of passing football with the Greatest Show on Turf and won a Super Bowl.

Lewis spent much of the last fifteen years working at Alabama State, Prairie View, the University of Arkansas at Pine Bluff, and Huston-Tillotson University, so he understands the HBCU culture.

"The nurturing we felt as students is why homecoming is such a big deal at HBCUs," Lewis said. "And we all felt like we went through something to graduate, whether it was financial aid, books being late, or trying to register.

"When you meet an HBCU grad it's like meeting family. Coming home reminds you of all those good times and you're bonded forever."

Coach Prime had been making a point about the offensive line when the phone rang, the first time all season a phone had interrupted a meeting.

"Who does that belong to?" Coach Prime asked angrily.

"Me, coach," Cam'Ron said softly.

"Get out!" Coach Prime shouted.

Cam'Ron, who quickly left the room, stared straight ahead to avoid eye contact.

Then Coach Prime turned his gaze toward Sy'Veon, who sat in the middle of the room. Five seconds, which must have felt like five hours, passed before the coach spoke.

"You get out," he said, "and take your earrings off while you're getting out."

Coach Prime's words surprised Sy'Veon.

"I forgot I had them in. Then I was like, 'Oh damn,'" Sy'Veon said. "I saw him look at me and he didn't say nothing, but when Cam's phone went off and he told him to get out. When he looked at me, I knew it was over."

Those who violated Coach Prime's rules learned there were consequences whether you were one of his sons, a star, or the last man on the roster. Neither player started against Campbell University.

"That's the complacency. We're getting comfortable. We're too durn comfortable. You're sitting right there by him and you let it go down like that?" Coach Prime said to no one.

"That don't make sense. That's supposed to be your dawg. You ain't see it, Santee?"

"I ain't see it, coach," he replied.

"You ain't see it Travis?"

"No, I wasn't paying attention," Travis said.

"So nobody saw he had an earring in his ear. No one on the team," Coach Prime said. "I'm the only one in here that saw that he had an earring. Yes or no?"

He repeated himself, this time with more of an edge.

"I'm the only one in here that saw that he had an earring," Coach Prime said. "Yes or no?

"There's a spirit of complacency in here, fellas. You're gonna go out there and get your butts kicked if you don't fix it. Right now, there's not a good spirit in here. You think you're already there. You think you've arrived. . . .

"We're supposed to be the dawgs, but we come in here with earrings and why do we even bring a phone into a meeting? Why? Who's calling you in here? Y'all know the rules. Why do we do that? Complacency. Complacency. That's what I see.

"Coaches, y'all check this bull junk in your personal meetings and get this spirit out of here because that's what in here right now. Complacency."

Coach Prime stormed out, walked across the hallway, and sat in a small room alone with his thoughts.

"My heart dropped into my stomach when the phone rang," Cam'Ron said. "I was just hoping Coach Prime would take it a little easy on me. He knows I try to be a perfect guy. I don't ever mess up like that.

"The first thing I thought about was coach just talked about me this morning."

Coach Prime knew Cam'Ron better than most because Cam'Ron had played for him in high school.

Cam'Ron devoted his life to playing in the NFL after his sophomore year of high school, when he moved from Birmingham to Dallas. New York Jets defensive tackle Quinnen Williams, a family friend, and his parents believed playing Texas high school football would change his life.

"There were so many days I wanted to quit," he said with a laugh. "When I was in Birmingham, I was good. In Dallas, I was sorry. Everything was moving so fast.

"I went from being 'the man' to being a regular guy."

Shedeur and Cam'Ron had each committed to Florida Atlantic. When Coach Prime asked him to join him at Jackson State, he politely declined. A week before Signing Day, FAU rescinded Cam'Ron's scholarship offer.

A couple of weeks passed, and Cam'Ron called Mathis and asked for an opportunity to play at Jackson State.

"I know how Coach Prime and Coach Mathis are," Cam'Ron said. "Once you say no, it is what it is. I understand that.

"I felt like I messed up. That's why when I walk in here every day I have a chip on my shoulder, because they didn't have to bring me back. I told them no, but they stuck beside me. They stayed true to me. Every day I'm going to give it to them."

During a team meeting ten hours earlier, Coach Prime had said, "Cam ain't wishy-washy. He's the same guy. He really doesn't get too high. He really doesn't get too down. He has the mentality of a base-ball player."

Coach Prime attacked complacency during the team meeting that morning. He saw it in practice when defensive players didn't enthu-siastically chase the ball. He saw it on offense when receivers jogged when they weren't the first read. And he saw it on the scout team when those players didn't compete hard enough.

"It's easy when you're winning to become complacent. It's easy when you're successful to become complacent," he said. "It's easy when you feel like you're not going to progress to a certain level or you're on the scout team and you think you're not going to play. It's easy to become complacent.

"You don't watch film. You don't even give a durn no more be-cause you've become complacent. You're satisfied. You feel like you've maxed out."

Now Cam'Ron, one of the team's leaders, just got kicked out of a meeting. As he walked toward the lobby, he bumped into Mathis, who had excused himself so he could stream his son's high school football game.

"I gotta sit you. That's just what it is. You're my dawg, but I gotta sit you. It hurt my heart, too," Mathis said. "It is what it is. It was out of my hands. I can't go there for you."

Sy'Veon and Cam'Ron sat in the lobby for about fifteen minutes to see if Coach Prime wanted a private meeting.

He didn't.

"I tried to avoid everybody," Cam'Ron said. "It was a hurtful feeling because I feel like the team depends on me to be perfect—nobody's perfect—but they expect me to do the right thing and it's like, 'Dang, I let everybody down.'"

On Tuesday, Coach Prime had informed the team that ABC's morning show *Good Morning America* was coming to Jackson State and that Michael Strahan, a member of the Pro Football Hall of Fame and Coach Prime's friend, would be on campus.

At the end of Wednesday's practice, Coach Prime told the players they were going to shoot a promo for *GMA*. Of course, the players practiced three times before Sam, Coach Prime's personal assistant, shot a video.

"Stra? You ready?" Coach Prime said.

"Good morning, America!" the players shouted.

The plan called for Strahan to go live Friday morning from campus with some band members, cheerleaders, Coach Prime, Shedeur, and Travis for a short segment. Strahan would also do a sit-down interview with Shedeur for Fox's *Big Noon Kickoff* college football show.

Good Morning America came on at 7 a.m. central time, which meant the camera crew arrived at 2 a.m. to lay cable and set up three huge strobe lights and cameras on JSU's practice field.

Lewis and Michael Rhodes, a member of Coach Prime's two-man security team, arrived at about 2 a.m. to ensure the *GMA* camera crew didn't have issues getting set up. Lewis arrived with two sixteen-ounce cups of black coffee and a plastic bag filled with sugar and creamer.

The band, cheerleaders, and curious folks arrived around 5 a.m. Blue and white balloons were set up all over the field, including a huge balloon awning with JSU spelled out in silver balloons next to large inflated footballs.

"*60 Minutes. GMA. Big Noon Kickoff* with Shedeur on Fox on Saturday morning," said Lewis, "and then our game on ESPN on Saturday. All that in seven days."

A few cheerleaders held yellow signs with blue words that read GMA.

Coach Prime, Shedeur, and Travis rode the coach's golf cart from the football facility about two hundred yards to the middle of the field, where they waited about ten minutes for the interview to begin.

That afternoon, Riddley and Taylor strolled on the plaza, part of their yearly routine, before it became too crowded. The plaza is a roughly half-mile-long strip in the middle of campus.

Normally there is a smattering of students going here or there. That day, a few hundred students and alums filled the plaza. A few hours later, a fifteen-minute walk would take an hour.

Reggie Johnson, a 1995 graduate and former director of basketball operations, said, "I've had a family member here from 1977 to 2012 in some capacity. This is home. This is family. This is heritage. You're a part of this atmosphere and this game. I don't care if we win or lose, it's still home."

Taylor and Riddley usually kept a low profile, but they couldn't on this day.

Every few feet one of them posed for a selfie. They passed out hugs like Halloween candy to a multitude of folks, though every person received their own brief conversation.

They bumped into several members of the Tiger Fund, a booster group that wielded some power in the athletic department.

The Sonic Boom was gathering so it could march down the plaza. At the other end, Coach Prime, Forsett, and Rhodes sat in a golf cart waiting for the festivities.

"Homecoming means love, tradition, honor, family, friends, alumni, and all things JSU," said Naomi Harris, Miss Jackson State 2022–23. "I love the love here. Coach Prime has done a lot for us. He's put us on the map. He's taken care of the football team. He's doing his best to take care of the community the best way he can."

Before they returned to the facility and headed to the team hotel, Taylor and Riddley wanted Philly cheesesteak egg rolls from a distinctive orange and black food truck.

"As an alum, as a former player here," Taylor said, "ain't nothing like this homecoming, baby."

While there were plenty of distractions during the week, Coach Prime was fond of saying, "Keep the main thing, the main thing."

Coach Prime decided he needed more from the defensive line, so he challenged them in front of their teammates.

Players never have to wonder what Coach Prime thought about their performance. He knew the defensive line needed to play well against Campbell, so he put all of them on notice.

"We have some guys with a lot of potential," Coach Prime said, "but they haven't lived up to it."

Campbell's Fighting Camels (4-2) had won three consecutive games while averaging 41 points and 505 yards per game, including 234.3 yards rushing. They did it with an up-tempo offense that relied on their opponent getting fatigued and not getting lined up properly.

Thurman had been disappointed with the selfishness that came from players trying to make plays instead of doing their job, and he let them know about it after Wednesday's practice. When guys tried to make plays, they created holes in the defense.

"We call something and you do what the fuck you want to do because it's all about me," Thurman said. "That's not how you play team defense."

Less than twenty-four hours before the game, Coach Prime was still focused on the defensive line.

"I'm an old-school coach. When that's said, it's directed at me, I take that personally," Weeks told the defensive linemen. "That reflects on me as a coach and that reflects on you."

Thurman spoke quietly, yet forcefully. He told the defensive line exactly what he expected against Campbell.

"We're going to be led by your example. There will be no more slacking. There will be no more half efforts," he said. "We are counting on you guys because when your bigs dominate, the other guys can't help but follow.

"You guys have to begin to understand how important you are to this football team and to our defense. I'm expecting each and every one of you who get in that game tomorrow to be a monster."

When Coach Prime left his office just before kickoff with Tupac's "All Eyez on Me" booming in the locker room, he still hadn't heard from God. When he finally made his entrance, like a championship boxer entering the ring, Coach Prime stood silent for seventeen seconds.

"I studied long and hard to come up with something to encourage you and motivate y'all and God didn't give me nothing," he said. "Back in the day when we were coming up when our parents told us to do something and it wasn't done, there wasn't a lot of conversation back and forth.

"I don't know who got old-school parents, but when mama look at you like that or your daddy look at you like that, you know you in trouble.

"Now, give me my theme music."

Silence. Uh-oh.

Coach Prime whirled around.

"Start it over. Get on your game because he ain't ready," Coach Prime said of the DJ. "He's new to this.

"Now, give me my theme music."

The music started instantly.

Campbell received the opening kickoff, and three plays into the game, they went for it on fourth-and-1 from their own 34. Lamagea McDowell burst up the middle for 27 yards before Travis dragged him down.

It was Travis's first game since the opener.

Three plays after McDowell's big run, the Camels went for it again on fourth down. This time Tru Thompson, making his much-anticipated debut, stuffed him for no gain.

Tru, a transfer from Florida State, had missed the first five games recovering from a knee injury he suffered in the spring.

Bartolone, the play-caller, wanted to make sure Travis touched the ball early, so the game's first two plays went to the freshman.

On first down, Travis circled out of the backfield for a 7-yard gain. Then he caught a hitch for 4 yards and a first down. The drive ended with Mata's 22-yard field goal and a 3–0 JSU lead.

Campbell's Hajj-Malik Williams capped a 13-play drive with a sensational 20-yard scramble for a touchdown that ended with a somersault over Travis into the end zone and a 7–3 Campbell lead.

"This team feeds on us doing what we're not supposed to do," Thurman yelled at the defense as it came to the sideline.

Second-quarter field goals of 25 and 26 yards by Mata gave JSU a 9–7 halftime lead.

"We found ourselves in a dogfight. We thought it was going to be a homecoming," Coach Prime said at halftime. "You thought they were just going to lay down for you. That's why we've been on your butt all week long about complacency.

"We were complacent. Then we started turning it on and playing like we normally play. We have one half left to play like Jackson State plays."

Jackson State seized control of the game in the third quarter with a play that had befuddled JSU's defense all week in practice. It starred tight end D. J. Stevens, a walk-on from Ridgeland, about fifteen miles north of Jackson.

Stevens had evolved from a bit player into a weapon. Two weeks into the season, Shedeur told Bartolone that he preferred any formation without a tight end to one with a tight end.

Stevens caught nine passes for 58 yards in the first three games. Against Alabama State, when he caught three passes for

52 yards with a long of 26. Then he caught six for 31 yards against Bethune-Cookman.

"What do you think about Longhorn?" Bartolone said to Brewster on the sideline.

"Call it," he replied. "Call the motherfucker and watch this."

Brewster put West Right Longhorn into the game plan, a play Brewster borrowed from San Francisco 49ers head coach Kyle Shanahan, who ran it when he was the Atlanta Falcons' offensive coordinator.

"Anytime we cross the fifty-yard line and we're on the left hash," said Brewster, "because we want the tight end running into the boundary."

The Tigers lined up in a shotgun formation with Shane Hooks on the right and Dallas Daniels on the left. Stevens lined up next to the tackle, while tight end Hayden Hagler lined up off the ball on the right.

At the snap, Stevens ran across the formation, moving quickly but not too fast so he'd get lost in the line of scrimmage, while Hooks baited the safety. As he neared the end of the formation, Stevens turned up the left sideline.

Shedeur, who had faked a handoff to Sy'Veon, rolled right, kept his eyes in the middle of the field, and gathered himself. Then he lofted a perfect pass to Stevens, who caught it at the 30 and sprinted into the end zone for a 15–7 lead and his first career touchdown.

"When you're that open the hardest thing is catching the ball," said Stevens. "Once you catch it, it's just a race."

Sy'Veon's 4-yard touchdown run made it 22–7 in the fourth quarter.

The 22–14 win pleased Coach Prime.

"DT is great. He's great on adjustments. We just started out slow. To get a feel for the fans, the game, and get a feel for the crowd," Coach Prime said. "We always have a lackluster start. We gotta figure that."

CHAPTER 18

GameDay *wants to come to Jackson.*
—associate AD Duane Lewis

Duane Lewis didn't recognize the phone number starting with an 860 area code at 9:32 Sunday morning, so he happily let it go to voice mail.

"I don't know anybody in Connecticut," he said. "So I didn't answer it."

Ten minutes later, a text arrived from *ESPN College GameDay* producer Drew Gallagher. ESPN is based in Bristol, Connecticut.

We're interested in coming down but we need to have Prime on set, the text read. *If you guarantee that, we're coming.*

It shouldn't be a problem, Lewis responded.

Adrenaline coursed through his body. His heart pounded. Lewis called athletic director Ashley Robinson, who had already been contacted by *GameDay.* Then Lewis phoned Sam Morini, Coach Prime's assistant, with details.

Ten minutes later, Coach Prime phoned Lewis.

"*GameDay* wants to come to Jackson," Lewis told Coach Prime. "The golden ticket is you being on the set."

"Let's do it," he replied.

Within thirty minutes, Jackson State had secured an appearance on *College GameDay* against Southern.

"Obviously, the magnitude of who Coach is speaks for itself, but what gets overlooked is the success he's had as a coach," said Lewis. "We've been dominant. Winning enhances everything else and that's what's happening here."

The Tigers had won 18 of 20 games and most hadn't been close. They had a dominating defense, a star quarterback, and the only five-star recruit in FCS football. They're the kind of compelling story *College GameDay* loves.

The show saw itself as a vehicle for telling college football's best stories—not just highlighting the best games. Obviously, it wanted to be at the biggest games, which is why Ohio State has 21 appearances, more than any other school. Alabama is next with 16 appearances, followed by Florida's 13.

But *College GameDay* wanted to see more than two highly ranked teams play every week, which is why it went to Appalachian State in Boone, North Carolina, after the Mountaineers upset Texas A&M and why it wound up broadcasting from Kansas after the Jayhawks started the season 5-0.

College GameDay wanted to cover every aspect of college football from Division 3 to the Ivy League to the service academies to HBCUs to Group of 5 schools to the Power 5 schools. Still, it had originated from HBCU games just four times.

It went to North Carolina Central vs. Alcorn State (2021), Hampton vs. FAMU (2018), and Grambling vs. Southern (2005) in Houston. *GameDay* went to the MEAC-SWAC challenge to kick off the 2021 season but that was at a neutral site.

"The magic of our show is the crowd," Gallagher said. "The energy and the fan base. The fan base is like another cast member on set. An HBCU environment with all that passion. That's going to be ridiculous."

College GameDay chose JSU and Southern in a week where Alabama played Tennessee, Ohio State battled Penn State, and Georgia played Kentucky.

"We like to go to the best story that week. And there are no rules," Gallagher said. "Jackson State has been a major story in college football all year. We don't want to ignore or not shine a light on big college football stories no matter where they might be.

"What he's doing here and Coach Prime as a character is what brought us here. It took a couple of outcomes to keep us going to a couple of other places. Game results definitely dictate where we go because that's how you tell the stories of the season, because it changes week by week. It's kind of cool. The thing is we can be nimble and react to the stories."

Having *College GameDay* on campus excited Coach Prime because he saw it as yet another confirmation that what he had been preaching to his kids all season was true: it's important to dominate. *College GameDay* knew JSU had eviscerated its opponents and wanted to see the destruction up close. ESPN had provided an opportunity to see what JSU football was all about—and Coach Prime loved it.

The football program was getting an eight-hour infomercial, if you counted pregame and postgame shows plus the game. *College GameDay* provided marketing and advertising for JSU that it couldn't afford even if they put it on layaway for a hundred years.

More important, the show shined a light on Southern and the rest of the SWAC, and Coach Prime wanted them to bask in it just like JSU. Coach Prime and Robinson held a conference call with Southern athletic director Josh Brooks and explained that they wanted Southern's cheerleaders, band, and football team to have the entire *GameDay* experience, too.

"His hire is probably the most important hire in the last ten years in college football," said Desmond Howard of *College GameDay*. "Does anything Coach Prime does surprise anybody? He's not going to do something unless he can dominate it.

"That's who he is. He didn't take the job just to be a coach at an HBCU. This is not a head coaching job for him. It's a mission."

Inside a navy blue box in the middle of his desk, surrounded by the organized chaos you find on every CEO's desk, Coach Prime pulled out a gold bauble.

"We just paid for these two weeks ago. Look at this," said Coach Prime, slowly sliding off the ring's face. "I don't really like rings, so we made it so the front can be worn as a necklace."

When the players arrived at the facility for their daily team meeting, they found five-foot-high red, white, and blue balloon columns outside both doors.

Inside the meeting room, several folks scurried about preparing for the presentation. Six cardboard boxes filled with foot-long blue boxes sat on the floor. Each box had a white label in the upper right corner with the recipient's name.

An eight-foot table covered with a navy blue cloth adorned with JSU's block logo sat in the front of the room.

The players had waited months for their rings, and they were thrilled about the moment of truth. Coach Prime wasn't nearly as excited because he wanted the guys focused on the present, not the past.

But he also wanted to celebrate their accomplishments, which is why he presented the players their rings on Wednesday. That allowed them to enjoy the moment and quickly shift their focus back to practice once the ceremony ended.

Jackson State's SWAC Championship in 2021 was their second in the last twenty-five years.

"Coach Prime, I want to thank you for bringing the legacy back to Jackson State University. I want to thank you for changing the culture at Jackson State University," Robinson said. "I want to thank you for bringing a winning record back to Jackson State University and building men on and off the field."

Robinson turned to Coach Prime, who used the moment to ask more from his players because yesterday had nothing to do with today.

"Are we done yet?" Coach Prime asked.

"No, sir," they replied.

"Are we done yet?" he asked again.

"No, sir!" they replied even louder.

They watched an 8:21 highlight video from 2021 narrated by Rob J, who did play-by-play for football and basketball. The video perturbed Coach Prime because it lasted too long. Coach Prime, a man of routine and structure, thought every minute devoted to the ring ceremony took away from practice and preparation.

When the video ended, the ring ceremony began. Rob J announced each player's name and he walked down to the front of the room, where Coach Prime or Robinson handed the player a box.

"Everybody who doesn't have a ring stand up," Coach Prime said. "Sit down for a second.

"All you guys who have a ring stand up. Now turn around and look at everybody sitting down. It's on us to get them a ring."

After the athletic department officials left, Coach Prime showed the team another video.

This one showed three members of Southern's football team in their locker room. They stared into a camera—the kind a TV station would use—while someone else filmed it on a cell phone camera. The thirty-five-second video full of profanity and threats angered Coach Prime.

"Guys, that's character right there. It starts at the top and works its way to bottom," he said. "You guys know durn well if one of you guys had looked in a camera in our locker room and said that about the opposing team you would no longer be a part of Jackson State's team.

"If somebody was comfortable enough to say that to a camera, you have a problem. That's why it's imperative, imperative, imperative that we're smart this week. We're not getting involved in that stuff because we have everything to lose and they don't. We're going to dominate."

But only if JSU played with an edge, something Coach Prime didn't see in Tuesday's practice. He showed the players video from the seven-on-seven portion of practice. After he ripped the offense, he showed plays from the team portion of practice and laid into the defense.

Every comment focused on effort.

"Is that what you're teaching down there, Coach Weeks?" Coach Prime asked.

"No, sir," he replied.

"I know it ain't. It can't be," he said. "I hear you yelling all day."

"Who are the two guys in the middle? Who are the two tackles? Who are the two guys in the middle?" Coach Prime asked. "The inside guys? Who are those two?"

"Ninety-nine and ninety-one," said a voice hidden by the darkness.

"Do not start them. No way. Fellas, if we go about our business, our job, our dreams, our desires like this, we're not going to get very far," Coach Prime said. "The only way you get to the next level is by dominating. Winning is not going to get you to the NFL. Dominating is going to get you eyeballs, get you looks. It makes people take note that have never noticed you before."

The rivalry between JSU and Southern began on November 30, 1929, with a 98–0 Southern win. As the video of Southern's players proved, this is not a friendly rivalry.

"It's intense. Southern has always had a very good team and Jackson State has always had a very good team and when we get together, it's going to be a battle," the fifty-four-year-old Rhodes said. "It's going to be nasty. For as long as I can remember it has always been a heated rivalry game.

"They feel like they're the best. We feel like we're the best and it's a constant competition between the football team and the band all game long."

Southern led the all-time series 35–31. Southern won 12 of the first 14 games. Then JSU won 16 of 20, including a seven-game win streak from 1977 to 1983 under W. C. Gorden.

Southern and its legendary coach Pete Richardson won 9 of 14 games. JSU won 6 of 8 and then Southern won eight straight—the

NCAA forced them to vacate wins in 2013 and 2014—until Coach Prime arrived.

He led JSU to an emotional win over Southern in 2021. It marked his first game on the sideline after missing three games from complications that nearly killed him after having two toes amputated.

A day after having surgery in September 2021 to fix a dislocated toe he suffered in the late 1990s, Coach Prime returned to the field. A few weeks later, Askevold noticed his toes were black, an indication they weren't getting blood flow, when she changed his bandage.

She insisted he go directly to the hospital after practice and he was admitted immediately.

The next twenty-three days were the most harrowing of Coach Prime's life. He conversed with death multiple times and his faith grew stronger as his body weakened.

Coach Prime returned to the sideline because Shedeur said he needed him there. Understand, the father had coached the son since he started playing football.

With the SWAC Eastern Division title on the line, the son wanted his father near him. Coach Prime coached the game from a motorized wheelchair. He positioned himself at the 20- or 30-yard line opposite from the action; a black-and-red blanket covered his legs.

"To make the decision to cut your toes off because you want to be on the sideline for the championship game, I didn't even know where you come up with a decision like that," Hart said. "To make the decision to cut your toes off and then wrap them up two weeks later, your wound isn't even closed and you have all those people around you, he got a point that was low."

Coach Prime wasn't interested in reliving that anniversary as the Southern game neared. The video by Southern's players upset him because he found it so disrespectful, especially after telling Southern's administration that he wanted them involved as much as possible.

"This game ain't just about football. It's about the bands, the fans: it's a whole lot going on," Balancier said. "The bands really go at it. The whole week the band was putting in work. It's two a.m. and I can hear 'I hate, I hate, I hate J State.'"

He understood the rivalry from both sides. So did Aarion Hartman, a three-time All-SWAC long snapper at Southern until transferring to JSU. Balancier, a graduate assistant who worked with the defense and a New Orleans native, played linebacker at Southern and went 2-3 against JSU.

"My first season in the spring I felt some kind of way and they beat us," Balancier said. "After that I was like fuck them, since they done whipped my ass."

Hartman left Southern because he chased a dream and JSU was the best place to achieve it.

"Once I had a kid, I knew I was on the clock to make some money, some way somehow, and Jackson State had way better resources," he said. "Way better. It's a better resume-builder for sure. I had to make a business decision. I didn't care what nobody thought."

His phone blew up the week of the game. Text messages. Phone calls. Direct messages on Instagram. His IG post a few days before the game made it clear where his loyalties lay.

"I made a little post on IG. The whole university was on my tail," Hartman said. "I knew my mission for coming here. Everybody didn't know my mission."

Fans arrived at the Vet about 4:30 a.m. Saturday. By the time the countdown to *College GameDay* started at 7 a.m., about a thousand sign-waving fans—the ones who received the most TV time—were jammed shoulder to shoulder behind the set.

The cheerleaders were there, as were some members of JSU's band, the Sonic Boom, and drill team. They kept the crowd energized, as did a pair of cameramen who occasionally gave a thumbs-up when they wanted more noise or excitement.

New York City DJ Rob Swift did his part by spinning some old-school sounds. Southern's band, the Human Jukebox, and cheerleaders arrived about an hour after JSU.

The crowd was thick and the air full of anticipation as Coach Prime slowly rode his motorized three-wheeler through the crowd to the stage. This is what the *College GameDay* audience craved and the hosts on set wanted: Coach Prime ready to entertain and dazzle the audience.

He crushed it.

Coach Prime discussed his vision for JSU when he arrived, what the phrase "I Believe" meant, and the coaches who influenced him.

Then he explained, again, his mission at JSU.

"I'm here for the people, man. I'm here for the shorties. I'm here for those kids that can't see their way up or see their way out. I'm their navigational system," he said. "I love coaching. There's not one day I don't wake up at three forty-five a.m. and say I don't want to do this.

"I can't wait to get to the office and get to work. It's not even work—it's play. I can't wait to get into play and have a good time with these young men and women."

When asked if he planned to stay at Jackson State, Coach Prime said, "First I have to stay focused and I have to maximize these moments and continue to dominate them," Coach Prime told ESPN's Rece Davis. "I have made no plans to move. I have made no plans to go anywhere. I have made plans to dominate today."

Coach Prime had been linked to several jobs, ranging from Colorado to Auburn. None of that fazed him.

"The good news for Jackson State fans," said Davis, "is that a guy like Deion Sanders doesn't have to do anything he doesn't want to do. It's not like he has to prove himself by climbing some imaginary ladder."

As the segment ended, Coach Prime turned to the crowd and took one more wonderful swipe at Alabama State and its coach, Eddie Robinson Jr.

"Who is SWAC, baby? Who is SWAC, baby?" he said to the crowd, which shouted it back in unison.

One of the coolest aspects of *College GameDay* is when Lee Corso makes his prediction at the end of the show and puts on a mascot head.

Jackson State's mascot was so old and worn that they contacted Anderson's in White Bear Lake, Minnesota, which specializes in this sort of thing, and spent $1,100 to rush order a new mascot head and Tiger suit, so it would look perfect on national TV.

Corso became ill during the week and didn't make the trip to Jackson. The rain, which had been forecast all week for Saturday, wasn't going to start until the second half.

He prayed the rain would hold off long enough so JSU and Southern could play at peak efficiency on a dry field and show the nation the best version of HBCU football. More than two hours before kickoff, a couple thousand folks were already in the stands.

"Can you feel the difference?" Riddley said. "I told you it was different."

And that was before Snoop Dogg arrived on the field about an hour before the game. Or Rick Ross found a seat in the Prime VIP area. Thirty minutes before kickoff, Snoop danced in the locker room with a variety of players.

The eyes of the nation saw JSU fulfilling a promise Coach Prime made when he arrived. As a player, Coach Prime lived for the biggest moments.

In his first Super Bowl, playing for San Francisco, he intercepted a pass. Playing in the Super Bowl for Dallas the next year, he caught a 47-yard pass to set up Dallas's first touchdown. In the 1992 World Series with the Braves, he hit .533 with four runs scored.

Pressure had zero effect on him. Pressure, he'd tell folks, is a single mom trying to feed her family with no money. Football, he'd say, is just a game. Before his team took the field, Coach Prime reminded his players that pressure existed only in their minds.

"You all wanted the lights. You wanted the camera. You wanted the action—and you got it. What you gonna do with it? What you gonna do with it? You wanted thousands to see you. Some of you didn't believe it could be done at an HBCU, but we've done it. Now, what you gonna do with it?" Coach Prime said excitedly.

"They just didn't come to see you show up. They came to see you show out. So what are you going to do with the moment? Let's maximize it. Let's dominate it. Let's take advantage of it. Let's subdue it. But fellas, I want you to have fun."

A 3-yard touchdown pass to Sy'Veon made it 7–0, Shedeur's 42-yard scramble for a touchdown made it 14–0, and a 12-yard touchdown run by Shedeur and a two-point pass to Coleman made it 22–0 with three seconds left in the first half.

As the Sonic Boom filled the air with a joyful noise, Coach Prime turned to the crowd and started vibing. He pumped his right first in the air. Then he moved rhythmically to the beat.

To and fro. Head bobbing. The crowd, mesmerized, swayed with him.

Surreal.

"I was feeling joy because I was feeling the heartbeat of the fans," he said after the game. "I was connecting with our fan base. I just wanted to give the same energy back to our fans that they gave us since six thirty this morning."

As the half ended, the players sprinted into the locker room. They laughed and congratulated each other and celebrated a victory that had not yet been finalized.

"What the fuck, dude?!" Thurman yelled. "The game is not over. We have another half to play."

The rain, held at bay for a half, turned into a torrential downpour in the second half. Twice, lightning delayed the game. When the teams returned the second time, a couple hundred folks sat in the stands.

When it ended, Southern had been vanquished 35–0 and a national TV audience had seen glimpses of JSU's dominance. Seven times in the three minutes that he addressed the team after the game, Coach Prime used the word "proud."

"That was total domination. And the sad thing about is we started off like hot garbage, did we not? Imagine if we put it all together. That's what I'm still chasing," he said. "But I can't take nothing away from this game but happiness and pure joy.

"I'm so happy to be your coach and be a part of this history. Today was history. You guys are so young you don't even understand it. Riding through that crowd for *College GameDay* and seeing the supporters—rain or shine—it was unbelievable. It was a natural high to see how much love and respect and appreciation that y'all have earned."

CHAPTER 19

We would be crazy to think these kids
aren't affected by a rapper dying.
—Coach Prime

Coach Prime has been friends with Snoop Dogg for decades and he has the phone numbers of as many rappers in his phone as he does CEOs.

He's welcomed rappers from Young Dolph to Key Glock to Gillie da Kid into the locker room, where they dance and vibe with the players before the game and, at times, at halftime in the locker room and on the sidelines.

None of that is surprising. Rappers love sports and athletes love rapping.

Some athletes, such as the NBA's Damian Lillard, are considered serious rappers who put effort into their lyrical expressions. Most guys simply have enough money to put snazzy studios in their homes.

In 1994, Coach Prime released a rap song called "Must Be the Money."

Coach Prime understands the role music plays in his players' lives. Rap music speaks to them. For some, the verses remind them of where they grew up. For others, it's the lyrics promising riches and women. Or the beats.

So when he walked into his team meeting on Wednesday, November 2, he wanted to discuss Takeoff's death. Takeoff, the youngest member of the Atlanta hip-hop trio Migos, was killed outside a private party in Houston following an argument about a dice game.

Migos, which earned two Grammy nominations, is credited with starting a new era of rap in Atlanta.

Coach Prime knew the shooting had been a topic of conversation among the players, or would be eventually. So he confronted it.

"We would be crazy to think these kids aren't affected by a rapper dying. That's their life," Coach Prime said. "Every time we step on the durn field their music is playing. When we're in the locker room the music is playing. I know a lot of these guys.

"I would be a fool not to address what everyone is feeling, what everyone is thinking, and not give my take and my spin on it. The next day a player's cousin was shot and killed in St. Louis. It don't stop. It just don't stop. I pray they get it."

He confronted the issue at the beginning of JSU's team meeting.

"Takeoff was killed in a dice game in Houston, where we're going," Coach Prime said. "So, that eliminates all y'all leaving that hotel, 'cause it ain't happening until I give you further notice.

"I'm sad because it always seems like it's us, but we wanna say we matter, we wanna say we keep it one hundred, but it's always us. You cannot kick it with the same dudes you kicked it with. You cannot associate in the same realms that you associated with. You gonna have to change if you expect change."

The players understood why Coach Prime limited their movement, but that didn't mean they liked it.

"I definitely understood it. The world is so crazy these days you just never know," linebacker Baron Hopson said. "I really appreciate coach for keeping those guys who would've been outside in the hotel."

Willis Patrick has family in Houston, including his grandmother.

"For me that was kind of like, damn, I can't see my family but we were there for business," he said. "It's his duty to look out for us and protect us. If something like that happened to somebody of that magnitude, who's to say it couldn't happen to one of us? A bullet don't care who it hits."

Jackson State had won its first eight games for the first time in school history, but Coach Prime wasn't all that impressed. Then again, it's difficult to impress him.

As a concession to his players this week, only linemen, linebackers, and running backs practiced in pads as they prepared for Texas Southern. He reduced the overall hitting in practice to ensure the players felt fresh for the game.

"We fly to the ball, we finish blocks. We work our butts off," Coach Prime said. "It's not just happenstance that we find ourselves in the situations we're in."

The same could be said for Coach Prime's job situation. On Monday, October 31, Auburn finally fired Harsin after a 9-12 record, making it the shortest tenure in the school's ninety-three-year football history.

Auburn fired him two days after a 41–27 loss to Arkansas. They named former Auburn running back Carnell "Cadillac" Williams as the interim coach. Some folks at JSU's football facility believed Williams was a test balloon to see if Auburn's fan base would accept a Black coach.

Five days earlier, Auburn legend Bo Jackson had given his blessing to a potential union between Coach Prime and Auburn.

"Deion can coach anywhere in the country—college or professional level—that he wants to," Jackson told *USA Today Sports Weekly*. "It's just whether or not the organization is ready for Prime.

"You can look at what he's done for Jackson State in the short amount of time he's been there. He has the charisma. He coaches old-school and you've seen the results."

Former Auburn star basketball player Charles Barkley endorsed Coach Prime, too.

"I personally want Deion Sanders because No. 1, he is going to recruit like hell. . . . Deion is going to win wherever he goes," Barkley told Yahoo! News.

Coach Prime is an expert multitasker who has lived his life in the spotlight for parts of five decades. Having his name bandied about on ESPN, sports talk radio, or the newspaper didn't affect him and he didn't believe it affected this team.

"They're not going to come and challenge me or ask me certain things because we're so focused," he said. "If I'm giving them signs and tendencies that I'm looking out the windows then they have a right, but I'm full steam ahead. I'm not taking my foot off the gas.

"I have both hands on the wheel and I'm driving this thing in a big old four-by-four Ford. We're going to finish this journey, man. It's Celebration Bowl or bust. There's nothing else to win."

Texas Southern had won four games, including three in a row, because coach Clarence McKinney maximized his team's talent in his fourth season.

The Tigers led 21–7 at halftime, and if senior receiver Cam Buckley hadn't dropped an apparent 50-yard touchdown pass in the end zone, JSU would've led by 21 points and there wouldn't have been any angst.

Buckley, a four-star recruit from suburban Dallas, played for TRUTH, Coach Prime's youth football organization, as a kid. His father, Cedric, worked in the equipment room. Cam began his career at Texas A&M before transferring to Indiana.

But he couldn't make the over-the-shoulder catch on Shedeur's best pass in weeks. Shedeur's sprained shoulder had prevented him from taking many deep shots because he didn't have the usual confidence in his arm strength.

Coach Prime lit into the team as soon as the players walked into the cramped locker room. The locker rooms at PNC Stadium are so small, the offensive players dress on one side, while the defensive players dress on the other. He wanted them all crowded into one room to hear his message.

He was weary of the missed assignments, penalties, poor snaps, dropped passes, turnovers, and mental mistakes. At halftime, Texas

Southern should've been deciding when to unfurl the white flag. Instead, TSU wondered whether it could beat unbeatable JSU.

"I expect a dominant half and I'm not playing. A dominant half," Coach Prime said. "That wasn't good enough and you know it. When are y'all gonna start holding each other accountable? Hold each other accountable and quit saying, 'That's OK'?"

As Coach Prime left the locker room, Shedeur immediately moved into the space his father had vacated.

"This is some bullshit, bro," he told his teammates. "Everybody shut the fuck up. Offense, we gotta do better than this shit."

At least one of his teammates was pleased Shedeur voiced his displeasure.

"He needs to do that more. I'm glad he did it. He's a natural leader," Patrick said. "But he's like me, he doesn't want to talk just to talk. He doesn't want to be that guy who's rah-rah, just talk, talk, talk, 'cause people stop listening."

After Shedeur spoke, Aubrey blasted the defense. Before the players left the locker room, Coach Prime said, "Fellas, you have one assignment: get locked in. The plane ride is always better when you dominate."

A touchdown run on a draw play by Jacorey Howard on third-and-11 pulled TSU within 21–14, igniting its crowd.

Suddenly TSU's players bounced around on the sideline because they had the most precious commodity—hope—any underdog ever has. That's when JSU asserted itself.

It began with a simple inside handoff to Sy'Veon, who burst off right tackle between Henry and Patrick and powered through the safety. The collision sounded like a thunderclap, igniting the sideline.

"He killed him!" backup lineman Tre'von Riggins yelled from the sideline. "He killed him!"

Then Shane Hooks, a bit player in the previous few games, caught a hook and turned toward the right sideline to escape one defender.

He hurdled another and sprinted down the sideline before being dragged down after a gain of more than 20 yards.

"I couldn't go inside and I couldn't go out of bounds. My immediate thought was just to jump. When I did, he shot for my legs and I just hurdled him," Shane said. "I wasn't going down from the first tackler. It was going to take the whole team to get me down."

Two plays later, Shedeur ran around the right end and bulldozed the safety at the goal line for a touchdown, pushing the lead back to 14 points.

It was JSU's most important drive of the season: seven plays and 61 yards of dominance at a critical moment. Sy'Veon's run lit the fuse, but Shane's play ignited the offense.

Not bad for a dude who claimed he was not supposed to be here.

The third of Karen Mingo's five children, Shane arrived on July 15, 1999, after twenty-eight weeks. A normal pregnancy lasts forty weeks. Karen's water actually broke three weeks earlier, landing her at Joe DiMaggio Children's Hospital in Hollywood, Florida.

"They stopped the contractions and I stayed for three weeks," said Karen, "until I started getting a fever, so they took him out before he got an infection."

At birth, Shane was nineteen inches long, which is fairly normal, but weighed only two pounds and five ounces.

"I was the size of a Zephyr Hills water bottle," said Shane, who spent nearly two months in the newborn intensive care unit.

"He had a little bit of jaundice as a baby," said Karen, who was in nursing school. "He just had asthma as a kid and it got better as he got older. They told me I didn't have to come see him every day, but I did. It was rough, but I understood most of it so it wasn't as scary as it could've been."

Well, Shane grew into a sinewy 6'5" 200-pound receiver who regularly made game-changing plays.

Shane played on an option-based team at Orlando's Olympia High School. In three varsity seasons, he caught 50 passes for

829 yards and 13 touchdowns. As a senior, he caught 24 passes for 425 yards and 5 touchdowns.

He signed with Ohio University, an option team coached by Frank Solich, who spent nearly twenty-five years at Nebraska, when the Cornhuskers were a power under legendary coach Tom Osborne.

"Ohio," he said, "was my biggest offer, so I took the opportunity."

Shane played one game as a freshman, but caught 26 passes for 515 yards as a sophomore on a team that averaged just 25 passes a game. The next season, he caught just 8 passes for 120 yards and a touchdown and entered the transfer portal.

"As a receiver I'm trying to get the ball, so I needed to get up out of there," he said. "I felt like I couldn't be who I always wanted to be at Ohio University. I felt I couldn't be that person because it wasn't with my people."

Shane caught 6 passes for 55 yards and a pair of touchdowns in the JSU opener against FAMU. He followed that with 9 catches for 93 yards against Tennessee State.

He spent the next several weeks searching for consistency. Taylor said Shane's inconsistent practice habits led to inconsistent play. Coach Prime said Shane didn't watch enough video of his opponents.

But when Dallas Daniels sprained his ankle against Southern and didn't play, Shane caught 2 passes for 25 yards against Campbell and 2 for 29 yards against Southern. The Tigers needed more, so Taylor met with Shane on Tuesday morning before practice began to make sure he knew that.

"With [Daniels] gone, you need to show that you can be that dude, too," Taylor told him. "I know it, but you need to show everybody out here that you can be that guy.

"He took it personally. He said, 'I'm going to show you, coach.' Then he went out and practiced his ass off."

Taylor said Shane's biggest issue was handling success. In the past when he had strong performances, he had a tendency to relax the next week at practice instead of increasing his intensity. That habit led to uneven performances, but against Texas Southern he reminded everyone how he can impact JSU's offense.

"Every week, everybody is hollering for No. 4 and Shane is the complementary guy, but he can be a number one guy," Taylor said. "What was shocking is that he actually went out there and did it.

"I know what he means to this offense."

While JSU's sideline erupted after Shedeur's touchdown, not everyone was impressed.

"Man, that just goes to show you what those motherfuckers could be doing every time they get the ball," Riddley said.

A seven-yard touchdown catch by Shane extended the lead to 34–14 after a missed two-point conversion. Later, Shane added a nifty catch-and-run where he made three different defenders miss as he zigzagged across the field. A nine-yard touchdown catch by Shane, who made a leaping grab over a defender in the back of the end zone, pushed the lead to 41–14.

"He had those same two opportunities at home against Southern and he didn't catch them," Taylor said. "You have to be that guy every week."

A dominant second half and a strong performance on offense and defense should've made for a nice uneventful ride home.

It wasn't. Blame Tony Gray.

He had returned from suspension against Southern, but didn't play. Devin Hayes started at left tackle because Demetri Jordan sprained his right knee against Bethune-Cookman. Tony would've been starting if he could've controlled his emotions, but he couldn't.

He always needed to have the last word. He often confronted coaches and rarely practiced hard.

"He wasn't really a team guy in my eyes. A lot of stuff he did I felt like he was trying to get eyes on him," Tre'von said. "Even him, some-times, being obnoxious was trying to get attention.

"I felt like he was a cancer."

Tony didn't play against Texas Southern and on the return flight to Jackson, he took a seat in first class.

Coach Prime approved the seating chart on each flight. An argument ensued after secondary coach Kevin Mathis told Tony to return to his seat. Understand, Tony was already in a precarious situation because he had pouted earlier on the trip. He wanted his own room instead of rooming with Tre'von.

He refused to share a room and after a couple of hours, Tracie Knight, frustrated with his boorish behavior, finally acquiesced. She had taken on the role of director of football operations for her big brother.

"He'll give me the room and give somebody else the key," Tre'von said. "He ain't never been my roommate. That joker is crazy."

The commotion awakened Coach Prime, who ordered Tony back to the coach section. Then he sent Dominique, the equipment manager, a text at 1:21 a.m.

"He almost never texts me after nine o'clock," she said. "So when I got the text, I was like, he's serious."

Coach Prime's text read, *Please clean Tony Gray's locker tomorrow. We're done with him.*

She replied, *Yes sir.*

On Monday morning, Dominique placed all of Tony's personal belongings in a green trash bag and set it in a corner. She took his shoulder pads and helmet, removed the logos, and returned them to the equipment room.

"Anytime Tony Gray has been kicked off the team," she said, "I always leave his stuff in his locker because I think he's going to apologize and everything is going to be OK."

Patrick and Shedeur were Tony's closest friends on the team. More than once they ventured into Coach Prime's office and vouched for their friend.

"The first time," said Patrick, "me and Shedeur went in there and begged and begged. 'Give him one more chance, he'll get it right. Give him one more chance.'"

Eventually, Coach Prime gave in.

"Every time Grown tries to stand up for him I say, 'You know he's the reason you had a fumble and a pick. He gave up two sacks in the Celebration Bowl. You know that, right?'" Coach Prime said.

"You don't work on your game enough to get on the field and protect your boy?"

Forsett joked that one day Tony will be Shedeur's bodyguard. The friendship between Tony and Patrick was built on Patrick's desire to understand Tony.

"I want to get to know people. Why are you like this? Why do you act this way? Once you get to know people you start to root for them," Patrick said. "You see the talent, but you see him not pushing himself to that potential, so I got frustrated with him."

On Monday, Patrick drove by Tony's apartment on his way to practice and noticed that his friend's car was still in the parking lot.

"I texted him, 'Where you at? You good?'"

No response.

So he called Tony. No answer. He called again.

And again. And again. And again.

"At this point, I'm pissed-off," Patrick said. "We're down on linemen. This is the week you can really get in and play. No response."

Patrick walked into the facility and something felt off. When Tony missed the meeting, Patrick assumed the worst.

"He ended up texting me back that x, y, z happened," Patrick said. "It's just disappointing. It hurts."

Shedeur felt the same.

"He didn't really want it for real," Shedeur said. "It disappointed me a lot."

Tony said playing for Coach Prime wasn't fun.

"It's like a job. You never know if you're doing good, but you'll always know if you're doing bad," Tony said. "Being able to enjoy the guys around me and fight for the person next to me was good.

"It's not even about Coach Prime. I've been around celebrities before. It's not just about him. It's about me, too. Some people get caught up trying to please the coach."

Tony struggled to explain why his season went awry.

"It's not about what I think," he said. "It's about what they think."

Coach Prime said Tony wasn't committed to excellence.

"Tony wants to be one of the guys," Coach Prime said. "Tony don't want to work out. Tony says he's hurt but never wants to go to the training room because we know ain't nothing wrong with you.

"That's the way you get over on people. Tony don't want to adhere to the coaches or instructions. He really don't wanna play football. He just don't know how to quit."

CHAPTER 20

*I figure I just have to keep on pushing because
at the end of the day there's a purpose.*
—defensive tackle Tru Thompson

The Monday after beating Texas Southern, Coach Prime traveled to Dallas, where his friend Mike Zimmer buried his son.

Adam Zimmer died from chronic alcohol use on October 31 in suburban Minneapolis. He was thirty-eight.

When Coach Prime joined the Dallas Cowboys in 1995, Mike coached him. They hit it off because Mike was hard-nosed like his college coach Mickey Andrews.

Mike's nephew Andrew Zimmer joined JSU's staff as an unpaid analyst in the fall.

This was Andrew's seventh year coaching, and he didn't want to volunteer again like he had at Eastern Illinois in 2021. Andrew's dad had suggested they call Uncle Mike to see if Coach Prime could use him.

If it didn't work out, Andrew would become a railroad supply salesman like his dad.

Adam, a safety at Trinity University in San Antonio, didn't have the height, weight, or speed to play in the NFL, but he had the acumen, work ethic, and bloodlines to coach in the league.

He moved quickly from assistant linebackers coach in New Orleans to the same position in Kansas City to assistant secondary coach in Cincinnati, where his dad ran the defense.

When the Minnesota Vikings hired Mike in 2014, he hired Adam as linebackers coach. In 2020, he promoted Adam to co–defensive coordinator.

The Vikings fired Mike at the end of the 2021 season. Adam couldn't find a job, so he settled for being an off-site analyst with Cincinnati.

"He was just really lonely and turned to something that he shouldn't have. He'd been turning to it a little too much lately," Andrew said. "You can't let the game become your life because it so easily can. This game had so many things for Adam but when it all ended he didn't really have an identity for himself."

Malachi Wideman, Justin Ragin, and Tru Thompson dealt with the death of their friend, former JSU basketball walk-on Geronimo Warner.

The twenty-one-year-old—Nimo to his friends—died suddenly while playing basketball in the Walter Payton Recreation & Wellness Center, the same building that houses the football offices.

Nimo, a management major from Arizona, was one of Justin's best friends. Justin arrived on campus teary-eyed on Tuesday morning for a 6:45 meeting with Reilly.

Justin, Nimo, and his girlfriend often spent evenings at Justin's home playing Uno and various drinking games.

"I've been getting better, but it was really hard the first two weeks," Justin said. "Whenever I'm at football, I try to keep football the main thing because my mind likes to wander."

Sadly, Justin knows how to compartmentalize death. Nimo is the third close friend who has died in the past five years.

Malachi played basketball with Nimo on JSU's basketball team.

Malachi played 14 games for JSU, averaging 5.6 points and 2.4 points in 13.1 minutes per game.

"I still have his basketball in my room," Malachi said a few days later, while relaxing in the players' lounge.

Tru, Justin's roommate, also took Nimo's death hard.

Tru dislocated his knee and tore his patellar tendon when he squatted 630 pounds in the spring. He had vacillated about red-shirting.

More than once, he threatened to quit. He lost confidence in the knee and gained weight, but the staff kept trying to boost his esteem. They believed in Tru more than he believed in himself.

Nimo's death made Tru question his existence.

"That hit me hard. We were just talking to him. It kind of scared me. My realization of life changed. I've been in the mood of what's the point if we're all going to go one day," Tru said. "I figure I just have to keep on pushing because at the end of the day there's a purpose. I wouldn't be here if there wasn't a purpose."

When Coach Prime arrived Tuesday morning, the building's water pressure was low, another reminder of the city of Jackson's never-ending water situation. He considered taking the team to Mobile, Alabama, for the Gulf Coast Challenge a day early.

First, though, he needed to help Bethune-Cookman's football team.

They were playing at Alcorn State in Lorman, Mississippi, on Saturday. Tropical Storm Nicole forced the football team to evacuate their campus and take a twelve-hour bus ride to Jackson. Coach Prime offered to let them use JSU's practice and dining facilities.

"I want to be a blessing to them. That's what we should be," Coach Prime said. "Let's be great hosts."

Bethune-Cookman's players arrived about 11 a.m. Coach Terry Sims spent much of practice in Coach Prime's golf cart.

At lunch, several players sat at circular tables with black tablecloths and bonded with Bethune-Cookman's players over football, girls, and rap music.

While the players discussed their usual topics, the coaches did the same. Many had already resigned themselves to the fact that Coach Prime would be at another school in the fall.

They were simply curious about where he was going and whether they'd be joining him. Most speculation centered on Auburn, but they also wondered about Nebraska, Arizona State, Colorado, and South Florida.

Bartolone and White had been through a similar situation in 2021 at Nevada and found it easier to wait for news instead of trying to figure it out.

"Who's he bringing? Who's in the boat? What rats are going to be swimming for shore when the boat crashes?" Reilly wondered. "Who's on the lifeboat? And who's swimming for shore?"

Coach Prime kept the team in Jackson until Friday. Three buses left at 8 a.m. to make the 188-mile trip down Highway 49 to Mobile.

The defense and its coaches rode on the first bus—Coach Prime says the defense carries the team—the offense and its coaches rode on the second bus and the support staff rode on the third bus.

Early in the week, JSU learned that Aubrey had been selected to the Senior Bowl game in Mobile. The college all-star game is held every February and most NFL teams send their coaching staff and scouting departments to the game. Aubrey would be told about his honor in the locker room after the game.

Dallas had been named to the East-West Shrine game, a college all-star game played annually in Paradise, Nevada.

Aubrey and Dallas would each have an opportunity, he figured, to go to an NFL training camp just like Isaiah Bolden and De'Jahn Warren. Coach Prime wanted a pipeline from Jackson State to the NFL like it was back in the day when the best African-American players played at HBCUs.

It wasn't until the late 1960s and early '70s that programs such as Alabama and other big-school powers in the South started signing Black players because they could help them win games, not because they cared about social justice.

Coach Prime has a forgiving spirit, but he forgets nothing, which is why he enjoys beating Alabama A&M coach Connell Maynor.

In Coach Prime's first season at JSU, Alabama A&M beat the Tigers 53–45. When asked what advice he'd give Coach Prime, Maynor said, "He should recruit some more five-stars."

In 2021, during the weekly SWAC media conference, Maynor suggested Coach Prime sought attention for riding a scooter after having surgery on his left foot.

"Coach Sanders, I hurt my ankle getting off the bus the other day," Maynor said on the conference call. "You got an extra scooter for me? If you've got an extra scooter, send me one down here."

Well, after JSU's 61–15 victory, Barstool Sports' Dana Beers, who directed the *Coach Prime* documentary series on Amazon Prime Video, left a pink scooter on the Bulldogs' midfield logo. Coach Prime tweeted about the incident.

> With love, #CoachPrime. I apologize for giving him what he asked for!!! I'm from FLORIDA y'all know how we get down. THEE I LOVE JSU!!!

This is why Coach Prime wanted to clinch the Eastern Division title against A&M in the Gulf Coast Challenge.

"I wanted to hit their coach in the mouth when I saw him because of bad blood," Weeks said. "I can't stand him.

"What they did and how they treated us the first year we played them. They deserve another ass-whupping and we're going to give it to them."

The rhetoric didn't make Jackson State play any better in the first quarter. For the fourth time JSU trailed after the first quarter.

Less than two minutes into the game, Maynor executed a fake punt on fourth-and-two from the A&M 48. The drive stalled at the JSU 8, but Victor Barbosa's 30-yard field goal gave A&M a 3–0 lead.

"I wanted to send a message we were here to win the game," Maynor said. "We believed we were going to win the football game."

Travis's first touchdown, a 20-yard pass from Shedeur, gave JSU a 7–3 lead. A leaping interception by Travis, his first, led to a 19-yard touchdown pass to tight end D. J. Stevens and a 14–7 lead.

Then Jeremiah Brown, Cam'Ron, and Aubrey changed the game.

On a read option with 1:24 left in the first half, Jeremiah forced the quarterback to pitch the ball. Cam'Ron launched himself at the ballcarrier like a missile.

He was parallel to the ground when he slammed into the quarterback, jarring the ball loose. Aubrey pounced on it, positioning the Tigers to score another touchdown before halftime.

For Aubrey, it was yet another tone-setting big play in a season full of them. He led with his play and his voice.

He's the dude who led a players-only film session the night before every game. He's the dude whose voice resonated in the locker room, but he was also a pleaser, who spent his youth trying to earn his daddy's respect.

The father taught the son to never back down from a challenge, and the value of hard work.

"When I worked out with my daddy," said Aubrey, "I always had to be the last one to leave the field. I could never let anybody outwork me. No matter how long they stayed."

He's spent a lifetime waging a war inside his mind to control his emotions. Three tumultuous seasons at Missouri that included three position coaches, two head coaches, and a knee injury that limited him to one game in 2019 is how he wound up in the portal.

"I had a bad start at Missouri. . . . I was big-headed. I had a bad temper and I made some bad decisions," Aubrey said. "I didn't talk to coaches the right way sometimes.

"I was very emotional. My mind was focused on the wrong thing. All the girls. Weed. Liquor. I wasn't used to that and it put a burden on me."

Aubrey Miller Sr. and Cedric Buckley played football together at Arkansas State. They thought JSU would be a good fit for Aubrey Jr.

Aubrey had been following Coach Prime on Twitter since 2017, so he wanted to play for him at JSU.

"His motivation and his words really moved me. That's really what made him my idol," Aubrey said. "It wasn't how he played—of course, he was a dominant player in all areas—it was the things he was saying that made me idolize him."

Aubrey has worked tirelessly to identify his triggers and harness his emotions.

"Prime is hard on all players but you can't take it personally. He and Prime had a horrible relationship. Use [the relationship] as motivation," Buckley told Aubrey. "I told him to keep the relationship on a player-coach level because once you form a personal relationship, if it doesn't go your way—now you hate him."

Aubrey remained on a journey to maturity. There was no question about his football prowess.

At 5'11" and 230 pounds, he is undersized for an NFL linebacker. The average NFL linebacker is 6'2" and 240 pounds.

He's fanatical about his body—he travels with a scale—and his stats. Coach Prime, Hart, and others have told him NFL scouts care considerably more about production than stats.

"I get a call from him most Mondays," said Lewis, "wondering why he was credited with one number when he believes he got another."

Aubrey's fumble recovery created an opportunity and Bartolone took it.

Shedeur, his sprained shoulder feeling a little better each week, threw a 35-yard touchdown pass to Shane, giving JSU a 21–7 halftime lead against Alabama A&M.

"We were in a zone and you're supposed to keep the ball in front of you," Maynor said. "They're eighteen-, nineteen-, and twenty-year-old players. Sometimes, they make mistakes."

A 21-yard touchdown pass from Shedeur to Willie Gaines on fourth-and-10 made it 27–10 early in the third quarter.

A blowout appeared inevitable. Then disaster occurred.

Shedeur, facing pressure on third-and-seven from the JSU 17, escaped the pocket and took off. He wanted to run over the defender in front of him and get the first down, which was cool.

The problem? He never saw the guy coming from his right.

"This not open, this not open, so I stepped up and I scrambled. Whenever you slide, they be marking you short," Shedeur said. "My thing was, we ain't been generating no offense, so I gotta get the first down.

"I ran over the dude and he fell backwards. The dude on the side hit me, and I was knocked out."

Shedeur lay face-first on the grass. For only the second time this season, the trainers rushed onto the field to check on a player. Coach Prime demanded players leave the field under their own power if at all possible because it instills toughness and gives JSU a psychological advantage over its opponents.

Shedeur spent a couple of minutes in a blue tent getting examined before heading to the locker room for the rest of the game.

Shedeur passed for 185 yards and 4 touchdowns. Before the shoulder injury, he averaged 345 yards passing with 17 touchdowns and two interceptions.

The combination of his sprained shoulder and defenses dropping eight defenders and rushing three frustrated him. Since the Alabama State game, he'd averaged 228 yards passing per game with 14 touchdowns and three interceptions.

His practice repetitions were limited, and he felt out of sorts.

"The whole middle of the season it just felt like I lost something," Shedeur said. "I lost the 'it' factor. The difference factor.

"After I hurt my shoulder. I was limited in the weight room, and all of that stuff starts to take a toll on you mentally. It made me think. When you're playing without thinking the game is easy. When you're thinking about stuff it's hard."

A 30-yard field goal at the start of the third quarter made it 27–13. Neither team scored again.

"Go win it this year," Maynor told Coach Prime after the game.

In the locker room, the equipment staff passed out hats and T-shirts for winning the title, while Robinson addressed the team.

When he finished, JSU legend Robert Brazile spoke.

"Hey, guys, we're not finished yet," he said. "If you're happy about this there's something wrong with you."

Then Brazile announced Aubrey's Senior Bowl news. His teammates celebrated loudly. Aubrey, who finished with a game-high 17 tackles, could not be found.

When he finally entered the locker room, his teammates surrounded him and a Senior Bowl representative handed Miller his official invitation.

Aubrey hugged anyone who entered his personal space, while left tackle Willis Patrick fussed at Shedeur for not sliding.

CHAPTER 21

There's a major disconnect with the defensive line coaches.
—linebackers coach Andre' Hart

Sophomore defensive end Jeremiah Brown had seen enough.

This time, he didn't keep his thoughts to himself. Nope, this time he made sure they heard him—and if they didn't like it, too bad.

Practice had just ended, and it was time to run a series of sideline-to-sideline sprints. Justin Ragin ambled slowly off the field toward the track surrounding it. Nyles Gaddy had removed his cleats, an indication that sprints weren't in his future.

Sure, those players were veterans, but Coach Prime had preached for weeks about players holding each other accountable.

Coach Prime had also talked all week about practicing with urgency and avoiding complacency as the Tigers moved into the final stretch of the regular season.

"When you win over, over, and over," said Shedeur, "you can get complacent."

The hardest obstacle for any team that has lost in a championship game is dealing with the monotony of the next season. You just don't fast-forward to the Cricket Celebration Bowl. This team had accomplished so much, but one loss, depending on when it happened, could wreck it all.

"We gotta dominate. We've been saying this from day one. We gotta finish. We gotta have a completion to whatever you start," Coach Prime told the players and coaches Tuesday morning. "You have to finish, whether that's schoolwork, whether that's football. Anything you start you have to try your best to finish."

When Jeremiah saw Justin and Nyles about to skip conditioning drills—they weren't done practicing in his mind—the morning message still resonated in his mind.

"It wasn't nothing personal, I was just trying to hold him accountable," Jeremiah said of Justin. "He always holds me accountable for everything I do. Mess up on film, he's quick to point it out and correct me.

"He's a great guy and a great leader, but it's football. It gets emotional every now and then."

Bench-pressing too much heavy weight had wrecked Justin's shoulders; his knees were worse.

He'd played much of the season with a torn posterior cruciate ligament that limited his mobility. The young man who once squatted 525 pounds abandoned the squat rack in July because his knees couldn't handle it.

He was twenty-two years old with a grandfather's gait. Why play?

"I have to finish what I start. A lot of people look up to me," Justin said. "It's an emotional roller coaster. I love the game but it's taken a huge toll.

"I feel like I could play better, if I had a better body, but I can't and I'm not happy with what I can do."

The goal for Thurman, Weeks, and Reilly each week is getting Justin to the game with a high energy level. Jeremiah wasn't privy to that information. Neither was Coach Prime.

You could certainly blame the coaches for not telling him but that's not really how it worked at Jackson State. Coach Prime is not the kind of control freak who wants to know everything about every player.

Coach Prime let the assistants control starters and rotations, then held them accountable for their decisions.

"I don't like it when guys who get the most reps in the game don't want to run," Jeremiah said loudly enough for Justin and Nyles to hear.

Jeremiah exchanged fuck-yous with Justin, who explained why his body wouldn't let him run sprints after practice and play well on Saturdays.

As the confrontation escalated, shoves turned into punches. The scuffle didn't last long before Coach Prime blew his whistle to stop it and motioned the players to gather around his golf cart.

"[Justin,] you go in practice and then you do push-ups on the sideline," Coach Prime said. "These folks don't like that. Then you want reps in the game."

"hurt," Justin said. "My knees are bad."

"if you're hurt don't play," Coach Prime said.

"nt me to play," Justin said of the staff.

"mise you that if you're hurt, you won't get on that bus te]."

days later, Coach Prime provided more insight into a up that created more consternation than any other on

they were the team's most talented position group—and the big st collection of underachievers. They lacked physicality, blew too many assignments, wilted under criticism, and didn't always play hard.

Every week, different guys screwed up, which resulted in a unit that played consistently inconsistent football. Coach Prime raised a sensitive topic while he criticized Justin and Nyles by proxy.

The defensive line, he suggested, as a group had an issue with Weeks and Reilly because they were white men in a position of authority.

"There's a major disconnect with the defensive line coaches," Hart said. "The shit that goes on down there. How they talk to each other. Ain't no way."

He wasn't the first coach or player to suggest that.

"Some of the boys needed some more fire lit up under their ass," defensive lineman Jason Mercier said. "Coach Weeks was just a little bit too lenient because he was so cool.

"Defensive line is a different thing. You gotta be a hard-nosed dude to deal with us. They needed Coach Prime's energy."

At an HBCU, where culture rules everything, there's a thought that the guys in the trenches need a coach who will instill the fear of God in them. Sometimes "please" and "thank you" don't work as well as well-placed cuss words.

Sometimes they need a dude just as big as they are with grown-man strength to persuade them to do their job instead of playing hero ball.

"If we were at a PWI [predominantly white institution], they wouldn't have a problem with Weeks or Trevor, but at an HBCU they see them as outsiders," Coach Prime said. "Weeks has coached in the NFL for years and Trevor was a guy who made it by hard work.

"Trevor befriends them. They take his kindness for something else. He tells them the truth but they don't want to receive it."

Jeremiah had been on edge all week because he didn't want to play defensive end, even though he was starting for the top defense in FCS football.

Reilly kicked him out of practice Tuesday after refusing to join a drill.

"If you're trying to be a leader, then you're not a leader. You gotta focus on yourself and do all the little things right before you can tell somebody else how to do their job," said Jeremiah, oblivious that sitting out of a drill looked bad.

"Young guys are scared to speak up because they feel like they're not doing enough on the field. But if you bust your behind in practice and you're working hard, I believe you have a say-so."

Jeremiah decommitted from Florida Atlantic after picking them over South Carolina and Kentucky. He yearned to play middle linebacker.

"I love that box. I like reading, filling that gap, and getting that tackle for loss. There's nothing better," a smiling Jeremiah said. "Sacks are great, too, but I just love hitting a running back square in the face—boom!—getting that tackle for loss and that adrenaline rush. I just love it."

Jeremiah, 6'1" and 220 pounds, is long and lean. Most inside linebackers are thick and stout. He was not built for the position no matter how much he loved it.

On Tuesday afternoon, Jeremiah sauntered into the office Thurman shared with Hart and stated his desire to play middle linebacker.

Again.

It didn't matter that he played his best game of the season against Alabama A&M with a season-high nine tackles, including two for a loss.

Thurman listened to Jeremiah before he told the young man a story about Thurman's career at USC.

Thurman had entered his sophomore season as a starting safety, but injuries forced him to play receiver. The point: the team's needs always trump an individual's needs.

"Do they think we don't want them to succeed?" Thurman said rhetorically. "We're putting them in the spots where they can have the most success and they're fighting us."

Then he shook his head and returned to playing *Jeopardy!* on his iPad.

"[Thurman] said we have so much talent," said Jeremiah, "that the best way to get me on the field was to play edge. I took it as a good thing. They trust me, so I trust them with my future and everything."

On Saturday against Alcorn State, he would need to trust Justin and Nyles, so the defense would thrive.

Alcorn State and JSU are rivals but not in the way Southern and JSU are rivals. This is more like family instead of enemies.

"When the game is over, it's not going to be a fight like it would be against Southern," Riddley said. "We'll just hug it out."

Jackson State led the all-time series 48-37-2, which pitted Mississippi's two largest HBCUs. It has been called the Soul Bowl since the mid-1970s.

Alcorn is in Lorman, Mississippi, a community in Jefferson County. The school is located just off Highway 61, a two-lane road about ninety minutes from Jackson. There's one way in and one way out. At times, traffic snarls and the road becomes a parking lot.

Leave Jackson too late and some folks won't get seated until halftime.

The trip to Alcorn State excited Coach Prime because he wanted a glimpse of the 22,000-seat stadium where Steve "Air" McNair's legend began.

In 1994, McNair finished third in the Heisman Trophy voting behind Colorado's Rashaan Salaam and Penn State's Ki-Jana Carter.

The Tennessee Titans picked him third in the 1995 NFL draft. He played thirteen seasons with Tennessee and two with Baltimore, passing for 174 touchdowns and running for 37.

Coach Prime played his last two seasons in Baltimore, retiring after the 2005 season. McNair arrived in 2006.

Now his older brother, Fred McNair, coached Alcorn State.

McNair led the Braves to SWAC championships in 2018 and 2019. He and Coach Prime became friends, bonding over ways to improve the SWAC.

"I love him, love him, love him," Coach Prime said about McNair during his Tuesday news conference with the local media. "I have so much respect for him and what he has represented during his career and what he has done for the SWAC for a multitude of years."

They met when Coach Prime took Shedeur on a recruiting trip to Southern Mississippi and they stayed in touch. Their bond grew closer in the spring of 2021 when Jackson State held a Pro Day and invited athletes from various SWAC schools to attend.

Coach Prime and McNair squeezed in a few conversations between watching their players work out.

"I feel like we've had a friendship ever since," Coach Prime said. "Coach McNair is a good man, a great man, with a great family. I love the way he goes about his job and his business. Coach McNair is one of the leaders and pillars of the HBCUs."

The undefeated regular season was only important to Coach Prime because it represented another step toward a perfect season.

"I don't think Shedeur lost more than five football games in high school or ten games in his life," Coach Prime said.

Jackson State was 21-2 with Shedeur at quarterback as JSU headed into the Soul Bowl. All but one victory in 2022 had been by double figures, but Coach Prime hadn't seen enough dominance—and that's all he cared about.

"Only once have we shown up all together—the first game—and we're still chasing that moment," he said. "Sometimes you win, win, win and people start thinking, this is easy. It's not easy although we may make it look like that. It's truly a task."

But it's a heck of a lot easier with Shedeur at quarterback.

Shedeur removed any doubt about whether he would play against Alcorn State with a tweet on Sunday night that said he'd be ready.

"He's good," Coach Prime said Tuesday. "He had a little setback but he's good."

Coach Prime spoke with his son on Sunday at their weekly meal, and implored him to start sliding whenever possible.

Multiple players—offensive and defensive—and coaches delivered similar messages during the week because Shedeur was the roster's only irreplaceable player.

"I told him he need to get his ass down," Patrick said. "Them extra yards ain't worth it. I almost had a heart attack when I seen it happen. I was sick the whole game after he got up.

"I saw it as it was happening. It hurt my heart to see him on the ground and it threw me off my game, and then I get in the locker room and he's smiling and laughing and talking about it. He's all right."

Shedeur took most of the practice snaps that week, an indication he wasn't having issues with light, noise, or equilibrium. All of those issues can result from a concussion or head trauma.

"Was I a hundred percent ready? No, I wasn't," Shedeur said a few weeks later.

When JSU's seven-vehicle convoy arrived in Lorman, there was surprisingly little traffic. That's not to say fans from both schools hadn't packed the side of the road leading into the picturesque campus.

The tailgaters had been there since the wee hours of the morning, smoking ribs and wings and other treats between guzzling sodas, beer, and the kind of liquid joy found inside pint-sized silver flasks on a chilly November morning.

Mata's 38-yard field goal gave JSU a short-lived 3–0 lead.

The Tigers' next drive was a disaster. Shedeur held the ball too long on consecutive plays, resulting in a pair of huge losses on sacks.

"Teams were switching up everything they'd shown all season," Shedeur said. "We're still busting routes, we're not playing with our minds, and you get to the game they're not doing anything they've done all season.

"Now it's hard to focus on keys because you're not comfortable with what they're doing."

Shedeur struggled on the next series with another sack. After the series, he sat in a metal folding chair next to the bench and stared straight ahead.

Coach Prime walked over and spoke animatedly; Shedeur's expression never changed.

"He's a player who thrives on rhythm and completions because his best trait—outside of his mind—is his accuracy," Bartolone said. "The more passes he completes, the more his confidence soars, the more rhythm he finds, and the better he plays.

"This is why it's hard for him to quit on a play by throwing it away."

Shedeur just knew he needed to play better.

"I do a lot of self-evaluation and I ain't like what I seen against Alcorn," he said. "I know quarterbacks are going to have games like that. I was thinking too much. I wasn't all the way there. I was just a little off.

"I missed one to Dallas early in the game. It just went downhill. I'm not a delusional person. I know if I'm doing good or I'm not."

This team, however, had been built on defense. Justin, still pissed from his fight with Jeremiah and Coach Prime's stinging criticism, had vowed to deliver his best performance of the season.

"When I got home, I was angry. I'm going to show them Saturday," he told himself. "I took my pills and my shot and got ready to ball out."

Justin started the cleansing process late in the second quarter when he chased down Alcorn State's quarterback for a 21-yard loss, knocking the ball loose. Of course, Jeremiah scooped it up and returned it to the Alcorn State 2.

Sy'Veon scored on the next play, giving JSU a 10–6 lead with 8:06 left in the half. Less than a minute later, JSU scored again.

On second-and-10 from the Alcorn 37, the Braves messed with Travis one too many times. They had thrown at him several times in the first half, and completed a couple for short gains.

Travis, playing right cornerback, bodied Alcorn receiver Monterio Hunt off the line of scrimmage, beat him to the spot on a comeback route, and intercepted the pass at the Alcorn 44.

Then the excitement began.

At the 28-yard line, Travis stopped—yes, he literally stopped—to let an Alcorn State player whiz by him. He picked up a key block from Cam'Ron at the 5 and cut inside for a touchdown and a 17–7 JSU lead with 7:39 left in the first half.

"They had got that play on me the drive before," said Travis, "so I told the guys that play was on me."

The 17–7 halftime lead didn't please Coach Prime, surprising no one.

"Thank God for the defense," he said. "Thank God for defense. Offense, you haven't done a got-durn thing.

It turned out that Travis was just getting started.

Jackson State held a tenuous 17–13 lead with 14:22 left in the game. Tension engulfed the sideline as the players realized their perfect season was at risk.

Football in its simplest form is about players making plays. The best players make plays at winning time.

Travis is one of those players.

Shedeur had a clean pocket for one of the few times on second-and-5 from the Alcorn State 47 and threw a ball that drifted toward the right sideline. Travis tracked the ball, slowed, and turned his back to the sideline before he leaped high and cradled the ball against his chest at the Alcorn State 17.

Two plays later, he made an even better catch.

Shedeur threw a perfect touch pass and Travis made an over-the-shoulder grab and dragged both feet to stay inbounds as he tumbled to the ground in the back of the end zone.

He bounced up, holding the ball aloft in his right hand. Then he immediately started pointing to the grass to show where he dragged his feet as Graham, Breaux, and Stevens celebrated with him in the end zone.

"The first thing I was thinking about was keeping my feet inbounds because I knew I was squeezing the sideline," he said. "I've caught the ball a million times. I don't even think about that.

"I know I'm going to catch the ball. I just wanted to make sure I dragged my left toe and kept my right foot up."

Initially, officials ruled him out of bounds. Officials studied the replay for several minutes before reversing the ruling on the field and setting off another JSU celebration.

Jackson State led 24–13.

It marked the second consecutive game in which Travis had scored a touchdown and intercepted a pass.

This was the dynamic player that JSU's fan base had waited to see. This was the guy Coach Prime had praised for his work ethic and athleticism.

"You kind of expect it in terms of the great plays," Thurman said. "The run was the most impressive thing about the interception. He didn't settle for intercepting the football. He wanted to put it in the end zone.

"He might have gotten a little fatigued on defense because he doesn't give up many balls. The ability that he showed to come back and make plays is what you look at.

"A lot of guys when they give up a play, it stays with them. He was like, 'You got me, I'm gonna get y'all.'"

It had been a trying season for Travis. As he worked back into the lineup, he needed to regain confidence in his ankle.

It also took some time for Bartolone to figure out how to use him on offense because the defense was always aware of him every time he was on the field.

"Travis Hunter, he's not getting the ball every time he's in the game. That's not good for him or anybody," Bartolone said. "We try to get him one reverse a week and let him do more as he grows."

Finally, they figured out the formula. Remember, Coach Prime was the NFL's first two-way player since 1960 and Chuck Bednarik, when he played receiver and cornerback for the Dallas Cowboys. Bednarik, a member of the Pro Football Hall of Fame, played center and middle linebacker for the Philadelphia Eagles.

In 1996, Sanders caught 36 passes for 475 yards and a touchdown for the Cowboys.

"He's [Hunter] a very confident individual and he likes the challenges. He's performing against ego," Coach Prime said. "We've had quarterbacks who could easily throw the ball on the other side of the field but ego says no, I'm not going away from Travis Hunter, I'm going to throw at him.

"It comes from homeys and teammates all during the week. Well, you saw the results. On offense, Travis gives you opportunity on fifty-fifty balls. The kid is just dynamic. He's truly dynamic. I can't wait to see him next year when he's truly healthy. He's still limping around a little bit."

Travis finished with two receptions for 49 yards and a touchdown. He broke up three passes in addition to his interception and touchdown.

Justin ended the next drive with a sack, giving him 3.5 for the game. He celebrated with a pelvic thrust.

As the final seconds ticked off, Justin sat in the middle of an empty bench, a wide smile on his face. Jeremiah dapped him up and sat to his left.

Then Nyles ambled over and dapped up each player before taking a seat to Justin's right. They were exhausted yet happy.

The fight six days ago seemed like six years ago.

PART IV

CHAPTER 22

*We have a chance to go down as the greatest team
to ever walk through Jackson State.*
—offensive lineman Tyler Brown

It was four days before Thanksgiving and Coach Prime had plenty to be thankful for, whether it concerned his football team or his life.

He was thankful to have four of his five kids either working with him or attending JSU. He was thankful for Tracey, his fiancée, who helped nurse him back to health after the blood clots nearly took his life in 2021.

He was thankful for his sister Tracie, who had taken over as director of operations, and her young son T.J. And he was certainly thankful for his mom and the foster care twins—Heaven and Nevaeh—she had pretty much raised since they were babies.

Coach Prime was especially thankful for God's abundance as well as his grace because the dull throb in his foot served as a regular reminder of just how close he came to death in 2021.

He was also thankful for a staff he trusted and a team that had managed to wade through the season undefeated and needed two more wins to achieve perfection.

But he knew it wasn't going to be easy. The rumors about him leaving for Colorado or South Florida or Auburn had increased and he was trying to keep his team focused on perfection.

"We have to finish what we started. We have to finish the dream. We have to finish the goal," he said.

The rumors weren't going away and the players weren't ignoring them. How could they? Social media is part of their daily existence. They spend several hours a day on Instagram, YouTube, Twitch, Snapchat, Twitter, TikTok, and others.

In his October 2022 interview with *60 Minutes*, Coach Prime made it clear that if he received an offer from a Power 5 program, he would listen intently.

"I'm going to have to entertain it," he told *60 Minutes* when asked about Power 5 interest. "Yes, I'm going to have to entertain it, straight up. I'd be a fool not to."

His players either saw or heard that interview. They understand the business of college football.

Many had already played at multiple programs. Sometimes it happened because their coach was fired. Other times it happened because their coach left for another job.

Some players transferred because they wanted more playing time or the scheme didn't fit them. A few left because of poor grades or off-the-field trouble. Others realized they weren't quite good enough to be starters at the Power 5 level.

They changed schools to find a better situation for themselves.

"Everybody's mind wanders. My mind wanders," Patrick said. "I'm an overthinker, but when you're on the football field you have to focus on the task at hand."

Still, they wanted some answers; they just didn't know where to find them.

Hart's linebacker room is different. Most of JSU's alpha dawgs reside in this room; Aubrey leads the pack. He's followed in no particular order by Nyles, Brown, Jurriente Davis, and Baron Hopson.

One day after their meeting ended, Hart was about to leave the meeting room when they asked him to stay and answer some questions.

"These motherfuckers were like, 'Coach, you're gonna talk to us today,'" Hart remembered. "'We need to know what's up with Coach Prime.'"

Their boldness surprised him.

"First," he said in his sternest daddy voice, "y'all need to lower your fucking tone. I'll tell you what I know."

Hart stood before his players trying to figure out what to say and how to say it.

They needed answers for their peace of mind, enabling them to focus on the SWAC Championship game and the Cricket Celebration Bowl. What he told them would quickly be spread to the rest of the team, so each word mattered. Lying or misleading them was not an option.

"What's going on? I don't know. I'll tell you what I do know. Are people calling? Yes. Has he accepted anything? No. Will I go? Yes. Will he have an opportunity? Yes. That's what I know."

For the time, they were satisfied. The players weren't the only ones questioning their future.

The graduate assistants and several position coaches weren't sure how they fit into Coach Prime's long-term plan. Sure, he always praised his staff publicly and JSU had just completed an undefeated regular season, but coaches know security isn't part of their lifestyle.

The staff knew Hart, Thurman, and Mathis would be on his next staff because of their personal relationships with Coach Prime. They figured Coach Flea would be on the staff because he was the assistant head coach, and he had replaced Coach Prime when he missed three games in the 2021 season.

Brewster figured to go with Coach Prime because he was the only other coach on the staff who matched his energy and had the charisma to captivate players when he addressed them.

"Shit happens every year. We dealt with it last year. In this profession, this is what happens with success," White said. "My job doesn't change. It's the players you worry about. You have to keep them focused. Nothing has happened. He's still here. There's just more noise."

Most of the players took a big-picture view of the situation.

"We're focused on winning a championship," Tru said. "Yeah, we're gonna talk about it, but the future is the future and it'll take care of itself."

Tyler Brown suggested his teammates focus on winning a pair of championship rings in the next three weeks.

"There are things out of our control. Why would you want to make yourself more anxious or sad thinking about those things?" he said. "We have a chance to go down as the greatest team to ever walk through Jackson State. That's what matters."

On Tuesday morning as Coach Prime laid out the week's schedule—it would be light since they had two weeks to prepare for Southern in the SWAC Championship game—he wanted to know what his players were thankful for as Thanksgiving approached.

Many players had overcome tragedies and obstacles. Few players had made JSU their first choice out of high school.

"This is a rehabilitation center in a lot of ways," Riddley said.

"A lot of times it's about the beholder. It's the coach. We have a lot of good football players who wouldn't be out here if the coach was better at their first stop."

For many, the opportunity to play for Coach Prime and at JSU, now one of the country's highest-profile programs, represented hope for a better future, whether that included the NFL or a career that would allow them to support their future families.

"I'm thankful for each and every one of you. I'm thankful for this wonderful coaching staff," Coach Prime said. "I'm thankful for this opportunity to come before you every day and I'm thankful we have like-minded men in this room with a common goal to be successful and dominate and to prosper and bless and encourage a multitude of others."

When he finished, he told the players he wanted to know why they were thankful. He started pointing at guys.

Quarterback Norm Douglas was first. He was thankful for his mom and Nugget, his best friend, who helped him get to JSU. Next was defensive end Antonio Doyle, who was thankful for the opportunity to play football and for his daughter.

"She's my motivation," he said.

Quay Davis, laughing to hide his nervousness, stood up and said, "I'm thankful for having my kids—all four of them—and I'm thankful to just be here."

Coach Prime, arms folded, looked directly at Quay and said, "You're going to be a great father to every last one of them."

He pointed to Tru, still working through Nimo's death, and said, "I'm thankful for all y'all. I love y'all. I'm thankful for my parents, but I'm just thankful to be here."

Tru was supposed to be a difference-maker for Jackson State.

He was supposed to stop the run and make plays in the backfield. Tru was supposed to do all of that because he was dropping down from a Power 5 school to an FCS school, where his skill set should've made him an elite player.

It didn't. Or he wasn't, depending on how you viewed his season.

Either way, the best you could say about him was that he made a few plays, but not enough to be noticed on a weekly basis. There was always something with Tru, which is not to say everything that kept him from realizing his potential was his fault.

"I can do it, but my body says I can't," he said. "The weight I trying to hit—630—I've done it before but the knee just gave out. I came down. The whole knee blew. I had trauma from that. The weight fell back and my kneecap ended all the way up in my thigh and my leg was just dangling."

He couldn't walk on his own for a couple of months, which led to him gaining about thirty pounds. The rehab was supposed to take six to eight months, which is why he didn't return to practice until October.

He was still overweight, which meant he couldn't practice as hard as he wanted or Coach Prime demanded.

"What messed with me mentally is that I wanted to go—I'm the kind of player who just wants to go, go, go but my body wasn't allowing me to," he said. "It was frustrating. You just feel hopeless because you're trying to do your best but all the muscle in my leg was gone."

Understand, Thompson was supposed to be a star.

Florida State offered the Grayson, Georgia, native a scholarship as an eighth grader after watching him dominate in a camp. Florida State fired coach Willie Taggart after Tru's freshman season and Mike Norvell replaced him.

He played sparingly the next two seasons, which was why he entered the transfer portal.

Reilly reached out to him and Coach Prime vetted him with his friend Taggart. Tru fit Thurman's defensive scheme because he had the bulk to play nose guard and the athleticism to be disruptive and create negative plays.

A week ago, though, he once again considered quitting.

The knee injury, the frustration of being in poor shape, and Nimo's death put him in a fragile mental state. He had started drinking Reign energy drinks for the first time before workouts to help power through them. Those drinks often contain taurine or other stimulants that can cause an increased heart rate.

As Tru's heart rate sped up, he began having a panic attack.

He went to the hospital and had an EKG, which provided peace of mind.

"It has been a tough year. I'm trying to get back to normal. I've been a little off," Tru said. "You have to keep going and keep pushing. My realization of life changed. I've just been in the mood like what's the point of everything if we're all going to go at one point.

"I just have to keep on pushing because at the end of the day there's a purpose of why I'm here. I wouldn't be here if there wasn't a purpose. I'm working out with a purpose. I'm doing class work with a purpose. I find the purpose for whatever I'm doing and do it. I'm going to live so I have to focus on what I want to do. It was like a wake-up call. Now I'm ready to go."

Coach Prime called on several more players, such as Travis and Donald Turley.

Max Gibbs, a transfer from Southern Cal, and receiver David Studstill said why they were thankful. Then it was Malachi's turn.

"I'm thankful for all of y'all. I see y'all like a family. I'm around y'all more than my family," he said. "I'm thankful for you, Coach. When I left Tennessee I had a lot of dirt thrown on my name and you took that risk of taking me in and letting me be part of this family and this journey.

"I'm thankful to my grandma who raised me. I'm thankful for a lot more but there's not enough words to say how thankful I am for a lot of things."

Quarterback Grayson Thompson, who played on Coach Prime's seven-on-seven team as a high school senior, spoke, followed by Hayden Hagler.

"This is my favorite team I've ever been a part of. Thankful for the coaches and thankful for my family," Hayden said. "I have the three strongest guardian angels watching over me."

Turning boys into men, the promise Coach Prime makes to the parents or guardians of every recruit, doesn't occur by happenstance or luck.

Coach Prime warned his players to be careful driving home, by adhering to the speed limit and not driving under the influence of alcohol or weed. He reminded them to be careful once they returned home because their success, real or perceived, could cause friends and family members to change.

Envy and jealousy run rampant in neighborhoods where hope is a precious commodity and despair resides on every corner. Several JSU players grew up in neighborhoods where tomorrow isn't promised.

"Everybody that's there for you ain't there for you," he said. "Everybody in your family don't love you. Some people ain't really down for what you're doing. You have an anointing on your life.

"You're gone, you've progressed, you're not who you were when you left. They're seeing you in the same light. Keep the peace, keep the love, keep the joy, keep the respect."

Being on time is about discipline, and it's one of Coach Prime's few rules. He typically arrives twenty to thirty minutes early for any appointment because time is a valuable commodity. He told his players to be back in Jackson at 2 p.m. on Sunday for a team meeting.

"Listen clearly," he said. "If any of y'all come back one minute late, I promise you your season is over. Your locker will be cleaned immediately. Immediately.

"Don't come telling me your flight got canceled, because I know it's going to happen. Don't tell me you had a flat tire. You should've left on time. I told you to be back Saturday.

"Somebody died, you better be in a picture right next to the casket. I'm serious. There's no excuses. Coaches included. Don't call me, we're going to move on."

CHAPTER 23

Only two people got a record: me and my son.
—Coach Prime

Bruce Feldman, one of the nation's top college football reporters, broke the news November 26 during a segment on Fox Sports' *Big Noon Kickoff*: Colorado had offered Coach Prime its head coaching position.

Feldman did not say Coach Prime had accepted the position.

"At Colorado, where they're desperate to pump some life into this program, CU has offered Deion Sanders of Jackson State the job," Feldman told Fox host Mike Hill, "and I'm told he has legitimate interest in becoming the Buffs' next head coach.

"He's 22-2 the last two years, but he hasn't really gotten much buy-in from Power 5 jobs and vacancies. I'm told if he can go there— the people at CU are optimistic—he would make this program nationally relevant for the first time in a long, long time."

Coach Prime had spent the entire season being transparent about his potential interest in a Power 5 job, and his name had been linked to multiple jobs for several weeks, so getting an offer wasn't surprising.

The news, however, was a problem.

He had to maneuver through a massive distraction no matter how hard he tried to snuff it out. He couldn't control this story or the narrative that accompanied it.

In his world, Coach Prime always has control because he's rich, powerful, and an iconic athlete and brand. Being an athlete known by a singular name is an honor reserved for the greats.

Ali. Jordan. Messi. Gretzky. Tiger. Venus and Serena.

Prime.

A few others exist, but you get the point. Most coaches crave control because they have trust issues or they're micromanagers. Coaches, they say, are hired to be fired. They demand control to ensure that if they get fired, it happened on their terms.

Coach Prime is involved in every football decision. Travel. Helmets. Uniforms. Practice gear. Coaches' attire. Championship rings. Facility upgrades. Grass. Turf. Nutrition.

Everything.

"Anything that involves football, I'm in it," he said. "If it has anything to do with the football program, it has to cross this desk. Anything."

Why? That requires a story.

The year: 1989. The site: RFK Stadium in Washington, D.C. The opponent: Washington Redskins.

From the Atlanta 34, Coach Prime had man coverage against Art Monk. The defensive play required him to play about eight yards off the line of scrimmage because the Falcons were blitzing.

"I looked in backfield and he stutter-stepped and ran right by me. Touchdown. I didn't even look back. I just ran off the field," Coach Prime said. "My coach said, 'What happened?' He beat me. Don't worry, it won't happen again.

"From then on, I bumped. Bumped. You gonna get me, you gonna get me my way. You're not gonna get me your way. You got me when I'm backed off, looking in the backfield. I can't give you credit for that. You got me, but I can't give you credit. I threw a shutout. They didn't catch another ball.

"If this program ain't gonna succeed, it's going to be my way, I know how to work it. I know how to run it. Ain't but two people gonna get the blame. Only two people got a record: me and my son. No one else is getting a record associated with their name."

The leak about Colorado's offer didn't come from Coach Prime's inner circle. They kept his toe amputation a secret, so they could certainly keep a secret about a job offer. Bottom line: Coach Prime needed to wade through considerable drama to win the last two games and achieve perfection. And that's before he walked into the Gordon meeting room at 1:55 Sunday afternoon.

The players were seated. Most of the coaches stood along the wall leading up the stairs. The players wanted to know what, if anything, Coach Prime would say about the Colorado offer.

The players and coaches had been given Thursday through Saturday off for Thanksgiving and were told to be back in Jackson at 2 p.m. Sunday for a team meeting.

By now, everyone and anyone had either seen it on social media or been told about it by teammates, family, or friends. Only one person was missing—and it wasn't one of the usual culprits.

Shilo Sanders was in the building but he wasn't seated in the auditorium. That made him late.

Uh-oh.

"Dang," Shedeur thought, "Shilo finna be late and it's finna be over. We don't have phones in the meeting room, so I couldn't call him or text him. It was in God's hands."

When Shilo walked into the meeting room and walked toward the stairway, his father said, "Get out!"

Shilo protested. "It's not even two o'clock yet."

"Get out," the coach repeated. "Clean out his durn locker."

Shilo wheeled around, muttering to himself, and walked briskly out of the meeting, which continued without incident. It was yet another distraction.

John Huggins, recovering from a high ankle sprain, had returned to practice but the staff didn't know if he was healthy enough to play. Huggins, 6'2", 205 pounds with 4.39 speed, was a good tackler and an NFL prospect.

Without Shilo and Huggins, JSU still had enough talent with Herm Smith and Cam'Ron, but they had been robbed of any depth.

Shilo, according to folks who know the family best, is closest to Coach Prime's personality. He drove his dad crazy during the season with a variety of shenanigans.

He washed his suit before one road trip instead of taking it to the cleaners, so he needed another jacket at the last minute. He rarely attended meetings while he recovered from a torn ACL he suffered in the spring, aggravating Coach Prime and Thurman.

Shilo figured he didn't need to attend meetings if he wasn't playing. Of course, Coach Prime and Thurman wanted him to be familiar with the scheme once he had been cleared to play. And when he rehabbed his ACL, he often ignored Askevold's instructions.

Then again, how could you criticize his rehab process when Shilo returned to the field six months after blowing out his ACL?

"He's an athletic freak," said Askevold, shaking her head.

Shilo embraced being the family rebel, but being late for this meeting had put his father in a bad spot. Coach Prime didn't want to suspend his son, but there was no way around it. Not after he made such a big deal about being on time and spelled out the consequences for being late before the team left for Thanksgiving break.

"It's one of the hardest things I've ever had to do in my life, but it is what it is. I had to put it down. He didn't give me no option," Coach Prime said. "It wasn't on me. It was on him. He did that.

"Hopefully, it gets him prepared for life and football. He has to make some different life choices so he won't be in those situations."

Bucky said his father was frustrated and embarrassed because Shilo was the only player late.

"You have to really enforce that. If it was five or six people and Shilo was included it might've been easier," Bucky said.

"It was a bad look. It was a bad feeling. And a feeling of betrayal, too. Like c'mon, bro. You tripping."

Each Monday during the football season, the SWAC hosted a conference call. Each coach answered questions during a specific ten-minute time slot. While Coach Prime failed to address Colorado's offer in the team meeting, he discussed it briefly during the weekly SWAC teleconference.

"The report is true. They're not the only ones, but the report is true," Coach Prime said. "I'm not going to sit here and tell all my business, but they're not the only ones. I would be a liar if I told you they didn't.

"You know they did, I know they did; everybody there knows they did, so it is what it is. That's not my focus right now. My focus is to win and to be dominant. My focus is right here in this beloved stadium to be dominant on Saturday.

"That's my focus and I keep the main thing the main thing. Everybody who knows me knows that about me. I have an innate ability to focus and keep the main thing the main thing."

The challenge was getting his players and coaches to manage the distractions the way he did.

"To someone else that hasn't been that dude, it's intoxicating. I've been Prime for a long time, dawg," he said on the teleconference. "Attention ain't nothing new to me, come on. I'm not being braggadocios; this ain't new to me.

"Being in the spotlight ain't new to me. I've got to just turn that light and channel it to my kids, channel it to my coaching staff, channel it to the support staff."

The questions continued. At his weekly news conference with the local media on Tuesday morning, Coach Prime answered more questions about his future.

"My team don't give a durn about that. Y'all care about that. My team cares about what we tell them and how we work," Coach Prime said. "Y'all act like these kids are crazy. You know durn well when we win this kind of stuff happens.

"That's part of life and I love that part of life for them and the coaches. They don't think like y'all think. You guys just sensationalize stuff instead of just asking the right durn question so I can give you the truth of the matter."

Actually, the team cared about his future because it affected their futures, depending on whether they followed Coach Prime to Colorado, remained at JSU, or entered the transfer portal.

"My phone has been on meltdown," Brewster said. "Kids calling. Blowing me up."

Would you like to return as Jackson State head coach? one TV reporter asked.

"That's a tricky question. I don't even want to go there because you know what that's going to start," he said. "I'm enthusiastically happy where I am. Truly happy.

"I'm proud. I'm pleased. I feel like this is the best fan base in FCS football by far. I think this is the best fan base in HBCU football in quite some time and we have work to do. We're not finished."

Tuesday brought more distractions because receivers Malachi and Quay each missed practice.

For Malachi, it wasn't surprising because he had often been MIA. Whenever Malachi missed a practice or arrived late to a meeting, he blamed it on being unable to secure a ride from his apartment.

"You know he could walk," White said.

Of course, Malachi didn't have a valid explanation for why he hadn't asked one of his teammates for a ride or why he hadn't called receivers coach Taylor for a lift, even if it meant chilling in the players' lounge before the morning meeting.

Quay missed practice because his phone broke. Quay said he didn't get a text that Tuesday's scheduled day off had changed because of potentially bad weather.

He was pissed that the other receivers hadn't made sure he wasn't late because they knew his phone had malfunctioned. Quay arrived at the facility around 11 a.m., about thirty minutes after practice ended. He spoke with Brewster, who suggested a conversation with Coach Prime.

"These niggas stay right next to me. They didn't say, 'Quay, we know your phone is fucked up. You good? Get up,'" said Quay, wearing a gray Jackson State hoodie and joggers while munching on two chocolate chip cookies in the players' dining room a couple of hours after meeting with Brewster.

"Fuck me? Fuck them. I'm really pissed-off at them niggas. They some bitches. They knew I was in there. They some haters. I would've woke them up if they were in my situation, but it's cool."

Quay had arrived on time for Sunday's team meeting and figured that would earn him some grace from Taylor, but it didn't. Taylor, like most of the coaches on Coach Prime's staff, is old-school. You don't get credit for doing what you're supposed to do.

Taylor wasn't investing any more energy into Malachi or Quay because he couldn't care more about their success than they did, especially with a roster of talented receivers doing what they were supposed to do.

After speaking with Taylor, Quay had turned in his equipment, effectively quitting the team five days before the SWAC Championship game.

"Ain't no point. I'm not going to play. I'm a real nigga. I'm not a sorry-ass nigga," he said. "I never disrespected a coach on this staff. I never missed a practice. I've always been on time."

A sign of immaturity is wanting credit for doing the minimum.

"I tried to come up here and explain. Other niggas who missed shit didn't do that," Quay said. "I'd love to stay but I turned my stuff in. Ain't nobody trying to understand me. Even though I give my all to those motherfuckers."

At this point, Quay vented as though he wanted to hear if his decision-making made sense when he said the words aloud.

"I love the team, I love the coaches, but y'all not gonna fuck me after I been loyal," Quay said. "Coach Prime ain't trying to hear what I'm about to say because he thinks I'm bullshitting. I'm just letting the devil get to me. Fuck it . . . I let my family down. I let my kids down."

That's why Quay felt conflicted. Playing football was the best way, the only way he knew, to create a new path for his children and his family.

Quay could transfer with three years of eligibility left. He thought it would be easy to find a new opportunity. After all, Rivals ranked him the fifth-best receiver and the 36th player overall in the Class of 2021 after he caught 40 passes for 857 yards and 12 touchdowns for Dallas's Skyline High School.

"I got too much potential. I got too much in me," he said. "Everybody knows me and Travis are the most athletic and the best players on the team."

But he comes with baggage—and it ain't Louis Vuitton.

When fall practice began, some coaches referred to Quay as Deebo, as in San Francisco's Deebo Samuel, who caught 77 passes for 1,405 yards and 6 touchdowns and added 59 carries for 365 yards and 8 touchdowns in 2021.

Quay is a powerfully built 6'0" and 195 pounds, with body fat in the single digits. Like a lot of players he wound up at JSU because of off-the-field issues. He accepted an offer to Kansas, but the school revoked his letter of intent in March after a tweet surfaced accusing Quay of domestic violence.

"Yesterday, after the allegations referencing a football recruit were brought to our attention, we immediately contacted individuals with knowledge on the matter to try and learn more about what happened," Kansas Athletics said in the release.

"Based on the information we were able to gather, KU football has terminated the recruitment of this individual and communicated to him that he will no longer be recruited to play football at the University of Kansas. While we do not know the full details of what occurred in this instance, we were able to learn enough information and decide that it is in the best interest of Kansas football that we separate from this individual. We condemn violence of any kind against women."

Malachi's teammates had grown weary of the excuses because he wasn't contributing anything. The dude who scored 12 touchdowns last year had only three catches and one touchdown.

"If No. 13 would've fucking shown up this year and poured something into us," said Bartolone, "he would've made us a better team."

A few weeks earlier, another coach pointed at Malachi and said, "This is the motherfucker we need. He hasn't given us anything all year. It would be nice to get something now. There's still time."

Malachi had become a nonfactor and the receiver room had decided they were better off without waiting for his immense talent to show itself. Quay was on his fourth position since the season began, which spoke to both his talent and his lack of production.

He played running back, receiver, slot receiver, and tight end.

"He's not really as good as he thinks he is," Reilly said. "He has straight-line speed but his hips are stiff. He's not fluid and he doesn't run good routes and he won't study and watch tape to get better. But when you turn on the fucking TV in the lounge his *Madden* profile pops up first."

Quay caught six passes for 33 yards and two carries for 12 yards in the regular season. For several weeks, he had been working with the tight ends, which seemed like a good fit because JSU could create mismatches against safeties.

Malachi and Quay each had playmaking ability and Coach Prime never wavered from the fact that he's loyal to winning. He believed each could help JSU win.

Coach Prime coached them hard, punished them when necessary, and gave them chances to prove their worth.

On Wednesday morning, Coach Prime and Taylor met with Malachi and Davis to discuss their future.

"A whole practice. A whole practice. I don't ever let them play the victim," he said. "I hold them accountable, and we have to figure out where we go from here because what you did is already done. It's over. It's in the books.

"You miss a whole day of practice and you have the audacity to blame others when everyone else is here? If you can't get a ride, you gonna notice that around seven a.m. and start blowing people up, right? That never happened. T. C. was blowing Malachi up until one or two o'clock. He's just lying."

Coach Prime told Taylor to decide the players' punishment. Taylor told the other receivers they could vote whether to suspend them for a game or let them play.

The players voted to suspend them.

Before Malachi and Quay missed practice, Coach Prime had planned to use them against Southern. He had decided to use Rico Powers at one receiver spot because he was a speed guy with big-play ability.

Dallas was returning to the slot after playing outside and Kevin Coleman and Willie Gaines were going to rotate at the other slot position when they used four receivers.

"I put both of them in the game plan this week. That's God speaking. It is what is," Coach Prime said. "Quay had three plays just for him and Malachi was rotating with Shane but that's just God's way of clearing things up."

Jackson State still had two games left to play and he needed their complete focus to win and finish undefeated. The words for the week were "focus" and "finish." With all the rumors regarding his future, Coach Prime needed his team focused on beating Southern.

He also had to make sure his players understood that Southern, their archrival and opponent in the SWAC Championship game, would play much better than it did a few weeks earlier when Jackson State blasted them 35–0.

This had been a championship-or-bust season from the start and Coach Prime wasn't about to let conversations about his future derail it.

On Tuesday morning he read his squad one of his favorite books next to the Bible. The book, he said, changed his life. He took a seat in his white chair, faced the team, and began reading *The Little Engine That Could*, written by Watty Piper in 1930.

It's the story of a little blue train engine that takes on a job to go over a mountain that other engines refused to do. It keeps repeating "I think I can" while going up the mountain and it ultimately succeeds because of its focus and determination. The engine then repeats "I thought I could" once it reaches the other side of the mountain.

Afterward, Coach Prime quizzed the players about the story.

"Give me one moral of the story?" he asked.

"It's about you believing in you," one player said.

"It's about taking a leap of faith," another said.

"Don't quit," Weeks said.

"Believe," Taylor said.

A couple more players added their thoughts before Coach Prime brought it home like a preacher when the organ starts playing just before he asks who wants to give their life to Christ.

"It was always about getting to the other side so they could make folks happy. It was never about the engine," he said. "Several trains passed him up because they were too good. Or they were too mighty. They thought it was a waste of time because he didn't fit the description.

"Ain't too many of y'all fit the description. Now, you sitting on the side of the track saying to yourself, 'I think I can, I think I can.' What are you going to attach yourself to make sure you get to the other side? You can bless a lot of people that have faith in you.

"This whole city believes in you. Many in the SWAC believe in you. . . . It requires focus and finish. I believe we have everybody in here that's going to focus and finish."

Although winning the Cricket Celebration Bowl was the ultimate goal, the SWAC Championship remained paramount. Lose it and there would be no redemption story.

"Some of these men have never won a championship from peewee to checkers to Monopoly," Coach Prime said. "Now they're getting a chance to win and understand the art and philosophy of what it takes to win.

"There are far more lessons about life than lessons about this game. We're trying to birth winners. It's so much higher than the game of football that we're trying to teach them at Jackson State."

A few hours before the All-Conference team was released publicly, Coach Prime asked Duane Lewis to announce the team to the players, but he pleaded with them not to let happiness or disappointment affect their practice effort or performance.

Second-team All-SWAC: receiver Shane Hooks, tight end D. J. Stevens, defensive lineman Justin Ragin, defensive back Isaiah Bolden, and kicker Alejandro Mata

First team: quarterback Shedeur Sanders, running back Sy'Veon Wilkerson, offensive lineman Tyler Brown, receiver Dallas Daniels, defensive lineman Nyles Gaddy, linebacker Aubrey Miller Jr., defensive back Cam'Ron Silmon-Craig

Freshman of the Year: Kevin Coleman Jr.

Defensive Player of the Year: Aubrey Miller Jr.

Offensive Player of the Year: Shedeur Sanders

Coach of the Year: Deion Sanders

Obviously, Travis would've been on the All-Conference team but he didn't play the minimum amount of games necessary to be eligible.

"Some of you guys on second team, I thought you should've been on first team," he said. "Some of you guys on first team, I don't know about a couple of y'all. But we're happy and blessed.

"Some of you guys should take this and say they've lost their minds and I'm going to show them how they messed up. I'm finna go out here and whup somebody. If some of y'all mad and upset, you should be."

Patrick was one of those players.

"It's my fault," he said. "I didn't play as well as I should have. I can't blame nobody but me."

As more nuggets about Colorado's offer trickled out during the week, including the $5 million annual salary, Coach Prime seemingly leaned toward taking the job. Reports surfaced that some players in the transfer portal had been told to wait a few days before making a final decision while Coach Prime made back-channel calls about potential staff members.

The rumors also started a social media firestorm. All sorts of folks weighed in on whether he should stay at JSU or leave.

Critics questioned his loyalty to JSU, which had given him an opportunity to coach, and whether he really supported HBCUs. Some questioned his faith and others said they were disappointed that he chased more money.

"Why is everyone so concerned with how my life fits in with theirs," he said rhetorically. "Sooner or later, you should ask yourself, what's best for him? Why does my life have to fit in with your happiness? What does he want?

"How can God speak to me in one realm but not in another? So God just stopped communicating with me? I didn't check with nobody when I left Atlanta for San Francisco. I didn't check with nobody when I went to Dallas, and I think that was a pretty good move.

"The Bible says a good man's steps are ordered."

Coach Prime's relationship with Aubrey is complicated. He liked and respected the player, but it took him some time to appreciate the person. Aubrey is a bundle of emotions, but Coach Prime isn't an emotional person or player.

The players viewed Aubrey as a leader, and he was the only player on the defense whose voice controlled the team. Coach Prime wanted to reward him for a terrific season, but couldn't figure out how to do it.

Before Friday's practice at the Vet, the players circled the block at midfield, like they do before every practice. Normally, Coach Mo Sims called out a player's number and that player addressed the team.

This time, Coach Prime addressed the players.

"Aubrey, come inside. Come inside. This is the first time that we're having this. Usually we have leaders and they have an *L* on their shirt," Coach Prime said. "Every leader ain't a dawg and every dawg ain't a leader.

"Correct?"

"Yes, sir."

"Hear what I said, every leader ain't a dawg and every dawg ain't a leader. This is our first time ever putting a *D* on somebody's shirt and he's going out there with the captains because we do have a dawg."

As his teammates clapped, Aubrey beamed, thrilled that he had finally earned the acceptance he craved from Coach Prime.

"Now, don't do nothing to make me snatch that *D* off your jersey," Coach Prime said. He was only half-joking.

A few days later, Aubrey reflected on the honor.

"It meant a lot," he said, "because I know I'm a dawg but I also think I'm a leader."

What's the difference?

"Being a leader is holding people accountable, making sure you do right, from extra workouts to the film study to knowing everybody position to making sacrifices," said Aubrey, "and hopefully everybody sees the sacrifices you make and they'll do the same.

"A dawg is going out there and annihilating people. It's getting to the ball being violent, being disruptive, and being dominant."

In twenty-four hours, he planned to prove he deserved the *D* on his chest, and he didn't care about any of the so-called distractions.

CHAPTER 24

In coaching, you get elevated or you get terminated.
—Coach Prime

By the time Coach Prime walked into the Vet at 12:42 p.m. on Saturday, everyone knew this would be his last game as JSU's football coach.

News broke late Friday night that Coach Prime was expected to become the twenty-eighth head coach at the University of Colorado Boulder. He didn't broach the topic with the players and coaches at breakfast, and the folks who knew him best weren't sure when he'd do it.

"He hasn't said anything," Forsett said. "He's waiting for God to speak to him."

Coach Prime will tell you his personal relationship with God allows him to see, hear, and feel his presence whenever he wants to talk.

Brewster, who played football with Colorado athletic director Rick George at Illinois, helped start the conversation.

"I thought Prime was the right guy for him to galvanize the situation and truly bring some positive energy and juice," Brewster said. "He was the right guy at the right time.

"Rick was one hundred percent bought in from the beginning with Prime. I had a lot of dialogue with Mike McCartney, the son of [longtime Colorado coach] Bill McCartney. My message to Rick was there's one choice for you: He's a ten-star recruit. You gotta get this done."

Mike McCartney has worked in various capacities in college and pro football, ranging from agent to coach to front-office executive for much of his adult life.

George calmed Coach Prime's apprehension about the cold weather associated with Colorado. One morning, George sent him a photo of a snow-covered football field. Later, he sent a picture of the same field except the snow had disappeared.

He acquiesced to any of Coach Prime's demands, including working with school officials to make it easier for Colorado to admit transfer students. The $5 million salary and pool for coaches' salaries eliminated every reason to stay at Jackson State.

With Coach Prime expected to leave, how well would JSU play?

"It ain't gonna make a difference today because we have a bunch of tough-minded guys who have been through a lot in their lives," Brewster said. "If they were different, it might be a bunch of crying and stuff. Coach Prime has kept them locked in."

Reilly, who usually had a good feel for how the team would perform, wasn't nearly as confident.

"If it were me, I'd feel some kind of way. It's kind of janky, like you got one foot in and one foot out," he said. "This happened to me and it happens to everybody in this business. It happens at most schools this time of year because somebody's getting fired or leaving for a better job.

"Our defensive coordinator [Matt Patricia] got hired to be the [Detroit] Lions coach and Philly hung forty on us in the Super Bowl."

Normally the players danced and joked in the locker room, while rap music created the proper environment. On this day, most players sat silently at their metal lockers.

When the players returned to the locker room before kickoff, Gillie da Kid and Wallo had arrived. Gillie, being Gillie, went live on Instagram and danced with several players.

Ten minutes before kickoff, Evis McGee, a member of Coach Prime's two-man security team, summoned Amari Ward to the coach's office. The freshman walk-on, who wasn't expected to play, pointed at himself to make sure he was the intended target.

He returned a couple of minutes later.

"I want this one bad," Coach Prime said. "I'm not thinking about me right now, I'm thinking about Amari. Where ya at?"

The 6'1" 310-pounder joined Coach Prime in front of the team. The coach put his left arm around Amari's neck.

A day earlier, Amari's life had changed forever.

At six thirty Friday morning, Amari's alarm went off in John W. Dixon Hall, Suite 717A. Five minutes later, he heard the suite door close.

He figured his friends, Flynn Brown and Randall Smith, were headed to the gym. Amari walked out of his room into the common area, then noticed that Flynn's door was cracked open.

"I see blood, so I peep my head in there and I see blood everywhere. It's all over the place, so I'm like dang, they must've went to the hospital," Amari said. "I see blood marks on the floor like somebody was being dragged out the room, so I peeped my head out the door and I see him pulling something in the elevator.

"I'm thinking that must be Flynn taking his stuff home 'cause he was going home the next day."

Amari walked into the bathroom and washed his face and brushed his teeth. Since they lived on the seventh floor, the guys often left the window open.

"I hear a dragging sound outside my window. I look down and I thought I saw Flynn dragging something down the stairs," Amari said. "I watch a lot of TV and that looked like a body."

Fear enveloped him. He phoned his dad, Jermaine Ward, and woke him up in Lake Wales, Florida.

"Hello," Jermaine said.

"Dad, I just saw so much blood," Amari said frantically. "There was just so much blood."

"What happened?" his dad asked.

Amari just kept repeating, "There was so much blood." Jermaine ordered Amari to go to the football facility and let the coaches know what had happened.

"I just threw some stuff in a bag and ran over and told coach," Amari said.

Coach Prime walked him down the hall to Rhodes's office. Rhodes immediately called the shift supervisor so they could assess the situation and determine whether it was an active crime scene.

"It really shook him up. I could hear it in his voice," Rhodes said. "He was worried about his roommates."

Amari spoke to authorities the rest of the morning. Several hours later, the police sent him home to gather his belongings. When he arrived, the room had been declared a crime scene.

"I told them I thought it was Flynn," Amari said, "but the lady said that was the suspect pulling the victim out of the room."

Flynn was the victim.

Suddenly the totality of what had occurred while he slept hit Amari with the force of a summer squall.

"What if I didn't take off running to the facility? What if I would've stayed there and called the police and he came back and saw me? What would he have done to me?" Amari wondered.

Authorities found Flynn, a twenty-two-year-old from New Jersey, dead inside a Dodge Charger. He had been shot in the head.

Randall, a twenty-year-old from New Orleans, was arrested and charged with murder.

Randall, Flynn, and Amari had played *Madden* on a Sony Play-Station and listened to music much of Friday.

"We were just chilling and having fun," Amari said. "We took a walk on the plaza and we went to Walmart."

They returned around 10:30 p.m., and Amari told his friends he was going to bed.

During a preliminary hearing, Randall said he killed Flynn in self-defense. He said Flynn had taken a doughnut from his hand

and began choking him until he couldn't breathe, so he grabbed a gun and shot Flynn in self-defense.

Video footage showed an unidentified person going to the Dodge Charger where Flynn's body was discovered at about 2:30 a.m. According to investigators, it appeared Smith tried to flee and cover up the scene.

Randall received a $200,000 bond.

Flynn had transferred from Lackawanna College in Pennsylvania in the spring of 2022 and had earned a roster spot on the 2023 football team. The day before Thanksgiving, Flynn texted Riddley just before midnight.

> Hope you have a Happy Thanksgiving Coach O, I'm still at school, so I won't be having a Thanksgiving but I know that being able to live another day & live a good life where everyone around you including family has love & care for you is all I need to be thankful for. I hope you are enjoying your time with your family & friends Coach. & I'll be ready for you in January.

Flynn's killing led Amari to survivor's guilt, sleepless nights, and anxiety. He spent countless hours trying to figure out how a day that began so well ended so tragically.

"A lot of things terrify me now," he said. "The other night, the housing director was knocking on the door for ten to fifteen minutes and I didn't open it because I couldn't see who was at the door."

A day after Randall's arrest, Amari received several phone calls from New Orleans's 504 area code. He sent them to voice mail. He also received a threatening text.

That night in Lake Wales, an eleven-hour drive away, someone sprayed the house across the street from Amari's parents with bullets. His grandmother lived in the house. She was not harmed.

"Somebody came up around two or three in the morning and just shot my house up," Jermaine said. "We don't know if this part of the situation. We just don't know."

Police investigated and found fifty-two spent shell casings. The shooting made the local news.

"We had to contact the FBI in Mississippi and the local sheriff's department down here," said Rebecca Cox, Amari's mother. "We weren't pleased that school didn't reach out to us a little bit more than what we felt they should."

Jermaine suggested counseling and Amari took his advice; his mother prayed for God to protect her baby.

"A lot of things trigger me. I've only been getting two to three hours of sleep a night because I'm up thinking," Amari said. "It replays in my head every day, especially when I'm alone. I just turn my game off and sit on my bed like, dang."

Amari wanted to feel normal. Standing on the sideline with his brothers allowed him to do that.

Apparently, Brewster knew what he was talking about. The Tigers played their best first quarter of the year in their biggest game of the year after a week full of distractions.

Nyles, a nonfactor for weeks, set the tone with two tackles for a loss on Southern's first series.

"I had to get my mind right and it was time to go. I came back locked in and ready to make something shake," he said. "I been tired of my situation with my playing time and not being in the mix as much. I was ready to hit something."

Nyles's production had dipped because of a sprained MCL he suffered against Grambling, and his attitude consistently pissed off the coaches.

Nyles wanted more playing time, which he believed would lead to more sacks, and more sacks would take him to the NFL.

After beating Campbell in Week 7, Nyles didn't agree with Reilly's assessment of his performance. Reilly suggested they review every play of the previous game.

It stemmed from Nyles being mad about his lack of playing time against Campbell.

"After the game, they felt as if instead of going in the locker room I should've turned up with the team," he said. "I wasn't too much in the mood to be singing on the field. I shook up some guys and told them I love them and ran inside.

"When coaches feel like they're right you have to ride with them. That's the thing I had to learn this season. Those are Coach Prime's coaches, so he's going to ride with what his coaches say. What they say goes. I just need to play ball."

When he challenged Reilly about his criticism, Nyles disliked the response, especially the part about a lack of physicality. Nyles sprung from his chair and nearly knocked over the seventy-inch monitor.

"He wanted to fight me. We have an understanding now. He plays three snaps of defense and he lets me coach him," Reilly said. "But you can't be late twice a week two weeks in a row. You used to be a captain and you sit in the front row. You know the head coach is looking for you as soon as he walks in the room.

"I've saved his ass four to five times with Prime and Pretty Tony. He's not a bad person, but he needs to be around good people, which is what worries me about his future because I don't want him to get caught up in some bullshit."

Nyles said he simplified his approach to the game and the coaching staff.

"Instead of focusing on what somebody else ain't doing or this and that, focus on me and just go," Nyles said. "If I make plays, everything else will take care of itself."

A tackle-breaking, crowd-energizing 35-yard catch-and-run by Shane on JSU's first possession set up Mata's 22-yard field goal and a 3–0 lead.

"We know what the fuck they doing," Shedeur said on the sideline. "They ain't changed shit. Let's dominate."

Safety Herm Smith made his best play of the season on Southern's next possession. He intercepted a pass and returned it 37 yards to the Southern 1.

"From the way he lined up and released, I knew that out route was coming," Herm said. "I was patient and just sat on it."

A one-yard touchdown run off left tackle by Sy'Veon made it 10–0. Touchdown passes of 14 yards and 40 yards to Shane and a pair of two-point conversions by Kevin Coleman made it 26–0 after the first quarter.

"Let's make these motherfuckers tap out!" Ricard yelled. "Keep being physical and have fun."

The Tigers led 33–10 at halftime, but Joshua Griffin's 39-yard field goal on the first half's final play meant Coach Prime wasn't happy.

He sensed the game's dynamics had changed because JSU couldn't stop Besean McCray, Southern's third quarterback. Jackson State's No. 1 defense wasn't playing like it.

"This stuff is real, fellas!" Coach Prime yelled as he walked into the locker room. "We're trying to be dominant, man. We're trying to make history and y'all think it's a game. This ain't no durn game to me. It's real."

He glared at the DJ.

"Don't play another durn note," Coach Prime said. "They ain't earned it."

Travis allowed a 32-yard completion late in the second quarter and headed to the locker room shortly before the half ended. As he entered the locker room, Taylor locked eyes with Travis.

"You good?" he asked.

"My body. My body is shutting down," Travis said.

"Don't worry about offense. You good," Taylor told him.

While his teammates prepared for the second half, Travis removed the tape from his cleats. As JSU took the second-half kickoff, Forsett probed Travis for answers.

McCray's 40-yard touchdown pass on Southern's first possession pulled the Jaguars within 33–17. At about that time, Travis returned to the sideline wearing a gray jogger and red Yeezys.

His eyes were distant, his expression blank.

"I didn't treat my body right during the week and it didn't perform well during the game," Travis said. "I didn't drink enough water and my lower body just gave out on me. After that tackle, I just got weak.

"I lost my strength. I felt very sleepy and tired. My mind definitely wasn't in it."

McCray's 42-yard run made it 36–24 as Southern scored for the fourth time in six possessions. Panic filled the Vet. Somebody, anybody needed to make a play.

Cue Willie.

He caught a 41-yard pass from Shedeur on third-and-four from the JSU 43, setting up a nine-yard touchdown pass to Rico and a 43–24 lead. Interceptions by Cam'Ron and Delano Salgado clinched JSU's second SWAC Championship.

As the game ended, the players poured onto the field with the kind of joy on their faces that can't be faked.

Coach Prime shook hands with coach Eric Dooley before he headed to the corner of the end zone, so he could acknowledge the band while it played "Jackson Fair," the school song.

Coach Prime had Tracey to his left and Shedeur to his right. His arms were wrapped around each of their shoulders.

While Tracey and Shedeur beamed at the crowd, Coach Prime had a faraway look in his eyes. He couldn't enjoy the moment because a private jet was scheduled to depart at 10 p.m. and take him to Colorado.

After the school song, Shedeur, wearing a white SWAC Championship baseball cap, grabbed a huge navy blue flag with a white *J* and waved it for several seconds at Southern's fans before planting it at midfield.

The offensive linemen met at the SWAC logo, where Markuson had told them on Friday they'd take a picture after they beat Southern.

"I ain't tripping," Evan Henry said. "He promised to make me a champion. He didn't promise me he'd stay."

Coach Prime joined Robinson, President Hudson, SWAC commissioner Charles McClelland, and other league dignitaries on the dais. More than once, Coach Prime gestured for the postgame festivities to be sped up.

He answered two questions from ESPN's Jalyn Johnson. Lewis said ESPN had agreed not to ask Coach Prime about the Colorado job during the postgame celebration.

"Jacksonians are resilient. They just needed a little hope," Coach Prime told Johnson. "They wanted someone they could believe in, someone they could trust, and someone they could ride with and be there for them. For that, we love you, Jackson."

Johnson asked Coach Prime about the Cricket Celebration Bowl.

"We haven't spoken about that all year," Coach Prime said. "Our motto all week has been focus and finish. We have one more to go to finish."

Aubrey, the defensive MVP, totaled five tackles, three for loss, a sack, and a forced fumble. Shedeur, the offensive MVP, passed for 320 yards and 4 touchdowns.

While Aubrey and Coach Prime were honored, Hart tried to convince a transfer portal linebacker to join him in Colorado as Aubrey Miller Sr. thanked him for developing his son.

"I've got a linebacker in the NFL with Detroit and I got one just named defensive MVP of the SWAC Championship!" Hart yelled into the phone. "I want to develop you the way I developed them."

That morning, Forsett told the coaches that Coach Prime wanted to meet with all players and support staff at the Walter Payton Recreation & Wellness Center at 8:30 p.m.

"Once we got to the stadium, it was reiterated in the coach's locker room," said graduate assistant Brandon Morton. "After the game, the players were told verbally by coaches to go back to the Walter Payton. Things got lost in translation because a majority of the players were still out on the field taking pictures and talking to family and friends."

Nearly an hour after the game, some players remained on the field celebrating with teammates and parents. Askevold drove Shane to the hospital because he had taken a helmet to the testicles hurdling a defender in the third quarter.

"I found out through social media. It was on Instagram and Twitter and every social media platform," Shane said. "I was in the examining room at the hospital. I knew he was going somewhere, it was just a matter of where he was going to go. You can't be mad at him. At the end of the day, it's a business."

Brewster and Reilly arrived in the team meeting room first. Reilly turned on ESPN just as one of its talking heads discussed Coach Prime's move to Colorado.

"Trevor, I don't think we should have this on," Brewster said. "The players are starting to arrive."

Trevor looked puzzled for a moment before he replaced *Sports-Center* with music. When the buses arrived, the auditorium filled up quickly. The Amazon Prime Video TV crew set up their lights, while their cameramen searched for the best positions to stand.

"[The players] been looking for answers all week and they didn't have any," Rashad Davis said. "The one thing Prime has always been is straight up. He ain't gonna sugarcoat or ease his way into nothing. He just gonna tell you how it is."

A few minutes later, Coach Prime walked in followed by Robinson. Coach Prime congratulated everyone on the victory and provided the schedule for the next few days.

Then he discussed his departure.

"I want y'all to hear it from me and not anyone else. It is what it is," he said, seated in his white leather chair. Robinson sat to his right in a folding chair.

"In coaching, you get elevated or you get terminated. Ain't no other way. You get elevated or terminated. Ain't no graveyard for coaches where they die at a place. It don't work like that.

"They're either going to run you off, or you're going to walk off. I've chosen to accept a job elsewhere next year."

He told everyone that he wasn't leaving for Colorado until after the Cricket Celebration Bowl. He also recommended Taylor replace him. As a Mississippi native and JSU alum, nobody would love JSU more or understand its culture better than Taylor.

"They know how I feel about T. C. . . . I would love for someone in-house [to get the job]," said Coach Prime, "because I don't know how some of y'all would act if somebody outside the house would come in not understanding how we function and how we get down. Let's clap it up for T. C."

After the applause quieted, Coach Prime made it clear that Robinson didn't have the authority to choose his replacement. Robinson would recommend a candidate to President Hudson, who would sign off on the coach.

"I would not be here if not for this man. You have no idea the trials and tribulations that we've stood back-to-back and worked out," Coach Prime said of Robinson. "I'm not tired of fighting whatsoever.

"But if I heard God's voice on coming, don't second-guess my hearing ability. I know God. I know when he shifts and moves, and I know how he gets down with me."

He spoke about the importance of showing how African-American coaches can thrive in FBS and that he'd still be turning African-American boys into men.

"My challenge is still to provoke change no matter where I am. I'm going to be me. I'm fifty-five and I don't plan on changing no time soon," Coach Prime said. "God made me like this, and I think God is pleased with what he's created.

"This is probably the toughest moment for me ever because it involves y'all. If it didn't involve y'all, I'm out," Coach Prime said.

"The thing holding me hostage is y'all's faces. This ain't easy. It's not about a bag. I been making money a long time. So it's not about a bag. It's about an opportunity."

Coach Prime spoke for nearly ten minutes before he entertained questions. Aubrey implored his teammates to dedicate themselves to winning the Celebration Bowl.

"I cried after that game because we gave it to them," Aubrey said. "Think about the team. Think about the guys you just won this with. We didn't have this last season. We lost two games. Just think about this story. We're still making history."

Santee spoke next.

"I appreciate you, coach, and everything you did," he said. "I love you."

Errick Simmons thanked Coach Prime for putting him on a winning team, something he didn't experience in high school. A member of the training staff asked for a rematch in Ping-Pong.

Evan thanked Coach Prime for an opportunity to make history. Hayden thanked him for the life lessons.

"A lot of us who came in from the portal were just betting on ourselves trying to find a better way," Hayden said, "and you showed us how not to just dominate in the game but dominate in life."

Antonio thanked Coach Prime for believing in him as a man as much as he did as a player. Several others spoke, including Justin, a former walk-on who evolved into one of the team's best players.

Coach Prime encouraged anyone and everyone to speak. No one uttered a negative word. Some were disappointed, but all understood the business of college football.

"At the end of the day it's his life. Life ain't fair. I'm glad for him," Nyles said. "He gets more money. He gets to show what he can do on a prime-time level, a Power 5 level."

The SWAC Championship trophy sat on the floor between Robinson and Coach Prime. Finally, Robinson addressed the room.

"Let's finish this thing and show people what we can do," Robinson said. "Coach is gonna be back here working on Tuesday."

Coach Prime grabbed the trophy, walked to the middle of the meeting room, and posed for pictures surrounded by his players. Brewster, who was starving, walked quickly to his black Chevy Silverado.

"I'm out. I'm not going to coach the Celebration Bowl," he said. "I'm going to be on the ground in Boulder making it happen. From day one, Prime said, 'Brew, do your thing and be yourself.' That's empowering, man."

As Brewster pulled up to the Green Taco, Coach Prime was headed to the airport. A new journey awaited.

CHAPTER 25

Baby, we're coming!
—Deion Sanders

Your belief is irrelevant to Deion Sanders. Coach Prime doesn't care, either.

Colorado, one of the worst teams in college football in 2022, was outscored 534–185. The Buffs lost three games by at least 40 points, seven by at least 30, and 10 by at least 20.

The Buffs fired Karl Dorrell in October, and Mike Sanford finished the season, which ended with a 63-21 home loss to 12th-ranked Utah. The 1990 national championship that Bill McCartney won seemed like forever ago.

The Buffs have had one winning season since joining the PAC-12 in 2011. None of that concerned Coach Prime.

The transfer portal reduced the time it took for any coach to overhaul a new roster. Colorado had one player on the All-PAC-12 team, and he was a second-team senior linebacker.

Coach Prime related to parents and coaches who had watched him play. Coach Prime related to players because he understood social media and lists rappers such as Snoop Dogg and Lil Wayne and influencers such as Desi Banks and Lou Young III as friends. Add high-energy recruiters such as Hart and Brewster and you understand why Coach Prime expected to quickly flip Colorado's roster and sign some of the country's best players.

He arrived in Boulder with his girlfriend, Tracey, his sister, Tracie, Bucky, Sam, Shedeur, Shelomi, Hart, Mathis, and Forsett on a private jet. At Monday's introductory news conference, Coach Prime introduced Shedeur.

"This is your quarterback," Coach Prime told the crowd. "He's going to have to earn it, though. Believe that."

At his introductory news conference, Coach Prime preened for the minicams. He matched the energy surging through Colorado and its fan base.

"We're not here to compete but to win. Not to show up but to show out. Not to be among the rest but to be the absolute best," he told the excited throng. "We're coming to work, not to play. We're coming to kill, not to kick it. Baby, I got to believe that we're coming. . . .

"Boulder, Colorado, you have no idea what you're blessing me with, the opportunity that you're giving me, and I feel like I owe you. So every day I'm going to work for you, I'm gonna strengthen for you, I'm gonna develop for you, I'm gonna commit for you, I'm going to do things that others wouldn't do.

"Baby, we're coming. So if anybody asks you something about 'when is he coming back?' you just say, 'I don't know, but I know he coming.'"

Jackson State was a mediocre program when Coach Prime arrived. Colorado's entire program needed to be razed.

No worries.

Coach Prime, the Buffs' fourth coach since 2018, specialized in provoking change and creating new environments.

Change is hard. It's inconvenient. It's uncomfortable. But change must occur because whatever took place with Colorado's football program hadn't worked. Some folks will have their feelings hurt. Others will be mad. Another group will complain—publicly and privately—and Coach Prime won't care.

He understood the process Colorado's football program must endure after losing 11 games for only the second time in school history. The Buffs are 5-21 in their last 26 games and have played in two bowl games since 2007. They won 10 games in 2016 under former coach Mike McIntyre, the first time they had done it since 2001, under former coach Gary Barnett.

"I truly understand what you want. All you want is the opportunity to win, to compete, to dominate, to be amongst the elite, to be amongst the best and darn it, I'm going to give you that," Coach Prime said. "We're going to outwork them, we're going to outrecruit them, we're going to outscout, we're going to outdevelop, we're going to get our education, we're going to graduate these young men.

"These young men are gonna be on campus, respectful and considerate and kind, opening doors for you and making sure everything is copacetic. . . . That's just the way I father, that's the way I parent, that's the way I coach. I'm old-school."

Coach Prime agreed to a five-year, $29 million deal. In 2022, he told anyone and everyone that any money he received to be a head coach at the Power 5 level wouldn't change his lifestyle but it would change the lives of his coaches.

Coach Prime made about $60 million as a professional athlete— $45 million in football and $13 million baseball—and countless millions as a spokesman for a variety of companies from Subway to Pepsi to Nike to Aflac insurance.

He advised his players to invest in dirt. He's shrewd with his money.

Coach Prime found himself under a wave of criticism for leaving JSU. No other coach in America was criticized for leaving his current coaching situation for a new gig the way critics hammered Coach Prime.

Then again, no other coach had Coach Prime's Q-Rating. And no other coach cared less about his critics. Some accused him of pimping JSU because he left for a significant raise. Others accused him of selling out the young Black men he professed to be committed to helping at JSU and the other HBCUs.

The anger and frustration from some fans and alums of JSU and of HBCUs in general is that Coach Prime cared more about himself than JSU and HBCU culture. After all, his critics claim everything he did at JSU was designed to help himself.

Coach Prime said he kept every promise he made to JSU fans and alums. He won games, graduated players, and brought more attention to HBCU football than it has ever had, while impacting the lives of the players he coached.

Some simply don't understand that Coach Prime's mission has always been to change the lives of kids through sports and discipline the way coaches changed his life. The day Coach Prime arrived at JSU, he was always going to leave. Whenever that day occurred, a portion of the fan base wasn't going to like it, and it didn't matter if he stayed three years, five years, or ten years.

The question is whether Coach Prime left JSU better than he found it.

Of the twenty-five FCS schools that changed coaches at the end of the season, only four of their coaches won at least 10 games. Jay Hill, 10-3 at Weber State, left to be the defensive coordinator at Brigham Young University. The University of the Incarnate Word's G. J. Kinne went 12-1 and left for Texas State in the Southland Conference.

Troy Taylor went 12-1 at Sacramento State and is now coaching Stanford. No one ripped him. Coach Prime left, and the questions came hard and fast.

"The thing that alarms me the most is just because I'm leaving Jackson, they think that I'm leaving African Americans. I don't know if you noticed or not, but I'm Black," Coach Prime said. "I can never leave who I am or what I am or how I am or how I go about being that.

"My calling is for young men, young women, people of all walks of life. Of all social climates and ethnicities. That's my calling. My calling is not built on a location. It's built on a destination."

Before he returned to Jackson, Coach Prime met with his new team. He didn't mince words. Coach Prime said most of them could hop in the transfer portal and suggested the ones who didn't would quit.

Most of his talk was psychological. Coach Prime wanted to prepare the players for a mentally and physically grueling offseason program, and he wanted those who didn't have the gumption to compete at the highest level weeded out.

He expected eight to ten players from JSU to join him in Boulder. "I'm bringing my luggage with me," he said, "and it's Louis [Vuitton]." He wasn't smiling.

For now, Colorado could wait. He needed to keep JSU together. It would be a massive challenge because JSU's players had seen their coach all over social media fawning over his new team's facilities and wearing their colors.

Could he get them to focus on meetings, practice, and their Cricket Celebration Bowl opponent, North Carolina Central University? Could he get the coaches who weren't going to Boulder to coach with the same intensity?

And could he get the coaches who were recruiting players to Colorado while preparing for NCCU to do both jobs equally well?

"I'm like, Lord, I hope he can get these dudes to Atlanta," Taylor said.

KaTron Evans and Josh Griffis, a pair of former four-star defensive linemen, entered the transfer portal. Each played about fifteen snaps a game and provided quality depth. Anthony Petty, a core special teams player, also entered the portal.

"Playing for Coach Prime was cool, but he didn't trust me to play for him like I wanted to," he said. "I knew the portal was going to be heavy, so I wanted to get my name in there and see what I could get."

A few players, like Antonio Doyle and Jurriente Davis, wanted to know if they could play for Coach Prime at Colorado. Others wanted to know if they should stay at JSU. In the second team meeting since taking the Colorado job, Coach Prime talked about finishing the mission.

"We have to complete it. We have to put a period. We have to put an exclamation mark," he said. "We have to finish what we started and we have more than we need to finish and be dominant."

Before the meeting ended, Coach Prime asked Taylor to address the team. He wanted the players to get used to hearing Taylor's voice in an authoritative role, and he wanted Taylor to get used to addressing the team.

"I have a problem with young men who don't finish the mission. The coaches matter. The block matters. JSU, the brand, matters," Taylor said. "Fight for your teammates. We're playing for the national title."

Coach Prime set the practice tone by keeping the same approach. He zipped around from one position group to another in his golf cart. Nothing escaped him.

"Sir, please roll up your socks so I can see the black," he told Tre'von.

Coach Prime turned his head just in time to see Shilo intercept a pass.

"Nice play, Shilo. Good job," he said loud enough for his son to turn his head and grin. "The ball always seems to find him."

He drove toward the sideline where Evan stood.

"So we're just gonna take our helmets off and chill out," Coach Prime said. "That's what we're gonna do?"

"No, sir," said Evan, quickly pulling on his helmet and buckling his chin strap.

Simmons, a walk-on who continually impressed Coach Prime with his work ethic, wore one green cleat and one red cleat. He made a nifty catch that drew a comment from Coach Prime.

"Every time I catch a pass," Simmons yelled across the field, "I'm gonna say Merry Christmas."

Practice seemed normal and that made Coach Prime feel good about the next couple of weeks. The next day, he continued to discuss managing distractions.

"We're steps away from holding that trophy. We're steps away from getting those hats, those sweatshirts, those T-shirts. All that stuff that comes along with victory and dominance," Coach Prime said. "What little things are you going to allow to interfere with that? Distractions? What I'm doing? What he's doing? No, no. If I can lock in, I know you can. Don't be distracted at a time like this.

"This is going to be the highest-rated game of your careers. Everybody is talking about Jackson State. They want to see what I'm going to do. They want to see what you're going to do. The curiosity is going to bring the viewers."

Coach Prime's recommendation that Taylor replace him as JSU's head coach hadn't shocked Taylor but that didn't mean he expected it, either.

"This is Deion Sanders," Taylor said. "For him to endorse you, I knew it was going to get crazy after that."

Not bad for a dude who wanted to be a game warden once it looked like football wasn't going to work out.

Taylor spent a year on New England's practice squad, but a hamstring injury compromised much of that season. He played in NFL Europe, but the Patriots cut him after that season ended. Detroit and San Francisco wanted him. He signed with the Lions and promptly tore his hamstring again.

Football was done; he was ready to be a game warden.

"I'm working at the department of wildlife. I never thought about coaching," Taylor said. "My boy at Coahoma Community College in the Delta said he needed an offensive guy to help him coach.

"I'm at a crossroads because I'm gonna go be a coach or a game warden."

Taylor helped Coahoma, a perennial loser, make the playoffs.

"I was OC, QB, RB, and WR coach," he said laughing. "The rest is history."

Taylor then spent two seasons (2012–13) at Texas Southern as wide receivers coach and recruiting coordinator before coaching quarterbacks and being the offensive coordinator from 2014 to 2018 at North Carolina Central.

He returned to Jackson State for one reason.

"They told T. C. it was his job before Prime came. The reason T. C. came back to Jackson is they told him it was his job," one JSU athletic department employee said. "Then they fired the other guy. T. C. knew they were trying to get Prime, so he could live with that.

"They told him Prime ain't gonna be here forever. Prepare while he's here and it's going to be your job."

Once Taylor learned Robinson wanted Coach Prime, he was pragmatic about it.

"This dude don't know you. You tell me I gotta keep those two coaches, that gotta be tough on his end," Taylor said. "The best thing we can do is shut the fuck up and do our fucking job well.

"That was motivation to me. I'm going to show you. I said hell, I'm here. I'm going to show you my value because I know you want to get rid of me but I'm going to make it hard on you."

Coach Prime and Taylor eventually bonded over bass fishing at Coach Prime's Mediterranean-style villa in Canton, Texas, a five-hour drive from Jackson.

"The stuff that comes out of [Coach Prime] is amazing. Every time he talks, I just freeze and listen. The dude is so loaded with knowledge," Taylor said. "He's a hard-ass, no doubt, but when he talks that's the word I needed every time I talk with him. This dude is touched.

"That's why God put me with him. I never told him that. Every time he talks to me it's this power and this energy and it just hits home."

Taylor said he has turned down opportunities to be a head coach at places like Winston-Salem State University. In his mind, he's ready to be a head coach. He wanted it to happen at JSU, but he was OK if it happened somewhere else.

On this Wednesday afternoon, Taylor was agitated. And frustrated. And anxious. Normally his baritone voice fills a room. This day, he spoke in hushed tones.

He wanted the job so badly, it drove him crazy. Robinson had offered him the interim tag, but Taylor declined it.

"I played here, grew up here, and I'm sitting right here," he said. "This is my alma mater. My resume is ready. I'm ready to go."

Robinson had said little privately and nothing publicly since the team meeting with Coach Prime. He needed to do the impossible and find a coach capable of following Coach Prime.

Nobody wants to be the man following "the man" because of the inevitable comparisons, expectations, and criticism.

Coach Prime's departure certainly didn't surprise Robinson, so he had candidates in mind. He wanted to explore all of his options before making a final decision. He even spoke with Hall of Fame safety Ed Reed, who turned down the job because he didn't want to follow Coach Prime.

President Hudson had a contentious relationship with Coach Prime, and he wanted a better relationship with the new coach.

While Taylor grappled with his fate, friends and colleagues like Tennessee running backs coach Jerry Mack, the former North Carolina Central head coach, blew up his phone. The text messages arrived so quickly, he couldn't respond to one before several more popped up.

Just so you know, Taylor was also recruiting for JSU, sending out offers and talking to potential players as though he expected to get the job. If he didn't recruit and Robinson hired him, he'd be screwed.

"The nation is ready for it," he said. "Everybody is pushing me."

You can include SWAC legend Doug Williams among those who thought JSU should hire Taylor. Williams coached at Grambling when Taylor terrorized SWAC secondaries and they had formed a relationship based on mutual respect.

"What in the hell are they doing?" Williams asked him. "This is unbelievable. How is this dragging along so long?"

Taylor didn't have an answer. One thing he knew for sure: God's plan always worked out.

He wasn't waiting on JSU to decide his future. If JSU didn't make him the Tigers' head coach, the new coach probably wouldn't want him on the staff. He had interviewed with Arkansas–Pine Bluff, and he thought he might get the job, if JSU didn't work out.

Practice ended Wednesday morning, and Thurman was pissed.

Nyles had been late for Monday's team meeting after arguing with his girlfriend in the wee hours of the morning. At some point he'd gone to sleep and she had tossed his keys, clothes, and equipment around the apartment.

"I went to sleep and she was still mad," he said. "I couldn't find my keys or none of my equipment in the morning."

He arrived at the facility at 7:35 but he was still in the locker room when Coach Prime began the meeting at 7:38.

Later he made the six-hour drive to Nashville, Tennessee, dropped off his girlfriend, and returned to Jackson. The damage, though, had been done. After conferring with Thurman, Reilly poked his head in Coach Prime's office and explained the situation.

"What do you want to do?" Reilly asked.

"Let's sit him for the first quarter," Coach Prime responded.

For Coach Prime, the standard didn't change even though he was going to Colorado in a week. Coach Prime believed in discipline even if it meant sitting a first-team All-Conference linebacker in the championship game.

On Wednesday, Nyles missed another team meeting. This time he met with Thurman immediately afterward.

Nyles, an admitted loner, was also an introvert. More than once he had removed himself from the defensive line group chat and missed important information. Reilly and Thurman had each spoken to Nyles's father numerous times.

"It's all about growing up and being a man and learning about life," Robert Gaddy said of his son. "The kid wants to be good. He wants to be great.

"Nyles owned up to his part. It could've been handled a little differently, but that was that man's team and he made his decision. I can't say it didn't hurt, but he had to live with it."

If Nyles had dominated on a weekly basis, the coaches might have given him yet another chance, but he was inconsistent. He recorded four sacks in the opener and four in the next eleven games.

Too many times he ran around blocks instead of being physical. Several staff members, including the head coach, didn't think he should've been named first-team All-Conference.

Missing another practice, for whatever reason, had jeopardized Nyles's roster spot. He met with Coach Prime, who told Nyles that he wouldn't make the trip to Atlanta for the Cricket Celebration Bowl.

Missing Wednesday's meeting used up all of Nyles's second chances. He blamed it on a miscommunication because he didn't know the team meeting had been moved from 7:45 to 7:15.

"I was asleep by the time they sent it out. I woke up early, too, around five o'clock put some stuff in the dryer and went back to sleep," Nyles said. "I woke up at six and was talking to my roommate. We went to our car to get our bags because the bags had to be loaded on the bus going to the airport before the meeting.

"I was in the building. It was seven eleven a.m. but the meeting started at seven twelve a.m. I take full responsibility. I ain't pointing the finger. One thing I understand about life is you have to be a man about shit. You have to own your own problems. What could I have done better?"

Actually, Coach Flea, who sends out the daily practice schedule in a text message, sent out a text at 4:35 p.m. on Tuesday with the new practice schedule.

He followed it up with a text at 7:53 p.m. that read

!! !! !! !! !! !! !! !! !!
team meeting 7:15

Aubrey, Nyles's best friend on the team, organized some players to speak on Nyles's behalf but the conversation never happened.

"Dang near the whole team was trying to talk to him [Coach Prime]," said Nyles, "but he wasn't really trying to hear too much. I ain't got no problems with Coach Prime. It's all love at the end of the day. Of course people are always gonna have misunderstandings and disagreements. That's life.

"You have to be a man. I appreciate everything he's done for me. I don't like everything that has transpired this week. He's the head coach. You have to respect what he says."

CHAPTER 26

Jack town, let's go.
—receivers coach T. C. Taylor

On Sunday, December 11, T. C. Taylor was sitting on the tan couch in the family room of his four-bedroom home relaxing with his wife, Dawn, when the phone rang at about 4:15 p.m.

Jackson State associate vice president and senior women's administrator Alyse Wells-Kilbert told Taylor the university expected to make a decision soon about its next head coach.

"Let me know. I'm here," Taylor said. "I'm not going anywhere."

Not unless Arkansas–Pine Bluff offered him its head coaching position. Arkansas–Pine Bluff had fired coach Doc Gamble in October after a 2-5 start, including 0-4 in the SWAC. Interim coach and offensive coordinator Don Treadwell went 1-3.

Taylor, one of forty-seven who applied for the position, believed his Zoom interview had gone well enough to land an offer. And if the job were offered, he'd take it.

The phone rang again. This time it was Robinson.

"Meet me at the president's house in about an hour," he said.

Taylor showered and pulled on a navy blue golf shirt with matching slacks and a navy blazer. He hopped into his black Ford F-150 pickup and made the fifteen-minute drive south to the president's home.

When Taylor walked into the president's home, he handed a binder detailing his vision, philosophy, and core values to President Hudson and Robinson. Taylor never opened his binder during the three-hour meeting. Two decades of planning had resulted in the information being stored in his memory.

As the conversation wound down, Hudson continued thumbing through the binder.

"He had a plan. He had a vision and a love and passion for the program," Hudson said. "He instilled the kind of confidence that said, 'Hey, I can make this happen. I can put my own stamp on the program, and I can keep a level of success going.'

"What he put on paper was good and honest based on who he was, his experience level, and it's not like I'd never heard of T. C. Taylor. If you're a JSU football fan, then you've been watching T. C. Taylor for twenty years. I've watched him as a player, I've watched him move up the coaching ranks, and he's a guy you can tell is ready."

Hudson asked Taylor to sit in the living room, while he and Robinson chatted. Thirty minutes passed before Taylor heard footsteps. Hudson handed Taylor a neatly wrapped package of cinnamon rolls from Sugar Ray's Sweet Shop and a small bag of glazed pecans.

"Excellent job," Hudson said. "I'm not saying you got the job. We're still talking to some guys."

"I appreciate everything," Taylor replied. "I just wanted the opportunity to get in front of you."

As he climbed into his pickup truck, Robinson joined him.

"It's a done deal," he said matter-of-factly.

On the drive home, Taylor phoned his wife with the good news. Next, he called Riddley.

"We got this motherfucker, O!" he yelled into the phone. "They gave it to me. God is so good, man."

When he returned home, Robinson phoned again. They planned a news conference for Tuesday, the day before the team departed for Atlanta and the Cricket Celebration Bowl.

"Whatever you need staff-wise, you got it. Me and the president are behind you a hundred and fifty percent," Robinson said. "Tell us what you need. If we ain't got it, we'll go get it."

When Coach Prime walked into the team meeting room Tuesday morning, he acknowledged a few more players were missing from the team meeting. Typically there weren't many open seats. On this day there were more than a dozen.

Most of the missing players were walk-ons or scout-team players who rarely played, if at all.

"Everybody wants to know what y'all are going to do. Everybody wants to think you're too distracted. Y'all don't understand our culture and how we get down," Coach Prime said. "Everybody in here has something going on, don't we? But you know how to compartmentalize, so you can stay focused on the main thing."

Coach Prime turned the meeting over to Robinson. First he congratulated the thirteen graduates, including the five players who were the first members of their family to graduate.

"We told you we'd give you an update on the next head coach at Jackson State. When you're successful and doing well you have to keep your house straight and you have to stay within your house," Robinson said. "I'm happy today to announce—"

Suddenly Coach Prime stood up and walked toward the door. "Let me see if they're ready to come in."

Robinson followed with, "Make sure he's ready to come in, Coach."

Coach Prime left the room.

"Bring him in," he said from the hallway.

"The twenty-second coach at Jackson State University," said Robinson, walking toward the door as though he were about to greet someone. "Are you ready to come in, coaches?"

Coach Prime said, "Give him his theme music."

Music blared.

"The twenty-second coach in Jackson State history is the one and only T. C. Taylor," said Robinson, pointing to Taylor, sitting in his usual seat at the top left corner of the auditorium.

Cheers and laughter filled the room. The players gave their new coach a standing ovation before engulfing him.

"T. C.! T. C.! T. C.!" the players chanted as he headed toward the front of the room. Weeks bear-hugged him.

The old king prepared his white throne for the new king. Taylor, wearing black joggers, a navy blue sweatshirt with JSU in red outlined with white, and a navy blue baseball cap with a white *J*, adjusted his cap and pounded his hands together.

Taylor leaned forward, paralyzed with glee.

"He about to cry!" one player shouted.

Taylor shook his head no, but the tears were close to flowing.

"Y'all just don't know, man. God." Taylor stood up and began pacing. "God is good, man. God is good."

He clapped his hands and gathered himself.

"Paid my dues. Been patient. Let God order my steps. Humble. It got me here today. Family. Y'all my family. My family at home. It motivates me. . . . Ever since I got into coaching this was a dream of mine," Taylor said. "Now, to say I'm the twenty-second head coach, it means something to me.

"My thoughts are all over the place because I just dreamed about this so long. Jack town, let's go."

For now, it was all good. The drama, however, was just beginning no matter how much Coach Prime tried to stop it.

Malachi had disappeared and Quay had returned to Dallas to take care of a rib injury. Malachi, who had not practiced in two weeks, phoned Taylor on Tuesday night to get the Celebration Bowl's itinerary.

Malachi said he had been away from the team working on his academics. Taylor told Malachi that he wasn't playing, because he hadn't practiced. His season, a disappointment from the start, was officially over.

Jacob Humphrey, a 6'4", 310-pound defensive tackle, had been ruled academically ineligible, meaning the Tigers were down yet another role-playing big body. Coach Prime remained confident JSU would win, and he hadn't changed his mind about Nyles not playing in the Celebration Bowl.

He didn't even want him on the trip.

The Tigers practiced Wednesday morning before taking their chartered flight to Atlanta. Coach Prime told the players they'd have Wednesday to explore Atlanta's nightlife. They had partied too much in 2021. Some players made it rain and received lap dances the night before the game.

"We kind of didn't want to mess up their mojo because they had been doing it all year and we were winning," Rashad said. "This year, it's over. It's a wrap. We putting them to bed and knocking on doors."

In Atlanta, Coach Prime and Mathis were chatting on the fourth floor of the CNN Omni Hotel when they saw Weeks. Coach Prime tapped him on the shoulder.

"Didn't we say Gaddy wasn't playing?" he asked.

"Yes, sir," Weeks replied.

"Then what is he doing here? How did he get on the plane?" Coach Prime asked.

"I don't know," Weeks said. "I never saw him get on."

"Me, either," Mathis said.

Coach Prime slowly shook his head.

"I didn't see him, either," he said. "How does he get on the plane and nobody see him? Well, let's make sure he's not on the sideline at the game. I don't want him infecting everybody else."

Pollock hadn't called assistant athletic director Alexis Stevenson to have Nyles removed from the flight manifest, which is how he was allowed to board the plane. Blame cell phones for the mystery of why no one saw Nyles boarding. Normally, coaches and players are on their cell phones talking, texting, posting on social media, or taking pictures, which in this case distracted them just long enough to miss Nyles.

"Everybody was calling my phone. I didn't know what I was supposed to do. From guys on the team to coaches to people in the staff room," Nyles said. "They were saying, 'You tripping, you need to come on.'"

No one on the coaching staff admitted telling Nyles to violate Coach Prime's directive.

"Hell no, and I really want to say fuck no," said Thurman, when asked if any of the coaches had encouraged Nyles to take the flight. "The answer would be a resounding no."

Actually, the coaches believed Aubrey was the only player bold enough to suggest Nyles take the flight. Plus, they were best friends.

"Prime is just a smart motherfucker," Reilly said. "Prime is like, Why would Nyles get on this plane? Who would tell him to get on? Weeks wouldn't. Andre wouldn't. Either he got on by himself or somebody told him. Who? It wasn't DT [Thurman], Kevin? That leaves one logical person."

Aubrey placed several calls from the plane to get Nyles a ride to the airport. Reilly confronted Aubrey and asked him who told Nyles to get on the plane.

"He talked to you," said Reilly, remembering the conversation. "Please, I didn't talk to anybody."

Nyles couldn't find a ride, so he drove himself.

"I'm driving eighty to ninety miles per hour and I'm hydroplaning, so I can make it," he said. "The only reason why I did it is my team said they needed me here and everybody is acting like I'm supposed to come.

"Everybody was cheering when I got on the plane. Coaches, too. It just threw me off how everything played out. I wasn't trying to disrespect nobody."

Nyles said he made the trip because other players have been suspended for a quarter or a game but had their punishments reduced or rescinded after showing good character.

"He's gonna get cut for this type of bullshit at the next level," Reilly said.

Coach Prime lit into his team during Thursday morning's practice at Georgia Tech. He's a stickler for running from drill to drill, sprinting to the ball on defense, and playing at a fast tempo on offense.

"I'm tired of the bull junk already. We're walking on the field. We're jogging on the field," Coach Prime said, "and some fool done went and told a guy that I looked in his eye and suspended to get on the plane and that pissed me off.

"I know who the fool is that did it. That pisses me off. When I look in a man's eye and say 'you're not coming on the trip' and he's on the plane because some fool done told him to defy what I said.

"We gotta get back locked in and get back focused. We're going to have a great practice and I'll deal with the fools. We good on that? Let's lock in and focus. Right now."

Nyles didn't want to become a bigger distraction, so he didn't eat with the team or attend any functions or meetings. He hung out in Aubrey's room.

"I wasn't trying to cause no scene. I wasn't trying to be a distraction to my team. I was just trying to give strong support and strong love," Nyles said. "I love them boys for real. We're at the Celebration Bowl. We're going to be national champions. I believe in them."

Aubrey missed breakfast Friday morning, nearly missed a team function, and sulked during the walk-through practice for defensive players. Afterward, he met privately with Reilly for about ten minutes and contemplated quitting.

"You can't quit this team twenty-four hours before the championship game. Do you know how many questions you'd have to answer? Prime would annihilate you," Reilly said. "Think about the kinds of questions you'd have to answer at the combine. Why the fuck did you quit? You think coaches are going to listen to you or other coaches? You get benched? Fuck it. Stand on the sideline and cheer for your guys."

Hart spoke to Aubrey at lunch.

"Don't let one man's mistake, that ain't got nothing to do with you derail you," Hart said.

While Miller and Hart worked through that issue, the anxiety that had troubled Tru Thompson in November had returned.

At about 2 p.m. Thompson texted trainer Lauren Askevold that he was having dark thoughts.

Tru had been searching for the meaning of life and his purpose since his friend Nimo died in November.

"I don't know if you can really look for your purpose or your purpose comes to you," Hart said. "How do you find that shit? I guess it's a feel or something overwhelming comes over you.

"That's how it came to me, because I couldn't find that motherfucker to save my life as a young man."

Tru was in his room on the seventh floor of the CNN Omni talking to Reilly and Thurman. Soon Askevold arrived.

"Tru was having some bad thoughts. It hasn't been the first time he's done that or had a panic attack," she said.

Tru is from Loganville, thirty-six miles east of Atlanta. Askevold gave him the option of calling his father. Tru's dad drove to Atlanta and picked him up.

"It was good. He gave me some tough love and I realized a lot of things changed for me after the injury," Tru said months later. "He told me to be myself and do the things I need to do to be the player I can be."

At 9 p.m., Tru phoned Askevold, asking to return.

"I feel better. I want to come back," he told her. "I don't want to let anyone down. I want to play."

That was no longer a consideration.

"At the end of the day I told him," Askevold said, "'You have to take care of Tru. You have to take care of you.'"

With Tru out for personal reasons, the reality set in that JSU had only four role-players at defensive tackle.

"We gotta play with what we got," Thurman said. "I will go to more of an odd look so we're not getting as beat up in there and put a little more on our linebackers."

Justin's versatility meant they could use him at defensive tackle but he'd wear down faster playing inside because of the pounding.

Linebacker Daelyn Dunn, a coach's son, was going to have to play Justin's defensive end spot.

"It's going to be a hell of a win, brother," Hart said. "It's going to be a hell of a story."

In their final team dinner of the season, the short speeches from the coaches felt different because everyone knew life was about to change for every person in the room. Several discussed the bond that players and coaches forged in Jackson during the water crisis, while they chased perfection.

"I've tried to be undefeated every single year," Weeks said. "This game is about what we do and how we prepare and what we've been through in Jackson, Mississippi, since we were bathing in a damn swimming pool."

The theme of the night, though, centered on life and football. The lessons learned during the season would carry some of these young men for a lifetime.

They learned accountability and responsibility and discipline. They learned about decision-making and consequences, good and bad, and disappointment. They endured tragedy and reveled in triumph.

They learned there's no shame in telling another man you love him, and they learned about prayer, and how it's OK to talk to God like he's your homeboy. Coach Prime pulled them to excellence, which is different than pushing them.

He set a standard, demanded they meet it, and then created an environment with everything they needed to achieve the standard.

"We've had people quit on us. Understand it's easy to have friends who want to smoke with you, drink with you, party with you, and chase women with you," Hart said. "That's easy. You need to surround yourself with people who can take criticism and understand you're trying to make them better, people who are not sensitive to the truths that shine darkness on who they are. If you do that you'll be successful."

When it was Taylor's turn to speak, JSU's thirteen receivers joined him in front of the team. They stood behind him, arms over each other's shoulders.

"There will never be another team like this," he said, "and I so don't look forward to Sunday."

A half a minute passed.

"This is a special group of coaches and trainers and players. We do a lot of laughing. We have a lot of fun. It has to come to an end and everybody has to go their separate ways and that bothers me," he said. "Come Sunday, 2022 is over.

"Some of you got plans. You seniors are done. Are you going pro? All I remember is the laughter. That's what I'm going to miss. We could just look at each other and bust out laughing because we're that goofy. I'm going to miss that because there will never be another 2022."

Then he turned to Coach Prime.

"I love this man. I love his vision. I love his consistency. Every day through sickness and health, he did his thing," Taylor said. "I chased that every day, Coach. Every day. That's why I don't want this to come to an end. I'm going to continue this shit. I'm not going to stop it.

"We owe it to him. We owe it to him. We owe it to him. Because he's done everything we've asked and then some. He's changed my life. He's changed these coaches' lives. He's changed your life."

Finally, Coach Prime spoke.

He thanked the people who contributed to the program's success, from the trainers to the film crew. He talked about how he had watched so many of the boys he recruited evolve into men, especially Aubrey.

"I don't want to go into the depth of how I feel because I know I'll get emotional because this is truly last call," Coach Prime said. "A lot of folks who started the journey with you are not here, so I applaud you. . . . It don't take long to be around us to understand we're a family. Families have focus. Families fight. Families have faith. Families have fun and families forgive.

"I rarely talked about my dreams, thoughts, and ambitions. My dream tomorrow is to truly be dominant from the start and finish with no exceptions. When we go out of the locker room we're going to be family and when we come back it's going to be history. Let's keep the main thing the main thing, and let's do our thing."

CHAPTER 27

Anybody could've caught it, I gotta be honest with you.
—tight end Hayden Hagler

A couple of hours before the Cricket Celebration Bowl at Mercedes-Benz Stadium, silence filled Coach Prime's office.

His business manager, Constance Schwartz-Morini, lovingly described as a pit bull in pumps, sat next to her husband. Jennifer and Leon Young were there, too.

Jennifer and Leon began regularly traveling to Jackson during Coach Prime's first year because Jennifer worried about him being lonely since he keeps his circle tight. They have known Coach Prime since their son played for TRUTH more than a decade ago.

These days, Jennifer and Leon managed Coach Prime's home and property in Canton, Texas, when he was not there. After games, Jennifer distributed meals to the players and coaches. Leon often held the three-legged portable stool Coach Prime used during games. Sometimes his foot throbbed so much that he sat down to alleviate the pain.

Jennifer understood his personality quirks. She could read his body language and quickly discern his mood.

"I don't need no new friends," Coach Prime often says.

On this day, Coach Prime was unusually quiet. The couples made small talk and fiddled with their cell phones, in between the moments Coach Prime reflected on his time at JSU.

He'd miss the players and support staff that didn't join him in Colorado. And he'd miss the folks he'd grown close to in Jackson. But he was also waiting for God to provide a scripture, a parable—something, anything he could drop on the players before the game.

"Do we need to leave and give you some quiet time?" Jennifer asked.

"No, my God don't work like that," he replied. "When God drops something in my spirit, he drops it. It don't matter where I'm at or what I'm doing."

While Coach Prime's mind zoomed down the Autobahn, the Tigers' locker room lacked its usual energy.

"What went on with our head coach—Coach Prime—announcing he was going to a new school, going to Colorado right after the SWAC Championship, talking to them and then we practice that next Monday like nothing happened. That felt weird to me," said linebacker Jurriente Davis. "People started to think about what's next instead of what's now. What's now is practicing and trying to win this championship. What's next is hit the portal. What's next is see if you want to stay with Coach T. C.

"This is the whole team. Not just the players. It was the coaches, too. Instead of putting an extra two hours of film into seeing what else we could do, they put that two hours into recruiting players to Colorado."

About ninety minutes before the game, Aubrey strode the length of the field and walked through NCCU's players. Trouble brewed. Jackson State officials escorted him back to the Tigers' side of the field before chaos ensued.

"When you get to the game, you walk around the locker room and you see how certain players prepare and they weren't doing those same rituals. It was just a little different," Taylor said. "I could literally look at certain people—the ones we were counting on like Aubrey—and they weren't quite themselves. Usually Aubrey already has that shit. He doesn't need anything extra."

A few players bobbed their heads to Kodak Black's "Walk." Most, though, sat at their lockers and listened to their personal playlists and waited for the game to start.

The locker room livened up once Gillie Da Kid and Wallo went live on Instagram.

It was moving toward the usual festive party-like atmosphere when the music changed and Tupac's "All Eyez on Me" started blasting. A few seconds later, Hart and Coach Prime walked into the locker room. They stood on a black crate so they could make eye contact with each player.

Hart prayed. Then Coach Prime spoke.

"Now . . . Now . . . Now . . . Now . . ." said an emotional Coach Prime.

"Let him use you, coach," a voice said.

"Now . . . Now . . . Now . . . Now . . . Thank you, Jesus. Thank you for each and every one of them," said Coach Prime, slowly shaking his head and sniffling.

"We love you, coach. We love you. Thank you, coach," anonymous voices said.

"Now . . . Not tomorrow . . . Now . . . Not the next day . . . Now . . . Not the next day after. We've done it together. Now, let's say it together. When I say now. All of y'all say gimme my theme music.

"Now!" Coach Prime shouted.

"Give me my theme music!" the players yelled.

DJ Willie B hit the button and Mystikal's "Here I Go" started blasting.

Coach Prime, surrounded by his players, clad in white jerseys with blue stripes on the shoulders and white pants, exploded.

"What! What! What! What! What!" they shouted to the beat before walking toward the tunnel, where they lined up before heading onto the field. The defensive linemen found a quiet corner and formed a circle.

"Day by day. Day by day," said Antonio, pausing long enough for his teammates to repeat his words.

"We get better. We get better," he said.

"We get better. We get better," they replied.

"We can't be beat. We can't be beat!" Antonio shouted.

"We can't be beat. We can't be beat!" they shouted.

It was time to win a championship.

The game's first play set a tone—and it wasn't a good one.

NCCU's Latrell Collier burst up the middle through a gaping hole for 10 yards and a first down. Just like that, NCCU's offensive line believed Jackson State's big, bad defense might just be overrated.

Davius Richard followed with a 5-yard gain on a quarterback run over the left guard. On second-and-5, E. J. Hicks beat Travis on a slant-and-go for a 42-yard gain.

Yikes.

The game was only four plays old, and JSU had breathed confidence into NCCU. The drive ended with Adrian Olivo's 32-yard field goal, which made it 3–0 NCCU with 11:37 left in the first quarter.

The Eagles stopped Sy'Veon for no gain on third-and-1 at the Jackson State 33, forcing a punt. Two series into the game and NCCU's offensive and defensive lines controlled the line of scrimmage.

A 21-yard run by Richard and a 31-yard trick play—a wide receiver pass from Hicks to Richard—set up an 11-yard touchdown run by Collier and a 10–0 NCCU lead. That was just about the time Tony Gray, wearing a canary-yellow sweatsuit, showed up on the sideline next to JSU's bench area. Nyles, who had been allowed on the sideline, saw him and smiled broadly.

Jackson State, on the verge of being blown out, needed a scoring drive. Shedeur capped a four-play, 67-yard drive with a 24-yard touchdown pass to D. J. Stevens.

"I told you we got you," Dallas told every defensive player he passed on the sideline.

An 85-yard touchdown pass to Kevin Coleman Jr. with 10:41 left in the second quarter gave JSU its first lead, 14–10, on its longest touchdown of the season.

It had been a frustrating season for Kevin, the other high-profile freshman. He finished the regular season with 25 catches for 338 yards and 2 touchdowns. He also returned 10 kickoffs for a 24.8 average.

"Personally, I feel like I didn't accomplish my goals for this season. I feel like the season was average for me," he said. "Overall, I did my job. Whenever the opportunity came my way, I did what I could do.

"Next year, I want to accomplish my goals. Team-wise I accomplished my goal, contributing to an undefeated team."

The day before the Cricket Celebration Bowl, Kevin used his second phone to text himself that he would return a kickoff for a touchdown. Then he sent another text that he would catch a touchdown pass.

Kevin, who had been one of the top high school receivers in the country, needed to run more precise routes and add strength. And as the only freshman with regular playing time he needed to understand when to speak and when to listen.

He played because Dallas, Willie, and Cam Buckley were the only true slot receivers on the roster. Dallas was the best, Willie had the most speed, and Cam was good against zones. Kevin was more complete than Willie or Cam.

Kevin's relationship with Cam slowed his progress.

Cam, a transfer from Indiana, had played three seasons at Texas A&M. He had been one of the SEC's promising young players after catching 51 passes for 756 yards and 4 touchdowns in his first two seasons, but he caught just 11 passes for 121 yards as a junior.

He sat out 2020 because of COVID-19 and played just two games for Indiana in 2021. Cam had become Kevin's big brother but he wasn't a positive influence.

"You might tell Cam to run a route at twelve yards and he might say, 'No, it would be better to do it this way. Jimbo [Fisher] showed me that at Texas A&M,'" Taylor said.

In early September, Kevin met with Coach Prime, who told the freshman to distance himself from Cam.

"Kevin was looking for direction, but he was being led the wrong way. Cam was making Kev into Cam," Taylor said. "I was not liking Kev because I saw him becoming Cam. Once Kev got away from him, he saw the self-destruction of Cam Buckley."

At the next receivers' meeting, Kevin moved his seat to the opposite side of the room.

"As soon as I went back in the room, I created space. When he told me that I knew it was time to be a leader—not a follower," Kevin said. "It wasn't hard at all. I knew it was to better me. God will use people to show you different things.

"When a great man like [Coach Prime] tells you to do something, you listen. He's trying to tell you something to help you out, so you do it. I already had that feeling—I know right from wrong—so if someone who's not even in the receiver room tells you that, you need to listen."

Jackson State's lead didn't last long. Every time NCCU ran the ball, it moved JSU's defensive linemen off the line of scrimmage. It embarrassed a unit that had dominated most of its opponents.

"Defense, we did what we could. We knew we were short," Aubrey said. "We knew a lot of people left."

The Eagles grabbed a 17–14 lead on a play symbolic of the first half for each team. J'Mari Taylor took an inside handoff and cut right. Aubrey met him in the hole—and Taylor should've been stopped for no gain.

Instead he ran over Aubrey, ran through an arm tackle by Cam'Ron, and shrugged off Jurriente at the goal line. Aubrey, still on his knees, put both hands to his head and then slammed them on the turf as Taylor rumbled into the end zone for a 17–14 lead.

As bad as the defense played, the offense was playing well. Shedeur's 7-yard touchdown run with thirty seconds left somehow gave Jackson State a 21–17 halftime lead.

"Do you motherfuckers understand championships are earned? They're not just going to give it to you!" Ricard shouted in the locker room. "Are you willing to scrape, crawl, scratch for that motherfucker?

"Make your mind up. Championships are earned, so you're gonna have to beat a motherfucker up and earn it. We're supposed to be the most physical team. Hit a motherfucker in the mouth. We worked too hard to go out half-assed."

Reilly diagrammed plays for the defensive linemen with a blue marker on the whiteboard in hopes they could stop NCCU's running game. Bolden, a fun-loving kid, hadn't addressed the team all season. But he screamed as he walked down a row of lockers.

"Stay together, bruh! All of us! One more fucking half, bruh! We're not going out like no bitch-ass niggas, bruh!" he yelled. "Straight up, I ain't going for that."

The Tigers led, but they weren't in control. Still, they had the ball first in the second half and a touchdown would give JSU an 11-point lead and the control it craved.

"Now is the time. Now is the time. Now is the time. You been waiting your whole life for this moment. It's now," Coach Prime said. "You been waiting your whole life to be undefeated. It's now. You been waiting all your life to make a play. It's now.

"We have a tremendous opportunity to finish and-O, but it's all based on what we do right now. I just want you to be the same person you've been all year, and guess what? We'll dominate now."

JSU managed just one first down before punting on their first possession. The Eagles used a 43-yard fake punt on fourth-and-4 from their own 33 to set up a 12-yard touchdown pass from Richard to Quentin McCall to take a 23–21 lead.

The four defensive tackles JSU had lost in the two weeks between winning the SWAC Championship and the Cricket Celebration Bowl had taken an even bigger toll on their depth than it figured. A defense that had entered the game allowing the fewest points (11.1 per game), total yards (233.2), and passing yards (135.4) in the country was pummeled.

The shock of being manhandled was too much for them to shake. The issues with gap control and discipline they never had fixed during the season showed up in the championship game. A 7-yard touchdown run and subsequent two-point conversion by NCCU gave the Eagles a 34–27 lead with 4:31 left.

The defense had now blown leads of 14–10, 21–17, and 27–26.

"Aubrey is usually in attack mode, he's supposed to be on go. He had that look of uncertainty," Morton said. "That's your toughest leader. Your general. He tried. Cam tried. It's like Spider-Man with no webs. What do you tell them?"

Even Taylor struggled to focus.

"In the third quarter, I just got to looking around thinking I could literally be coming back next year as the head coach and be in this same moment," Taylor said. "Oh, let me put that shit aside and get back locked in because we gotta win this game."

At one point in the third quarter, an exasperated Thurman asked the defensive players what defense they could execute.

"I kept feeling like the defense would put it together sooner or later but they didn't. You have to give credit to them," Coach Prime said of NCCU. "They played their butts off. They ran three plays the whole game, but they were very effective with those three plays."

It became obvious in the fourth quarter that if the Tigers were going to win, Shedeur had to lead the way. He wanted the pressure. Needing a touchdown drive to tie the score and force overtime wasn't a big deal. Besides, he had Travis.

"We have to go to our best player. That was Travis. Those two dudes are going to find a way to make it work. Throw it to Travis and he's going to figure that shit out and let's be done with it," Taylor said. "He's the number one player in the country. We wanted to get ourselves in position on that drive and then take your shots with Travis."

For Shedeur, he did what he was born to do.

"There's no difference between fifteen minutes and fifteen seconds you just go through your reads. I was reminding myself," said Shedeur, "you're in this spot for a reason. You wouldn't want anyone else to be in this position."

On fourth-and-7, Shedeur rolled right to avoid pressure and found J. D. Martin, who made a leaping catch in the middle of the field for a 10-yard gain and a first down.

Two incompletions sandwiched around a 12-yard gain to Coleman moved the ball to the 19. Three more incompletions made it fourth-and-the-game from the NCCU 19.

At that point, it was about players, not plays. The ball must go to Travis.

Shedeur, operating from the shotgun, took a three-step drop and lofted a pass to Travis, who tracked the ball at the 10-yard line. He backpedaled into the end zone and snagged the ball with both hands, tying the score at 34–34 as time expired.

"There was a lot of chaos. Travis is Travis Hunter. He's here for a reason. When I threw the ball, I just needed to put air under it and he was going to do the rest," Shedeur said. "It wasn't really hard. Travis did all the work.

"Travis has been doing it all season. We just had to find the right time to put him on the field. We have a lot of receivers in Blurr Nation. It's not just Travis's season. The receivers nicknamed their unit Blurr Nation because several receivers hailed from Florida. In their home state, when a receiver catches a deep ball or makes a leaping catch over a defender, the crowd yells, "Bluuuuuuuur!"

The sideline went bonkers after Travis' catch.

"Let's go! Let's go!" student trainer Asia Lamkin shouted, tears streaming down her cheeks.

Filmanati, usually too busy shooting video to get caught up in the game's emotion, made an exception.

"I believe!" he yelled.

The game, however, wasn't over. The score was tied.

"Everybody thought we won the game," Jurriente said weeks later. "I stood up on the bench knowing they got another possession. We haven't fucking won."

On NCCU's first overtime possession, Richard scored on a 1-yard run as the Eagles claimed a 41–34 lead. He completed 15 of 20 passes for 175 yards and a touchdown, and he ran 22 times for 97 yards and two touchdowns. Collier added 98 yards and a touchdown on 17 carries.

"We just ran out of juice," Reilly said. "We weren't mentally strong enough or physically strong enough to stop them."

Jackson State faced third-and-goal from the NCCU 1. A touchdown would tie the score.

Bartolone called Baconator Left Playboy, a naked play-action pass designed for the tight end that had worked for a touchdown in Week 1 against FAMU. The Tigers lined up with two receivers and two tight ends. Sy'Veon was the lone runner. Hayden, a tight end, lined up in the backfield between the left tackle and guard.

"I probably practiced with the first team more than I had all week," Hayden said. "I prepared like I was going to play like that all week."

It was just his second snap of the game. Graduate assistant Andrew Zimmer and Pollock sat in the press box, so no one actually coached the tight ends during the game. Brewster watched the game from Peckish, a wing spot near campus, in Boulder after he had spent the week recruiting in Colorado, Iowa, and Nebraska.

"It was a lonely feeling. I felt like these are my guys and I'm supposed to be there," Brewster said. "I almost thought I should've flown in there Friday to be part of it—even if I wasn't coaching.

"I checked into flights. I don't know why I didn't, but I didn't."

At the snap, Shedeur faked a handoff to Sy'Veon around left end before rolling right. Hayden ran across the formation and snapped his head, looking for the ball as soon as he reached the end of the line of scrimmage.

Shedeur, pressured heavily, lobbed a perfect pass. Hayden, wide open, extended his arms to grab the ball, but it bounced off his hands, tumbling to the ground.

"The moment didn't get too big for me. I wasn't nervous or shaking," Hayden said. "It's just a little freaky thing that happened. Anybody could've caught it, I gotta be honest with you."

Hayden deserved a better fate.

The 6'4", 222-pound redshirt sophomore tight end from Sulphur, Louisiana, had already experienced enough grief to last a lifetime. His story is one of faith and perseverance.

It's why he started at Marshall and wound up at JSU. As a high school player, Hayden used direct messages on Instagram and Twitter in an attempt to connect with Brewster when he coached tight ends at Texas A&M and Florida, respectively.

"I was just reaching out to him to get my film in front of him. I wanted to play for him. That's how God works," Hayden said. "We laugh about it now."

When it didn't work out, he settled on Marshall.

On November 14, 1970, a chartered flight carrying Marshall's football team after a 17–14 loss to East Carolina crashed into a hillside about two miles from Tri-State Airport in Kenosha, West Virginia, killing everyone on board.

The crash killed 36 players and 39 administrators, coaches, fans, spouses, and flight crew. The rebirth of the football program was the subject of a 2006 movie, *We Are Marshall*, starring Matthew McConaughey.

"The whole city—not just the football team—plays for its lost brothers," Hayden said. "I lost my three brothers. It's kind of like here. It just seemed like they were playing for something bigger than themselves.

Hayden caught two passes for 8 yards as a redshirt freshman but coach Doc Holliday's contract expired at the end of 2020 after a 7-3 season. New coach Charles Huff didn't want Hayden, so he hit the transfer portal.

"I just had a feeling from God that I needed something new in my life. I trusted my talent and bet on myself," Hayden said. "I wanted to be a part of something bigger than me and that's the kind of culture Coach Prime is building."

Hayden lost his first brother, Randall, a twenty-three-year-old former marine, to suicide when he was seven. Four months later to the day, his twenty-one-year-old brother, Billy, died when he was ejected from the vehicle in a car accident.

Two years later, nineteen-year-old Hunter died from an accidental overdose in Houston.

"His friends tried to calm him down so they put some Xanax in his alcohol . . ." Hayden said. "He wound up aspirating in the middle of the night."

Hayden's mom, Lisa, was at home when Randall died and she was riding in the car when Billy died.

"I remember driving from Lake Charles to Houston, when we heard my third brother was in ICU," Hayden said. "She was screaming and crying. I yelled, 'Mama, stop' and she started praying and it really helped me turn to my faith.

"Whenever I'm having a hard time. I just try to turn to God. He's pulled me out of the bottom of the bottom. God blessed me with all this talent. If I can make it one day, my story can help out somebody else who isn't doing all that good and thinks all the odds are against them. I just want to affect one person."

After his third brother died, Hayden's father left the family. Hayden said his father used alcohol to soothe his grief. The couple reconciled in 2020 after a decade apart.

Lisa said she lost her real estate business, her home and, eventually, her car, while she grieved.

"Jesus sent messengers along the way to let me know that like Job in the Bible, he was going to restore everything Satan had taken from us," she said. "I held on to that faith."

Occasionally, Hayden asked his mother when God was going to fulfill His promise since they often slept in a gray, four-door Honda Accord that required prayer to start some mornings.

"Me and my mom were actually homeless, bouncing around," Hayden said. "We stayed in her car. We stayed at a couple of her friends' houses, but it was all temporary."

A church blessed them with a seventeen-foot camper trailer. They couldn't afford the propane to heat it, but it was home.

"We stayed there, and we made it out," Hayden said. "She ended up making it. I seen her and that's what I had to do."

On fourth down, Shedeur, under pressure, sailed a pass over Kevin's head. Game over.

NCCU 41, JSU 34.

"I didn't even see the confetti fall. I ran in the locker room. I was bawling my eyes out," Jurriente said. "It was an emotional game for me to handle. Even if we had won I would've cried because it was a historic season."

Orange, blue, and white confetti dropped from the roof and the pyrotechnics exploded as NCCU's players celebrated. Jackson State's players wandered aimlessly around the field.

Last year they had partied away an opportunity to win. This year they made too many mistakes.

Long snapper Jacob Politte, a West Texas native who drove his truck 760 miles from Lubbock to Jackson for an opportunity to compete, squatted in front of his helmet like a baseball catcher and stared straight ahead.

Herm Smith, Willis Patrick, and cornerback Tayvion Beasley hugged on the sideline. Jency Riley walked up the tunnel with his right arm wrapped tightly around Hayden's neck.

"I dropped a touchdown pass earlier in the season against Tennessee State and there was no one to do that for me," Jency said. "I knew how I felt in that moment, and I would hate for him to feel those same emotions and think he was by himself.

"I got up and felt like shit. I went to sideline and it was me by myself. I know how that feels. It's all right, man. We still love you. It happens. It's not your fault we lost the game."

Quinton Williams Jr., a sophomore student assistant, sat on the bench next to Herm, an arm around his neck while he patted him on the left shoulder.

Forsett spoke softly to Tyler, who stared at the ground, while Coach Prime limped down the sideline. He embraced Tayvion, who sobbed in his arms. As Coach Prime made his way down the sideline, he hugged Smith and walked another ten yards and tightly embraced Mercier.

"I wanted to comfort them," Coach Prime said. "A lot of them were emotional because we didn't fathom a loss."

This is a side of Coach Prime most folks never see.

Coach Prime is a man who gives kids multiple chances. Coach Prime promoted a running back from walk-on to scholarship player because he loved his work ethic in practice. There are countless stories of Coach Prime helping kids in a million different ways, because he loves them.

"I don't play or coach for legacy. I coach for kids," he said. "I coach for love and passion. It's not a job for me."

Inside the locker room in Atlanta, each player experienced his own personal hell. None more than Hayden.

He sat in his locker wearing a sweaty, sleeveless white compression shirt and football pants. A white towel covered his head. Bartolone put his right hand on his knee and his left hand around his shoulder for about fifteen minutes.

"He was at one of the lowest points in his life. That kid had already been through enough in his life," Bartolone said. "He didn't try and drop the pass. In that moment, Hayden needed people to bring him up."

D. J. walked over and whispered in Hayden's ear. So did Kevin. Aubrey said he wasn't leaving the stadium until Hayden walked out with him.

"Man, I've been praying for this my whole life, and I just fumbled the bag," Hayden said to himself. "I wasn't trying to be easy or hard on myself. I was trying to be as real as possible.

"I'm thinking about Aubrey. I'm thinking about all the seniors leaving. I knew it was the last time. Coach Prime was going to be leaving. I knew that team would never be together again."

Shedeur gathered his teammates near the front of the locker room, while the coaches dressed or lingered on the field. Shedeur spoke about a lack of urgency at the beginning of the game and a lack of belief at the end.

"Emotion. Emotion. Emotion. We should feel like that the whole fucking game," he said. "We get to the end of the game and we score, everybody's cheering like we just won the game back there. Like we ain't been here before. Like we ain't even supposed to be in that position type shit. . . .

"Now, we get to the end of the game and everybody got sad, sad, sad faces. The game wasn't fucking over. We're a family, bruh. We gotta lean on each other. It's nobody's fault, bro. None of that. Defense, y'all carried us the whole season. I missed throws. We ran the wrong routes. We had drops. We missed blocks. Everything. It's not just one part of the team that ain't do it. Love y'all, boys."

Then Aubrey spoke.

"Y'all stuck this shit out and that means so much to me. We're forever locked in," he said. "I can't even cry right now, bruh. I'm trying to be strong. Pick y'all heads up. We still made history. We went undefeated. It's a learning experience."

As the players drew closer to break it down one last time, Nyles, standing near the back, spoke.

"I just wanted to apologize to y'all for me making some selfish decisions that hurt the team," he said. "I love y'all, boys."

Aarion Hartman, the Southern transfer, sat in front of his locker in shock. Every few seconds, defensive lineman Devonta Davis said, "Fuck."

The thud of shoulder pads tossed to the ground and the ache of despair emanated throughout the locker room. No one spoke.

Finally, Coach Prime addressed the players. He stood on a black folding chair, ensuring eye contact with his players. Hart, wearing a red T-shirt with I BELIEVE across the front, stood next to him.

"Come tighter. Come tighter," Coach Prime said. "We're still a family."

Hart prayed through an avalanche of tears before Coach Prime addressed the team.

"I consider it a time in life where we missed our opportunity. A time in life where we had it right in the palm of our hands. A time in life where we may have taken something for granted," he said. "A time in life where we really didn't focus on what we needed to focus on. A time in life where there were distractions. A time in life where you allowed those distractions to distract you. . . .

"We accomplished some tremendous things. Yes, we fell short. Yes, we did. We had some wonderful young men who graduated. They did not fall short. We had some wonderful young men who earned accolades. They did not fall short. We had some wonderful men in here that made changes in their lives that no one even knows about. They didn't fall short.

"So let's not blame one man for falling short because you don't know what he's come through."

Then Coach Prime shifted the conversation. One last time, he wanted the players to hear how much they meant to him.

"We love each and every one of you in this locker room. Yes, we chastise you. Yes, we punish you sometimes," he said. "Yes, we discipline you sometimes. We're just trying to prepare you for life."

EPILOGUE

The quest for perfection had ended with another disappointing finish. A national championship had eluded Coach Prime for the second consecutive season.

It was time for players, coaches—everyone—to deal with reality. Or the finality.

Either way, life as they knew it had changed.

A couple of hours after it lost, 41–34, to North Carolina Central, the 2022 Jackson State football team scattered.

Literally.

Coach Prime, Shedeur, and Shilo and several members of the coaching staff headed to Boulder to officially start their new lives at the University of Colorado.

T. C. Taylor, JSU's head coach, and the bulk of the team took the eighty-minute flight home to Jackson, where the players and coaches contemplated their choices.

For some, like linebacker Nyles Gaddy and receiver Rico Powers, who were poised to move into high-profile starting roles, it made sense for them to stay at Jackson State. Others, who had been drawn to the cameras and Coach Prime, figured it was better to leave because football at Jackson State just wouldn't be the same. Another group of players were undecided.

Hayden Hagler spent the night in Atlanta, replaying the worst moment of his athletic career.

"I knew I was coming back. I couldn't leave like that. God didn't do this for no reason," he said. "I've caught that ball a million times in practice. I don't remember dropping that ball one time all year.

"I've got all these eyes on me saying, what's he going to do now? What's he going to do now? I want those eyes on me. I knew it wasn't going to be the end for me. It was just another hump. It was another trial and tribulation I had to get through."

After the game, Hayden returned to the Hilton Hotel, where his mom and girlfriend went right after the game, to ensure their safety. They had received death threats on social media. Hayden picked up a large pepperoni pizza and took it to them. While they ate, he walked to the parking garage, sat in his girlfriend's white Jeep, and contemplated how that dropped pass had changed his life.

"He needed to be alone," Lisa Hagler, Hayden's mom, told me. "I'm always there to comfort him, but sometimes you need to be in your own head space. I think he felt like he let himself down and his brothers down. His brothers used to teach him if you touch the ball, you have to catch it. I think he went into the car to have some time with himself, with Jesus, and with his brothers."

After a while, Hayden actually left the car and walked the pass route a few times against imaginary defenders. Each time, he caught the pass and scored. After a few minutes, he returned to the car and his thoughts.

Hayden ignored loved ones who suggested in texts and voice messages that he make his social media page private or turn off the comments. He looked at the vitriol on Twitter and Instagram and forgave those who issued death threats or made crass comments. "This whole city, we been through a whole lot to get to this moment. If anybody has any kind of say-so or opinion, they deserve to get it off their chest," he said. "I've never been a big social media guy, so it wasn't that big a deal to me."

He watched clips and highlights of the play on social media to see what he did wrong and how he could improve. In the process, he missed Brewster's phone calls.

"I tried calling Hayden ten times that night because I wanted to hear his voice," Brewster told me. "I talked to his mom. That's when it hurt me to my core that I wasn't there."

Taylor finally reached Hayden after the flight landed in Jackson.

"He was broke up pretty bad," Taylor said. "I hate that the people blamed that game on him. For him to persevere says a lot about that dude."

Hayden credited his three angels.

"I was down on myself, but I've been through much worse times," he said. "I needed to go into that hotel room and hug the people I love. I knew I had overcome worse.

"When people heard a little bit of where I came from, it helped people be a little more understanding. That's all I wanted. People I don't even know on campus will come up and give me a hug or dap me up."

That's because he refused to let a dropped pass define him. He embraced that moment. He didn't hide from it or the disappointment. He used that mistake to fuel his offseason workouts, which began alone at a park until he felt comfortable enough to work out on campus with the fellas again.

Football had always been more than a game to Hayden, just like it had always been more than a game to Coach Prime. Hayden saw the game as a way to honor his brothers and, ultimately, touch lives by sharing his story of tragedy and triumph. Coach Prime saw football as an opportunity to change his mama's life.

It was the main reason he always searched to find his players' why. Players, he said, will quit on themselves and they'll quit on a coach, but they won't quit on their why because that's their true motivation.

Meanwhile at Colorado in his new role as head coach, Coach Prime's mission remained the same: turn boys into men and win football games, and ultimately, championships.

He quickly switched his mind-set from Jackson State to the challenge at Colorado because he's a man who controls his emotions. He takes pride in that, in fact. A quote from Coach Prime on his office wall says, "My emotions ain't qualified to make a decision, but I am."

This is the same man who has often said, "I never love anything that can't love me back."

His job at JSU certainly fell under that category. While he would miss the players and support staff—they could love him—it was easy for him to move on from the job. Besides, Colorado demanded his entire focus.

The only way he could do it was to surround himself with a staff loyal to him, so he brought most of his JSU crew with him. It made sense considering the Tigers went 23-3 in his last two seasons. On the Colorado side, Coach Prime only kept staff members committed to change because, clearly, in his mind whatever had taken place before he arrived had failed dramatically. This is what happens at most college programs when there's a coaching change or when a business brings in a new CEO. They come with their own people. Mostly for one reason: trust.

"Most people that fail in life or have setbacks are caused by somebody close to them, real close to them," he said. "So you gotta trust. Trust is everything. You try to build a collection of people you trust. Some people we have to get out of this building because I don't trust them. They were here before us and they're not with our movement, so I don't trust them."

Could the support staff he didn't trust ever earn it?

"No, because they're not built like that. They're not built for where we're going," he said. "They may be built for where we are, but not where we're going."

With him to Colorado, Coach Prime took defensive coordinator Dennis Thurman, linebackers coach Andre' Hart, secondary coach Kevin Mathis, and defensive ends coach Trevor Reilly. Thurman was moved to director of quality control, which meant he helped the defensive staff wherever it needed him. Reilly coached special teams.

Offensive coordinator Brett Bartolone, running backs coach Gary Harrell, tight ends coach Tim Brewster, and special assistant

Michael Pollock joined him from the offensive staff. So did offensive line coach Mike Markuson, but he lasted only a few weeks as an analyst. He resigned and Gunnar White replaced him.

Coach Prime hired Mo Sims as strength coach. Graduate assistants Rashad Davis, Anthony Balancier, and Andrew Zimmer also joined him in Boulder.

Trainer Lauren Askevold came with Coach Prime, as did student trainers Darshena Marion and Asia Lamkin. He also brought recruiting assistant Alexys Ellis and personal assistant Tysha Stewart, who planned most of his team events, whether it was a recruiting weekend or a summer block party.

Coach Prime's sister, Tracie, was named assistant to the head coach, and Craig Campanozzi was named director of sports video. Of course, Ray Forsett was named chief of staff.

He even took his security team of Evis McGee and Michael Rhodes with him.

He hired Mississippi Valley head coach Vincent Dancy as an analyst, and he asked childhood friend James Chaney to leave his job as head coach at Fort Myers's Lehigh High School to be director of player development.

Reginald Calhoun, whose son played for TRUTH, owned a successful logistics company and an outsourcing company in Dallas. But when Coach Prime asked the retired army first sergeant to be Colorado's director of football operations, Calhoun accepted the position.

Sound familiar?

In addition to people Coach Prime trusted from his circle of friends and his JSU years, he hired Alabama's Charles Kelly to be defensive coordinator and persuaded Sean Lewis to leave his job as Kent State's head coach to be offensive coordinator and quarterbacks coach.

Then there were the players. His sons Shedeur and Shilo naturally followed Coach Prime to Colorado, along with receiver/cornerback Travis Hunter, defensive end Jeremiah Brown, safety Cam'Ron

Silmon-Craig, receiver Willie Gaines, cornerback Tayvion Beasley, kicker Alejandro Mata, and long snapper Jacob Politte.

Changing the team culture toward a winning one would be a process, Coach Prime predicted—no harder or easier than he expected.

"Nothing is a surprise. Everything I thought it would be, it is," he said. "That means there's a lot of work to do."

Coach Prime used the offseason workouts in January 2023 to evaluate the roster. He demanded the players practice at a faster pace and forced them to work harder than they believed they could.

He created excitement in the community by signing a recruiting class that was ranked 21st overall in February 2023.

It was highlighted by Cormani McClain, a five-star corner-back, he flipped from Miami. Coach Prime flipped four-star running back Dylan Edwards from Notre Dame and four-star receiver Omarion Miller from Nebraska. He also signed four-star receiver Adam Hopkins.

Colorado easily signed the No. 1 transfer class in college football.

The excitement created from the players he signed and the transfers expected to arrive before the 2023 season is why Colorado's spring game drew 47,277—the most ever at the school. The game was televised on ESPN and 551,000 people watched it, the second-most-watched spring game since 2016. Season tickets sold out in April. It marked the first time since 1996 that Colorado had sold out season tickets.

"I was amazed," Coach Prime said after the spring game. "It was one of those moments that you will never forget."

Coach Prime created space for the new players he was adding through the transfer portal by cutting some players. Others left because they recognized they didn't have a future on the team.

The players who were cut had the option to keep their scholar-ships and remain students. A couple of weeks after the spring game ended, Colorado had a staggering number of players in the transfer portal, including Beasley, which created a controversy. Observers wondered what it meant that so many players were abandoning the program that Coach Prime was leading. When the transfer portal closed on April 30, Colorado had 56 players enter the portal, the most in college football. Ole Miss had 33, Texas A&M and Oregon had 31, and Arizona State rounded out the top five with 30. Most of the players in the portal had small roles, if any, for Colorado in 2022. Coach Prime wants big-time talent and work ethic.

"I'm looking for players who can compete for starting jobs at Georgia and Alabama. I want guys who can compete at Ohio State because those are the teams consistently playing for the national championship," he said. "That's the level we want to be on. Those are the types of players we're adding."

You won't find a more competitive person than Coach Prime. At Jackson State, he wanted to dominate and win the Cricket Celebration Bowl. Nothing has changed but his address. He wants to dominate and win a national championship at Colorado.

Back at JSU, Taylor, four months after he took the job, still didn't have new office furniture. In fact, the wall behind his desk still had all of Coach Prime's quotes painted on it.

"You know how the administration is," he told me. "It'll get done sooner or later."

The bigger issue Taylor faced was maintaining the program's momentum. Otis Riddley moved from player personnel director to assistant head coach/tight ends and Brandon Morton moved from grad assistant to running backs coach. Defensive tackles coach Jeff Weeks left JSU in February 2023 to coach high school football in Texas, and special teams coach Alan Ricard joined the University of Alabama at Birmingham in the same capacity. Several other key players who had been seduced by the bright lights, cameras, and Instagram fame created by the environment Coach Prime fostered left JSU because they didn't like the environment without it. Or they wanted NIL money that didn't exist. Or they wanted to play at a higher level.

"Ain't nothing changed," Taylor said. "We're still Jackson State and we're going to win football games."

He'll have a tough road.

Jurriente Davis transferred to Texas A&M University, Shane Hooks transferred to Auburn University, and Kevin Coleman went to the University of Louisville. Safety John Huggins went to New Mexico State University, Devin Hayes transferred to Middle Tennessee State University, and Herm Smith transferred to Idaho State University.

All started or were considered key role players.

Sy'Veon Wilkerson entered the transfer portal after the spring game, as did Nyles Gaddy, Malachi Wideman, and Trevonte Rucker, also a projected starter.

Sy'Veon asked the coaching staff for a car deal and they told him he'd have to find one on his own. He wound up in Colorado with Coach Prime.

"I haven't lost any sleep over it," Taylor said. "We can find a running back."

Nyles transferred to Missouri, but Trevonte and Malachi were still in the portal heading into June.

Before the spring game, Taylor admitted he wasn't sure whether Nyles would stay at Jackson State. Nyles was pressing the program for NIL money, but they wouldn't commit to it because of his conduct and performance in 2022.

"Every day," Taylor said of Nyles, "it feels different."

Cornerback Isaiah Bolden, drafted in the seventh round by the New England Patriots, was the only HBCU player selected in the NFL Draft. Hours after the draft, linebacker Aubrey Miller Jr. signed with the Miami Dolphins, receiver Dallas Daniels signed with the Denver Broncos, and cornerback De'Jahn Warren signed with the Chicago Bears. Offensive lineman Tony Gray signed with the Edmonton Elks of the Canadian Football League.

The difference in attention JSU's program has received without Coach Prime is in stark contrast to what it received with him.

It felt, for better or worse, like the Coach Prime chapter had closed and there would be little evidence he'd ever been at Jackson State in a couple of years.

Their spring game, with Coach Prime as head coach, was televised on ESPN in 2022 and had more than 41,000 people in attendance. In 2023, without Coach Prime, only about 1,000 people attended the spring game. If you choose to be generous, maybe 2,000 showed up in all, to try to enjoy the revelry of the atmosphere. Thunderstorms had been expected on game day, which school officials said kept some fans at home. Whatever the reason, the turnout was disappointing.

Defensive tackle Tru Thompson had lost about forty pounds and made a couple of nice tackles in JSU's spring game. Afterward, the smile never left his face.

"I'm finally back to being me," he told me. "I worked hard to get my confidence back in my knee and to get in shape and be the player I know I can be."

Tru had battled through the storms of his life and pushed through to see the rainbow on the other side. Now that it was over, it didn't seem like the storm had lasted all that long.

But that's what football and life are all about.

Coach Prime believes football teaches young men so many things about how to live. The game, if they let it, he says, teaches them self-discipline and the value of hard work. It teaches them how to weaponize adversity and overcome it. It teaches the difference between pain and injury and how to create mental and physical toughness.

The game teaches how to handle disappointment and failure as well as success and victory.

The game teaches how to win in life.

That's what Coach Prime passed on to his players, even though JSU lost its last game. Coach Prime gave his players, coaches, and support staff a game plan to win in life. They simply needed to execute it.

Like Tru was doing. And like Hayden did.

On the day he graduated with a degree in professional interdisciplinary studies, Hayden proposed to his girlfriend of four years, Ashley Patin. He had executed the first part of Coach Prime's game plan and he was ready to start his own family before beginning a career as a coach, where he could shape the lives of young men just like Coach Prime.

ACKNOWLEDGMENTS

As soon as I hung up the phone with HarperCollins in June 2022, I texted Deion Sanders with a cryptic message to call me when he had a chance.

A couple of minutes later, the phone rang. I told him about the offer I had been presented to write about a book on Jackson State's 2022 season.

"Have you signed the contract yet? If not, hurry up before they change their mind," he said laughing.

"Man, you know I gotta make sure you're good with me doing this before I agree to it," I replied.

"I got you," he said. "Whatever access you need, you got it."

Total phone time? Less than three minutes. And that's how I wound up writing a book about Coach Prime, the 2022 season, and his quest for perfection, while developing a roster full of men who will one day contribute to society as husbands, fathers, and businessmen.

A project like this doesn't get done without a ton of people helping me along the way. They either provided opportunity, time, or support for this project.

You can't do a project like this without the unwavering support of your family.

Thanks to my girlfriend, Brentavia, for grinding through this project with me. I love you for it.

I want my kids, A.J. and Jasmine, and my grandkids, Allanah and Eylan, to know how much I love them and how much they inspire me. I appreciate their mother and GiGi Lorraine, for filling in gaps while I spent five months in Jackson.

Dad, Carol, Kee, Lauryn and Ellison and Cinque and Addison, I love and appreciate you beyond words.

Then there are my dudes, starting with my workout partners Zues and Keith, who heard more about this project than they wanted during our 5 a.m. workouts once I returned to Dallas. Calvin, Clarence, and Joe served as sounding boards and helped keep my mind right.

Howard Bryant, one of the smartest men I know, is a brother and a mentor, and helped connect me to Rakia Clark.

I have to thank Mariner vice president and publisher Peter Hubbard and executive editor Rakia for taking a chance on me a couple of days after my *Sports Illustrated* cover story on Coach Prime and the Jackson State program dropped. Special thanks to Harper-Collins's director of international sales, Dan Vidra, for encouraging Rakia to find a writer on this topic. She set her mind to finding me. I'd never done a project like this, but Rakia guided me through it and gave me the confidence that I could produce a quality book. I wanted to give readers an intimate look at Coach Prime and JSU's program by taking them inside the locker room, meeting rooms, and players' lounge. I wanted to take them on the sideline, on the team buses, and to team dinners where they couldn't go.

There's no way to do a project like this without Deion providing complete access to the program, which he did. He granted that because of a close relationship built on respect and trust that we've established over nearly thirty years that goes beyond football. I can't thank him enough.

He never asked what I was writing or who I was interviewing. He just asked me to tell the truth and write with integrity.

No problem.

I also have to thank Constance Schwartz-Morini, the cofounder and president of SMAC. She's Deion's business manager. I have a lot of respect for the woman Deion calls "a pit bull in pumps" because she created a lane for herself and has dominated it. Sam Morini, Deion's personal assistant, was beyond helpful.

I want to express my sincere gratitude to the coaching staff who welcomed me into their meeting rooms, offices, homes, and automobiles. Dennis Thurman has taught me so much about football and life while working on this project. I talked to him almost every morning for ten to fifteen minutes, while he played *Jeopardy!* on his iPad and explained why players and coaches did what they did.

Otis Riddley spent much of his time explaining to me the backgrounds of players so I could understand why they behaved the way they did, good or bad, and I used that information to better connect with the players. Most of those enlightening and funny conversations with Coach O occurred on the sidelines during practice.

When you understand who you're talking to, the interview flows better. I couldn't have written the book I did without that kind of insight. His assistant Gabby Mossop was equally helpful.

Nobody understands Deion better than Andre' Hart and Kevin Mathis. They explained his approach to coaching and personnel and why he made the decisions he did about whether to give a player another chance or kick him off the team.

Their trust and honesty were crucial to understanding Deion and why he's become a successful coach.

Ray Forsett, Pretty Tony to the world, was equally helpful with his insight into players and Deion. Nobody laughs like Ray.

T. C. Taylor is another coach who provided so much background on players that it allowed me to go deeper in my interviews with them. He was especially open with me, expressing his vulnerability, anger, frustration, and, ultimately, happiness, through the process that wound up with him being named head coach.

Tim Brewster provided a wealth of information and as someone who hadn't known Coach Prime that long, he had unique insight into the man. Brett Bartolone was so helpful when it came to explaining the offense and what made Shedeur Sanders such a good player. I texted him often with detailed questions, and he always answered quickly and thoughtfully.

My dude Trevor Reilly kept it real every time we talked. You want unfiltered truth, ask Trevor. He was never short of opinions and I appreciated that. The other coaches—Gary Harrell, Michael Pollock, Mike Markuson, Jeff Weeks, and Alan Ricard—gave me their time when I asked.

Grad assistant Brandon Morton is another coach who became my dude and explained to me what made different players good. Or what made them tick.

Much thanks to grad assistants Rashad Davis, Anthony Balancier, Gunnar White, and Andrew Zimmer and analysts Kendall Adams and Trevarius Clark.

No way could I write a book like this without buy-in from the players. They were all eager to talk about playing for Coach Prime and their experience at Jackson State. And they trusted me enough to share the intimate details of their lives. I valued that trust and hope I told their stories in a way that makes them proud.

What I appreciated most was their honesty, whether it was Nugget Warren and Norman Douglas discussing how many friends and relatives they had lost to violence or illness—each needed two hands to count—since arriving on campus. Or uplifting stories like D. J. Stevens going from having his scholarship revoked to becoming one of the most important players on offense.

Special thanks for the conversations with Shedeur Sanders, Sy'Veon Wilkerson, Willis Patrick, Tyler Brown, Evan Henry, Shane Hooks, Dallas Daniels, Malachi Wideman, Tony Gray, Aubrey Miller Jr., Nyles Gaddy, Antonio Doyle, Jurriente Davis, Travis Hunter Jr., Jeremiah Brown, Cam'Ron Silmon-Craig, Shilo Sanders, Sam Johnson, Donald Turley, Alejandro Mata, Khalil Arrington, Anthony Petty, Tre'von Riggins, Justin Ragin, Tru Thompson, Amari Ward, Devin Hayes, Jency Riley, Hayden Hagler, Devonta Davis, Kevin Coleman Jr., and John Huggins.

I also want to thank Ke'Vric Wiggins Jr., Zack Breaux, J. P. Andrade, J. D. Martin, Caleb Jolivette, Quay Davis, Willie Gaines, Rico Powers, Greyson Thompson, Matthew Ricciardi-Vitale, Herm Smith III, Isaiah Bolden, Jalin Hughes, Tayvion Beasley, Lane McGregor, Jason Mercier, Delano Salgado, Jacob Politte, Santee Marshall, Gerardo Baeza, Glenn Misiak, Michael Thompson, Marquis Johnson, Daelyn Dunn, Kobe Paul, Andre Hunt, Julian Smith, Baron Hopson, Carlton Goodell, Zach Breaux, Aarion Hartman, Trace Shumans, Deontae Graham, Kirk Ford, Demetri Jordan, Julius Reynolds, Jacob Humphrey, Jeremiah Williams, Errick Simmons, Tayari Sherwood, Christopher Smith, J. J. Weeks, Dazerick Patton, Frankie Dunn, Donavan Hunt, Reginald Swinton, Kevin May, Emari Matthews, Jackson Barry, Alvin Brumfield, King Mwikuta, Kejuan Barbee, Timontre Graham, Josiah Laban, Elliot Blackmon, Zyon Walker, Kaseem Vauls, Jasper Friis, David Studstill, Cam Buckley, Max Gibbs, Julian Smith, Kris Cassel, Julius Reynolds, and Jelani Davis.

A few parents, such as Lisa Hagler, Karen Mingo, Tamillia Lowery, Ferrante Edmonds, Angelia Mikel Brown, Robert Gaddy, Jermaine Ward, and Rebecca Fox, helped with the project by providing details about their kids.

Athletic director Ashley Robinson was an invaluable resource, as was associate AD sports/media Duane Lewis, who also served as a constant sounding board for ideas and insight into the HBCU community.

There are also a number of supportive people around Jackson State's program who helped me complete this project. I need to thank trainer Lauren Askevold, always a willing resource, and her staff. The same for strength and conditioning coach Mo Sims and his assistant Joseph Stone along with Dominique Jasmin-Pasley and Cedric Buckley and the equipment room staff. Campo, who's known Deion for more than thirty years, had so many stories that didn't make the book. Bucky was incredibly thoughtful when discussing his dad and his brothers.

Malone Silver, associate athletic director for academics and compliance, shared many examples about Deion making academics a priority.

Tracie Knight, Deion's sister, deserves a special thanks for trusting me to interview her and her and Deion's mom, Connie. Tracie doesn't like dealing with the media but after numerous conversations, she finally relented. Once she did, she was forthcoming and honest. In the process, she revealed her brother's vulnerable side.

Michael Rhodes and Evis McGee, Deion's security team, were beyond helpful.

Special thanks to Leon and Jennifer Young and C.C. and Yolanda Moore. I'd also like to thank Greg Manogin. The former Sonic Boom drum major provided so much detail into the program and its history, while serving as a terrific sounding board. Ken Clark also deserves some love for teaching me about JSU.

I loved the stories from Miss Jan and Quonte Salley and the morning Lakers talk from student assistant Quinton Williams. Rob J was great too.

I appreciate Thomas Hudson and his Jackson State staff for making themselves available. Thanks to Rob Sale.

To anybody who helped me with the book that I didn't acknowledge, understand I appreciate whatever role you played because you were all critical to the project being completed. Please blame it on my head, not my heart.

CREDITS

No one writes a book alone. Many people behind-the-scenes did their best to make sure the book I wanted to write came to life. These are the folks at Mariner Books who made it happen.

PRESIDENT
Liate Stehlik

PUBLISHER
Peter Hubbard

EDITORIAL
Rakia Clark
Ivy Givens

CONTRACTS
Christine Cox

SALES
Ed Spade
Rio Cortez
Jessica Montany
Carla Parker

Mary Beth Thomas
Kelly Roberts
Joshua Hankins

DESIGN
Chloe Foster
Lucy Albanese
Mark R. Robinson

COMPOSITION
Miranda Ruoff

PRODUCTION
Laura Brady
Pam Barricklow
Christopher Andrus
Paige Jesionowski

PUBLICITY
Kelly Cronin
Maureen Cole

MARKETING
Jen McGuire
Tavia Kowalchuk
Bridget Kearney
Jeffrey Freiert
Ben Steinberg

COPY EDITOR
Thomas Pitoniak

PROOFREADER
Theodore W. Kutt

LEGAL
Mike Bzozowski
William Adams